CINEMA AND LANGUAGE

 The American Film Institute

The American Film Institute Monograph Series

Ann Martin
Supervising Editor

CINEMA AND LANGUAGE

Edited by

Stephen Heath
and
Patricia Mellencamp

University Publications of America, Inc.

The American Film Institute, established in 1967 by the National Endowment for the Arts, is an independent, nonprofit, national organization dedicated to advancing and preserving the art of the moving image.

The opinions expressed in this Monograph *are those of the authors and are not necessarily those of* The American Film Institute.

LCCCN 83-17020
ISBN 0-89093-583-1

The American Film Institute *Monograph* Series is published by University Publications of America, Inc., Frederick, MD, in association with The American Film Institute.

The American Film Institute
2021 North Western Avenue
P.O. Box 27999
Los Angeles, California 90027

Library of Congress Cataloging in Publication Data

Cinema and language.

(The American Film Institute monograph series; v. 1)
Papers presented at a conference held Mar. 27-30, 1979 by the Center for Twentieth Century Studies of the University of Wisconsin-Milwaukee.
1. Moving-picture plays—History and criticism—Congresses. I. Heath, Stephen. II. Mellencamp, Patricia. III. University of Wisconsin-Milwaukee. Center for Twentieth Century Studies. IV. Series.
PN1995.C4863 1983   791.43'75   83-17020
ISBN 0-89093-583-1

Table of Contents

Preface

The papers collected in this volume constitute one record of a conference on 'Cinema and Language' held from March 27 to 30, 1979 by the Center for Twentieth Century Studies of the University of Wisconsin-Milwaukee. The conference could not have taken place without the support, from inside the University, of the College of Letters and Science nor without that, from outside, of the National Endowment for the Arts (through the constantly encouraging Don Druker and Perrin Ireland) and of the Cultural Services of the French Embassy (through Hugues de Kerret). The organization was done by the staff of the Center and coordinated by Carol Tennessen, whose work was largely responsible for the success of the conference.

One record . . . During the conference, much took place: many papers were given and lengthy discussions occupied a large part of the time. Only a little of all this could be included here and we have simply brought together some of the papers that, though diverse in topic and different in approach, lend themselves to a coherent presentation of current aspects of the question of 'cinema and language'. The book thus moves from initial discussions of theories and problems (Heath, de Lauretis) to specific consideration of the place of the spectator in the meaning of film (Doane, Le Grice), and then to three particular 'case-study' areas: Marx Brothers' films (Mellencamp), Japanese cinema (Burch, Kirihara, Bordwell) and Surrealist film (Oswald, Williams), coming back via the matter of 'figures' in film (raised by Oswald and Williams, taken up by Andrew and then by Willemen) to the more general treatment of theories and problems (Willemen and Rosen).

A central feature of the conference was discussion, with the participation of the makers, of a number of films: Chantal Akerman's *Jeanne Dielman, 23 rue de Commerce, 1080 Bruxelles* and *Les Rendez-Vous d'Anna;* James Benning's *Grand Opera: An Historical Romance;* Bette Gordon's *Exchanges;* Malcolm Le Grice's *Emily;* Babette Mangolte's *The Camera:Je/Le Caméra:I.* The key participation of a number of other speakers and discussants should also be acknowledged: Raymond Bellour, Janet Bergstrom, Dick Blau, Keith

Cohen, Robert Cohen, Steven Fagin, Pamela Falkenberg, James Fleming, Sandy Flitterman, Vivianne Forrester, Douglas Gomery, Bruce Kawin, Annette Kuhn, Mary Lydon, Elisabeth Lyon, Annette Michelson, Constance Penley, Jonathan Rosenbaum, Don Skoller, Maureen Turim, William Van Wert, Miriam White and Alan Williams.

This was the fifth International Film Conference held by the Center, and like all the others, it had been enthusiastically supported from its very beginning by the Center's Director, Michel Benamou. His death in the summer of 1978 left the preparation of the conference without his help and guidance and we can only state our continuing sorrow at his loss.

Patricia Mellencamp   Stephen Heath
January 1980

We very much want to acknowledge our gratitude for the timely, efficient editorial contributions of Ann Martin, Assistant Director, Education Services, The American Film Institute.

Contributors

DUDLEY ANDREW, University of Iowa, is the author of *Major Film Theories* and *André Bazin;* he has contributed essays on, for example, color film and Japanese cinema to numerous periodicals.

DAVID BORDWELL, University of Wisconsin-Madison, co-authored *Film Art;* he has written extensively on Japanese cinema for *Screen* and has published essays in *Yale French Studies* and other volumes.

NOEL BURCH, Paris, France, is the author of *To The Distant Observer* and the recently reprinted *Theory of Film Practice.* He has contributed essays to *October* and *Screen.*

TERESA DE LAURETIS, University of Wisconsin-Milwaukee, has written a book on Umberto Eco and co-authored *The Cinematic Apparatus.* She has contributed essays to *Screen, Ciné-Tracts* and *Yale Italian Studies.*

MARY ANN DOANE, Brown University, has written theoretical pieces published in *The Cinematic Apparatus, October, Ciné-Tracts,* and *Yale French Studies.*

STEPHEN HEATH, Cambridge, England, is the author of *Questions of Cinema,* a collection of essays from, among others, *Screen* and *Ciné-Tracts*; he is the co-author of *The Cinematic Apparatus.*

DON KIRIHARA is a graduate student at the University of Wisconsin-Madison writing a dissertation on Japanese film.

MALCOLM LE GRICE, St. Martins, England, is the author of *Abstract Film and Beyond* and an independent filmmaker. His films include *Blackbird Descending* and *Emily.*

PATRICIA MELLENCAMP, University of Wisconsin-Milwaukee, edited 'Conditions of Presence' for *Ciné-Tracts* and has published articles in *Enclitic* and *The Structurist.*

LAURA OSWALD, Mundelin College, has published articles in *Semiotics* and for the Semiotic Society of America.

PHILIP ROSEN, Clark University, has published essays in *Screen, October* and *The Quarterly Review of Film Studies*.

PAUL WILLEMEN, British Film Institute, has written essays on, for example, Raoul Walsh, Jacques Tourneur and avant-garde practices. He edited a volume on Max Ophuls.

LINDA WILLIAMS, University of Illinois, Chicago Circle, is the author of *Figures of Desire*; she has published articles in *Screen* and *Ciné-Tracts*.

Language, Sight and Sound

Stephen Heath

'Cinema and language' has been in many ways the great theoretical impetus for work on film over the last few years: the attempt to pose with regard to cinema the fact and the analogy of language, to determine similarities, connections, terms of interaction. In many ways again, we seem now to be emerging from the hold of that impetus, from the kinds of questions it produced; emerging *from* them, it should be stressed, *on the basis of* the demonstration of their limits, and then, perhaps, *against* them, with different questions, or with some of the old questions differently. What follows is a brief account of something of the present context of 'cinema and language', a consideration of one or two points that are important in its current discussion.

Fundamental to this present context is, of course, semiology and its relation to cinema in the work of Christian Metz, whose immediate question, in his initiatory 1964 essay entitled 'Le cinéma: langue ou langage?', was exactly that of how to pose and define cinema as language. Rigorously worked through, the question was answered in terms of the difficulty of the linguistic model or analogy in respect of cinema: cinema as a language without a language-system, 'un langage sans langue'.[1] Question and answer, however, at the same time that they serve to emphasize the difficulty of cinema as language and hence its difference from language, also effectively function to enclose cinema in the given assumptions of language, in the Saussurian model of *langue,* the system or code of a language, and *parole,* the instances of the use of that system or code, with *langage* as the overall term, the sum of *langue* and *parole.* Its films so many messages, cinema is clearly a kind of language but, lacking a system or code equivalent to a *langue,* is unlike language in the linguistic terms of which it is nevertheless precisely then defined, as 'un

1

langage sans langue'. The model determines the conception and treatment of cinema.[2]

This enclosure can be readily seen in the to-and-fro of the argument of *Langage et cinéma*, the book in which Metz exhaustively explores from a linguistic perspective the notion of cinema as language. 'Cinematic language is different—rather than "distinct"—from what a language-system, a *langue*, *would be*, but takes its place (for here no *langue* exists)'. The thesis of something that takes the place of a language-system gives at once a difference, 'cinematic language has neither the same cohesion nor the same precision as a *langue*', and a closeness, the very difference being within this constant exploration of cinema through the *langue/parole* model which is thus always definingly near to hand, always the analogy or framework for description, as, for example, in the distinction between film and cinema, where the former is 'on the side of the message', the latter 'on the side of the code'. While it stresses cinematic language as constituted by the combination of a number of codes, as codically heterogeneous, the argument also finds occasion in such a film/cinema distinction to adopt 'provisionally' the 'fiction' of 'a unitary system': '*cinematic language*: set of all the general and particular cinematic codes, inasmuch as one provisionally neglects the differences separating them and treats their common trunk, by fiction, as a real unitary system'; to which unitary system can then be opposed the film as message and the *langue/parole* model retained, confirmed.[3]

The 'lock' of that model is not just a problem for the semiology of cinema, for thinking about cinema as language. What is at stake in Saussure's model is the reduction of the social fact of language to a stable system of signs available for free exchange by speaking subjects in individual uses of the common, normative code for the communication of particular informations: the individual utterances, the instances of *parole*, actualize the abstract reality of language as *langue*, the system as contract or horizon or ground for every subject, a social unity. As against which can be stressed the radical necessity to pose social and individual and linguistic together in their complex process, the necessity not to abstract the social into an underlying unity of language but to reappropriate the *action* of language in and into the social; and this without denying the specificity of language, the terms of the individual in its relations, while insisting nonetheless on the question of the ideological to language and individual.

For cinema, that necessity can be heard today as many varied points of interrogation, grasped in the pressures making for the development of this or that new strategy and practice, touching in different ways on what is classically elided in the semiological conception of cinema and language, crossing its limits. Thus, for example, the return of a stress on the body, on 'not moving away from the body', on engaging language in its nearness to that, the body-in-and-through-and-in-resistance-to-and-in-excess-of-language, putting *that* to cinema, 'not assigning language [or cinema with it] to a code, even if it might be agreed that it always secretes one more or less; its life has priority over its code and not the reverse';[4] the insertion of political issues of language and cinema, cinema and language, of 'analysis with image and sound';[5] the attempt to locate in cinema, *as* cinema, problems of representation and sexual difference, the question of language, for instance, in Mulvey and Wollen's film *Riddles of the Sphinx*, 'If we had a non-patriarchal symbolic order, what would the language be in that situation? What would the non-patriarchal word be?';[6] the concern, an old concern coming back anew in the context of the critique of semiology, with the idea of inner speech in respect of cinema, exploring something of the reality of Eisenstein's notion of the passage on screen, in cinema, of 'all phases and all specifics of the thought process'[7] (it might be remembered that Eisenstein would always talk of constructing, and not of using, a cinematic language). These points of interrogation and pressure are cited somewhat pell-mell, so many different indications, but also as crucially important, to be taken up in what follows.

'A language is not an inert material';[8] an emphasis from the wish not to assign language to a code that is found too in the more recent, psychoanalytically referred work of Metz, running over 'the paradox of code':

> in the final analysis, the code can owe its characteristics, and its very existence even, only to a set of symbolic operations (the code is a social *activity*), and yet is a code only insofar as it gathers up and organizes the 'inert' results of those operations.[9]

It is indeed against the 'inert' of *langue* or code that psychoanalysis has become important in current theoretical discussions of questions of cinema and language: psychoanalysis is exactly an attention to language in action and process, in its material effects and operations. It is sometimes said that Freud, unfortunately, lacked an adequate linguistics, missed what would have been the decisive support of Saussure and Jakobson ('Geneva 1910, Petrograd 1920 suffice to explain why Freud lacked this particular tool', as Lacan puts it[10]), but perhaps also it was not so unfortunate, not simply a liability to have had no equivalent to the conception of the *langue/parole* model. Freud worked more interestingly than is generally allowed with a 'linguistics' of the word as knot of meaning, semantic-affective complex, and with a specifically historical orientation, seeking to develop for psychoanalysis the thesis of the repetition by ontogeny of phylogeny, plunging into the history of the individual in the history of language to demonstrate the involvement of the unconscious in the repetition of linguistic material and effects from the origins of language to the present day (this is the purpose of such directly linguistic papers as 'The Antithetical Meaning of Primal Words'[11]). With that linguistics and concern with language as subjective process, without Saussure's model or with Lacan's use and displacement of Saussure through Freud, psychoanalysis, the 'talking-cure', is always in language; it is there that it locates and traces the movement of desire, follows the interminable constitution of subjectivity. The discovered unconscious is not some place, some 'where', but an implication of language, language as 'the condition of the unconscious',[12] the uncon-

scious structured as and from a language: 'it is the whole structure of language that psychoanalytic experience discovers in the unconscious'.[13]

What is significant for the moment is the way in which that experience
and its theorization in these terms cut across, disturbing, the system/individ-
ual set of *langue/parole*, and Lacan has used the expression *lalangue* to
specify the instance of this cutting across, this disturbance. Where *lalangue* is
a formal system to be described and *parole* its individual uses by communicat-
ing agents, *lalangue* names the subjective activity of language, the very
'object' of psychoanalysis, near to the 'basic language', the *Grundsprache*,
heard by Freud in the Schreber case history or in that of the Rat-man;[14]
lalangue as the articulation in the language of a given linguistic-system, in the
matter of a language, of the movement and insistence of desire, with its figure
(for psychoanalysis) maternal language, the mother tongue—the language
par excellence which supports desire in its initial objects: look, voice, breast,
excrement. In short, psychoanalysis comes with a whole different version of
language, of what exists as 'a language':

> A singular mode for the equivocal, that is what a language is amongst
> other things. Thereby it becomes a collection of places, all of them
> singular and all of them heterogeneous; from whatever way one consid-
> ers it, it is other to itself, ceaselessly heterotopical. Thereby it becomes
> just as well substance, possible matter for fantasies, inconsistent set of
> places for desire. The language is thus what the unconscious makes in
> and of it, lending itself to all imaginable games for truth to speak in the
> movement of words. *Lalangue* is all that; one grasps it negatively away
> from usual reference terms—*langue, langage*.[15]

If psychoanalysis then importantly enters current discussion of cinema,
it cannot be as the coherence of a new model to be applied in this specific field,
though in practice the attraction of a static appeal to this or that psychoanalytic 'theme' (mirror stage, fetishism, etc.) has been great, but as the insertion
of a question, the question of language and meaning and the process of
subjectivity, that breaks up some of the certainties of 'cinema and language',
ramifies that 'field' in different directions, so many shifts from any given
unity of description.

Take, to begin with, something of a context for that insertion, elements
of the idea and practice of sight and sound, instances of their opposition,
cross-opposition, inversion and double-inversion—inversion and inversion
again—from psychoanalysis to cinema on this question of language.

Psychoanalysis has been defined here as bound up in language, its
experience as an experience of language, its very situation one of the development of a veritable apparatus of language (analytic practice as a kind of
optimally functioning language theater, language given a hearing). Cinema,
often, has been assumed and defined as essentially separate from language or,
a different emphasis but on the same grounds, as universal language, enthusiastically ('la langue universelle enfin trouvée!' of the first Lumière spectators)
or dismissively (Leavis' 'species of amusing and informational Esperanto'[16]):

cinema as minimally linguistic, as visual, things as words (this was Freud's distrust of cinema and his wish to avoid it dealing with psychoanalysis in these terms: the simplistic visualization of a complex and highly structured linguistic process). This conception, indeed, the assurance of its ideological currency and effectivity, can be grasped in the very treatment of verbal language in the developed commercial cinema and the regulation in respect of that treatment of the multiple possibilities of sound. What determines is the standardization of the sound track for speech for the image, with verbal language and sound reduced to that visual intelligibility; hence, *inter alia*: synchronization, mixing for the achievement of an acceptable—accepted—level of clarity of dialogue, elaboration of the sound track in visible terms (sound 'in' or 'off'), attention to the creation of proper sound 'perspective' (sound anchored in and contributing to the maintenance of the representational space of the image), sound editing in the interests of smoothness of image flow (for example, the sound of one shot is very slightly run over the join of the next shot, hiding the interruption of the cut, preserving the illusion of an undivided presence), studio dubbing of the sounds 'in' the image (the sounds heard on the sound track are selected in relation to their 'visibility' in the image and recreated according to codes of verisimilitude in sound recording studios), even the very *size* of the image on screen and the power of its investment over sound (compare the difference in the economy of sound and image when watching a film on television, the latter recasting sound/image 'size').

This containment of language and sound, moreover, is part of a complex and entangled history in which cinema condenses and intersects a whole series of issues of sight and sound and language. Thus, again simply citing one or two aspects of that history, sound is both very early and very late in cinema; *early*, Edison's initial interest was in moving pictures as accompaniment for his phonograph, the very first years of cinema saw a host of sound-for-film projects (the work of Eugène Lauste, for example); *late*, the well-known story of the time taken for sound to be finally developed and adopted in cinema, the delay until the mid nineteen twenties. Sound, when it comes, loses for a while, foregoes the possibility of, mobility of camera and outdoor location shooting, a certain freedom of vision, but gains an immediate unity of the image as 'scene', a certain theater of sight; in the balancing out of loss and gain an economy of sight and sound is founded which henceforth constrains the terms of its modification (for example, with the recovery of the mobility of the camera after the introduction of the blimp) and of its difference (alternative orders and practices of cinema, defined as other *from* that economy, that standard: for example, documentary or independent avant-garde films). Sound is intensely modern in its technical foundation, the electronics of the twentieth century, very far removed from the nineteenth century image machinery of the film camera; and yet at the same time, given the massive modern investment in the image and its reproduction, often seemingly able to be envisaged as something more or less archaic or marginal, potentially and radically other to the current image; Adorno and Eisler, in their treatise on film music, written in Hollywood, give one symptomatic expression of this:

> The human ear has not adapted itself to the bourgeois rational and, ultimately, highly industrialized order as readily as the eye, which has become accustomed to conceiving reality as made up of separate things, commodities. . . . Ordinary listening, as compared to seeing, is 'archaic'; it has not kept pace with technological progress.[17]

One catches up here a vertiginous spiral of turns and oppositions and overlaps. What sense could we give today to the idea that hearing has not progressed with technology? But then how do hearing and sight 'progress'? The point is constantly the appeal to some other standard of the image and its 'optical sound', which, moreover, is to cut across psychoanalysis, the notion of the archaicity of hearing, finding, important resonances and difficulties in respect of analytic conceptions. Lacan, for instance, stresses hearing, or more exactly the invocatory drive, as closest to the experience of the unconscious, while Freud always regards the visual as most archaic, visual imaging as the register of unconscious presentations (but then again these terms of 'archaic', 'closest', 'visual' need to be examined in their specific meanings and arguments here). In the midst of all of which, returning to film, sound determines the final *property* of cinema: the world domination achieved by the Hollywood industry and the secured relation of that industry to the sources and mechanisms of finance capital; and the law of the speaking subject, the artistic and legal fiction of the creation of a film, its very sense, the ground of its language.

Consider, following out from this context, two issues in the thinking of sight and sound that can come back on the question of cinema and language: the emphasis sometimes put against the convention and conventions of cinema and the visual, on the voice; the distinction between 'thing' and 'word' presentations in Freudian theory and its implications with regard to the reference to psychoanalysis in current work on cinema.

The coming of sound in cinema is the coming of language through the voice; the sound track is developed in the end for that: synchronized visible speech, dialogue that makes scenes for the order and flow of the images, to which other possibilities of sound are sacrificed or subordinated. Yet in speech, running through language, the voice is also a certain deposit of the body, a certain 'grain', something else again, in excess, which the standards of Hollywood learned to pacify (and first and foremost by the very selection of voices, voices that conformed, that 'recorded well') and in specific instances to exploit (the presentation of this or that voice, often crystallized in the theatrical staging of a song, the voice of a Marlene Dietrich or a Lauren Bacall). It is this potential excess that has become the point of emphasis, the voice used towards a heterogeneity in and against the image; the work of Straub/Huillet (*History Lessons, Othon, Moses and Aaron, Fortini/Cani*), its uses of reading or recitation of written literary texts or of sung diction and performance, is only the most obvious example in contemporary film practice. Equally, the voice is assumed against the visual, against the look, and in particular in feminist writing; thus Hélène Cixous: 'What is important is the vocal, the musical, the language at its most archaic and at the same time most highly wrought level'.[18] Something of which idea of language in the vocal-musical at its most archaic and simultaneously elaborate level is the practice of Marguerite Duras (*India Song, Son nom de Venise*). That assumption, moreover, is found again round the question of 'femininity' in psychoanalytic theory today, the thesis that 'the eroticization of the voice and the discourse it vehicules is more present in feminine sexuality': 'mythologically, there is something which links femininity with the voice'.[19] Certainly, look and voice, scopic and invocatory, are given by psychoanalysis as in 'total distinction': 'the distinction is total', comments Lacan, who goes on exactly to stress the invocatory as closest to the experience of the unconscious, the unconscious never closed to the force of the auditory.[20] (This proximity of voice and unconscious in its descriptions would be an aspect to be taken into account in considering the effective situation for psychoanalysis of the voice/feminine conjunction—the implications of the suggested relation: feminine-unconscious-archaic).

In fact, Freud's own formulations seem directly contrary to this (it is worth noting moreover the relative absence of treatment of voice and vocal in his extensive writings), seem directly involved—with the distinction between thing- and word-presentations—in a nonlinguistic, much more visual version of the unconscious. Part of Freud's argument from that distinction is precisely that it is the visual which is more primitive, more archaic than the auditory (though both visual and auditory—Freud is very Hegelian here—are still much further advanced than the tactile, the olfactory and the gustatory). Dreams are described as essentially visual (and this, of course, is just what has led to attempts to equate cinema and dream, cinema as like dream); language found in them as speeches, utterances, is not worked up, not elaborated in the dream but is simply reproduced from matter heard during the day, is daytime material (it *must* be this because the unconscious does not know the logic of syntax, tenses, identity, and so on, is not linguistic).[21] Yet at the same time, what has to be grasped is that the visual of dreams is thing-*presentation*: interpretation, listening to the turns of unconscious desire, does not stop on 'things' (does not *show*), it breaks up and extends these presentations (seeks to find what they *say*). The visual in any sense of some purely visual realm (itself a quite imaginary notion) is finally non-existent in the Freudian description of the unconscious; the visual is always in a production of meanings and run through by language, by a language history, which has determinations in that production of visual-in-meaning. Freud's linguistics of the word is not a pre-Saussurian *pis aller* but an important focus on this mesh of meaning production that is the very definition of the unconscious; the word, to borrow from the stress of Freud's early monograph *On Aphasia,* as 'a complex presentation constituted of auditory, visual and kinesthetic elements'.[22] The focus holds against the reduction of the operations, relations, constructions of meaning—hence against the reduction of the unconscious—to a secondary, systematized delimitation of an object 'language', exactly the level at which the *langue/parole* model is cast. Insisting on speeches in dreams as daytime material, Freud is insisting on the radical eccentricity of dream productions to the stable order of subject to meaning in the given social forms of a language and its institutionalized practice; utilizing a distinction between 'words' and 'things' and assigning the former to the register of the secondary, the latter to that of the primary processes, with the emphasis then on dreams as visual, thing-presentations, Freud is resisting the linguistics idea of the word, fixed units of subject-conceptual meaning. The unconscious, and the 'visual' of dreams with it, is very much in language, on condition that language is understood in a transformation of the terms of the object 'language' of linguistics (and, for example, in the context of a history of the individual as subject in language and in which language itself is a history 'repeated now every time the development of speech has to be gone through in an individual'[23]).

Which is to come to the reason for a concept such as Lacan's *lalangue:* the unconscious is a movement, a work, a history, a repetition and so on in and through a symbolic function which, for Freud as for Lacan, is always implicated in language—neither verbal nor preverbal, the unconscious as a *drift* in language, in the matter of language. Thus Freud, at every moment that he operates the distinction between 'thing' and 'word', the antithesis of 'visual' and 'verbal', everywhere finds language; as though involved in a forceful resistance to and reassessment of Wittgenstein's note that 'what *can* be shown, *cannot* be said',[24] resistance and reassessment around the whole idea of 'language', 'meaning', 'saying'.

It is in relation to these problems of thing and word and saying that Freud looked from the very beginning towards the development of a conception of inner speech, near to what Eisenstein would call 'the quivering inner words that correspond with the visual images'.[25] In the course of his work on aphasia, Freud had come to posit that

> understanding of spoken words is probably not to be regarded as simple transmission from the acoustic elements to the object associations; it rather seems that in listening to speech with understanding the function of verbal association is stimulated from the acoustic elements at the same time, so that we more or less repeat to ourselves the words heard, thus supporting our understanding with the help of kinesthetic impressions.[26]

The argument there is merely for an 'inner' join of word and thing, the former being the *closure* of the latter (word-concepts are closed, object-concepts are open, which is an initial premonition of what will become the 'thing-presentation = unconscious/word-presentation = conscious-preconscious' emphasis of Freud's psychoanalytic work, which emphasis itself is thus in turn a remnant, a left-over from the early work on aphasia): word and thing are linked by the sound-image alone and inner speech is the constant— or not, as in aphasia—link of the two, the point of transmission of their relation (the sound-image engages kinesthetic impressions that are the very history for the individual of object- and word-concepts, of their production). With the discovery of the unconscious and the elaboration of its theory (psychoanalysis), the knot of this link, this relation, tightens and is displaced from a simple question of transmission; the history of language, the terms of the development of thought and consciousness and the process of the realization of the individual as human subject become coincidental, with the unconscious—and inner speech with it inasmuch as such a concept can stand in psychoanalysis—the fact and the demonstration of that coincidence, of its effects. Evidently, it is here, round the problem of this history, the interiorization of history as repetition, the balance from individual to universal subject-form, that the Marxist critique of Freud and psychoanalysis is made most strongly, and through a consideration of language; as, for example, by Vološinov in his 1927 essay on 'Freudianism': 'Processes that are in fact social are treated by Freud from the point of view of individual psychology...', but,

> this 'content of the psyche' is ideological through and through; from the vaguest of thoughts and the dimmest and most uncertain of desires all the way to philosophical systems and complex political institutions, we have one continuous series of ideological and, hence also, sociological phenomena.[27]

The idea of language in Marx begins indeed from its stressed reality as social activity: language is 'practical consciousness', a term of the relation of men and women in social process, material production. At the same time, however *(therefore)*, 'language is as old as consciousness',[28] which is exactly the problem developed by Freud, the area explored in his psychoanalytic experience and theory. For Marx, the three basic aspects of sociality—the satisfaction of needs, the satisfaction of further new needs and the reproduction of life—'have existed simultaneously since the dawn of history and the first men, and still assert themselves in history today'.[29] For Freud, the unconscious is a kind of archaic present in language, the assertion of a history; thus the idea, briefly referred to earlier, of a material established during the historical development of speech and which has to be repeated in the case of the development of speech in each individual. What is strongly in evidence here, again, is the 'ontogeny recapitulates phylogeny' conception that is part of a historical thinking in the nineteenth century common to both Marx and Freud (one might remember in this respect the admiration shared by the two men for the work of Darwin). Moreover, just as Freud sees the origin and foundation of language in the sexual (itself an emphasis to be found in Darwin), so too Marx can regard the division of labor as 'originally nothing but the division of labor in the sexual act',[30] thereby joining the sexual, the social and language ('as old as consciousness', 'practical consciousness') in an original and actual concomitance.

Simply, Freud offers to pose the question of language as a question of subjectivity and to grasp the sexual there, as sexuality (very different from 'the sexual act'), in that history of the construction of the individual against the possible extrapolation from Marx of some notion of an instrumental clarity of consciousness to language for a given subject-agent (language merely a tool for communication that has no constitutive role in the production of consciousness and its terms) or, on the other side, against the reduction of language to ideology (language merely a superstructural category, merely the area of a false consciousness and so equally without real constitutive force). Freud finds, that is, the productivity of language, its articulations, its divisions, its matter (recognizes what Marx intimates as the absence of ' "pure" consciousness', mind afflicted with 'the curse of being "burdened" with matter, which here makes its appearance in the form of agitated layers of air, sounds, in short, of language'[31]), but does so with no idea of historical transformation (this is the final blockage of the ontogeny-phylogeny conception, moving from species universal to individual with nothing between but recapitulation, and where Marx, even as he retains something of that same thinking, separates from it in the working out of a new social-historical science, historical materialism): no idea of historical transformation save only for the individual in consciousness, the practice of the cure, the psychoanalytic situation—the room, the couch, the silence—set up to suspend, to bracket out, history, the social, to engage the sole history of the individual, the person, in every sense an *inner* speech.

It is that interiorization that Vološinov is concerned to challenge, insisting that processes treated by Freud from the point of view of individual psychology are fully social, that the content of the psyche is through and through ideological. Paradoxically perhaps at first sight, one of the strategies of Vološinov's argument against Freud is, in fact, an appeal to a reality of inner speech. What psychoanalysis describes as the unconscious is redefined as an aspect of the conscious, an 'unofficial' aspect that is in conflict with the 'official conscious'; the conscious is linguistic, that use of language which is inner speech ('consciousness is in fact *that commentary* which every adult human being brings to bear on every instance of his behaviour'[32]); thus, as an aspect of the conscious, the unconscious (as Freud would call it) is linguistic and, since linguistic, a social and not an individual phenomenon. The argument, so to speak, has something right in its intention, wrong in its terms. Freud's account of the unconscious is itself, as has been said, not non-verbal in the way in which Vološinov suggests in order to expunge it in the interests of the linguistic and hence social, and the conflict between the 'official' and 'unofficial' aspects of the conscious is left without adequate explanation or content: Vološinov can see the area of the conflict as 'the sexual' but this is now outside of any theory of sexuality (hence, typically, one has no right at all to speak of infantile sexuality other than as meaning 'a set of strictly defined physiological manifestations'[33]) and tends towards a simple notion of social repression. The stress that 'the psyche in its entirety' is 'in every respect determined by socioeconomic factors'[34] remains unhelpful in its blanket generality and its imprecision with regard to what 'determined' might mean and to the mechanisms of the operation of such determination; the problem of the individual and subjectivity is not resolved by collapsing everything into the 'socioeconomic'. Certainly, the terms of the descriptions provided by psychoanalysis—'the content and composition of the unconscious'[35]—need to be understood and questioned historically, considered in relation to 'historical time and class';[36] certainly, it is necessary to recognize that there is 'no fundamental dividing line between the content of the individual psyche and formulated ideology';[37] but all this is not a reason (on the contrary) for erasing the specific domain of concern identified and approached by psychoanalysis, that of the construction of the individual, of the 'individual psyche',—or, to put it in a more Marxist perspective, of *the individual history of* historical construction.

Inner speech is still a valid point of exploration in this connection. Its theoretical development is, of course, not only in Vološinov. Initial psychological investigation is carried out in France in the late nineteenth century in the work of Egger *(La Parole intérieure)* and Ballet *(Le Langage intérieur)* and is bound up with the attempt to define the status of an inner speech as the carrier of thought, the point of the exchange of thought into its external expression.[38] It is indeed in Soviet psychology, however, that inner speech is decisively introduced and worked through, most notably with the researches of Vygotsky and Blonski (and in a context which includes in the nineteen twenties an active presence of psychoanalysis: Pavlov himself had been favorably interested in psychoanalysis from as early as 1913; Luria— student, collaborator and friend of Vygotsky—was the secretary to psychoanalytic circles in Kazan and Moscow; and so on).

Vygotsky's treatment of inner speech is set out in *Thought and Language,* published posthumously in 1934. His concern is the relation of thought and language, and inner speech enters the argument in the terms of this concern as a kind of monitoring of thought, as 'the living process of the birth of thought in the word': 'Thought is not merely expressed in words; it comes into existence through them'.[39] As such, inner speech can be given a genetic description: in the beginning thought and language are independent activities, thought proceeding without language in very young children, as in animals (equally, the child's cooings and other vocalizations are speech without thought, mere acts to attract attention or whatever); around two years, pre-linguistic thought and pre-thought language meet and join to initiate a new kind of behavior, verbal thought; at about seven years, after a period in which the child engages out loud in both social speech, for and with others, and egocentric speech, talking for itself in an activity of language that is in fact its use to direct and produce thought, the child learns to distinguish the functions of speech and internalizes the thought function of language, thus establishing inner speech. The latter can then be described as 'a specific formation, with its own laws and complex relations to other forms of speech activity', Vygotsky indicating 'the extreme, elliptical economy of inner speech, changing the speech pattern almost beyond recognition'; 'a simplification of syntax, a minimum of syntactic breaking down, expression of thought in condensed form, a considerably smaller number of words', (inner speech is characterized by a basic predicativeness, the omission of the subject and the parts of the sentence related to it, and by a contextual sense of words, an intellectual and affective intensity beyond what Vygotsky calls their 'objective' meaning).[40]

Certain of the arguments of *Thought and Language* were criticized by Blonski in his *Memory and Thought* published in the following year. Blonski opposes the idea that thought and language have separate genetic roots and proposes instead the recognition of a common source, work: 'both speech and thought have developed from work; primitive speech was really action; primitive intellectual operations were actions'.[41] Equally, he challenges Vygotsky's hypothesis regarding the evolution of inner speech from the child's egocentric speech, placing as it does the origin of inner speech at a very late stage of development (six or seven years, well into school age) and thus leaving the child in a prior state of the absence of any such mechanism. For Blonski, inner and social speech are simultaneous, the former developing in relation to the latter as the initial activity of the repetition of speech heard, listening accompanied by an internal echoing to aid understanding (Blonski is here near to Freud's account of inner speech in *On Aphasia* mentioned earlier). This 'accompaniment' continues as the permanent reality of the process of thought for the individual, with the actual characterization of inner speech then coming back to a similarity with that given by Vygotsky:

> An extremely rapid and changeable flow of thoughts, making little sense for an outsider because of its jumps and incompleteness of reading and judgements, continually reverting to fragments of phrases or even to individual words which would surprise the listeners.[42]

It will be clear that inner speech functions as a concept within a general context of the investigation of the nature of thinking, hence of the relation of thought and language. As such, it has a history which is longer than that of the psychological work outlined above, as long indeed as Western philosophy and with perfectly idealist emphases (Socrates in Plato's *Theaetetus* has a version of inner speech as 'the conversation which the soul holds with itself in considering anything'). Again, however, it has a real importance as a concept in connection with the problem of thought and language which is a fully, and necessary, materialist area of concern (the question jotted down by Lenin in the margin of Hegel's *Logic*: 'History of thought = history of language?'). What sense is to be given to—what are the operations and implications of—language as, in Marx's expression, 'the immediate reality' of thought? Vološinov, Vygotsky, Blonski engage, in different ways, that debate, the 'battle for consciousness' of the twenties and early thirties, the specification of the issues involved in moving 'from the social to the individual', grasping language and thought as 'subject to all the premises of historical materialism'.[43]

The debate is historically and theoretically important in cinema, is to be heard, for instance, in Eisenstein's 'all phases and all specifics of the thought process'. A more or less constant ambition for Eisenstein is the grounding of cinematic practice in the processes of psychological functioning and the establishment of the laws of the former from those of the latter. Inner speech is taken up in just these terms: 'the laws of the construction of inner speech turn out to be precisely those laws which lie at the foundation of the whole variety of laws governing the construction of the form and composition of art-works'.[44] The most important theoretical statement and assertion of inner speech is in a 1935 address, delivered to the All-Union Creative Conference on Cinematographic Questions, in which Eisenstein refers to work—probably by Luria—in the Moscow Neuro-Surgical Clinic and no doubt has Vygotsky's book very much in mind (Eisenstein appears to have been a member of a discussion group that included Luria and Vygotsky[45]). The tendency of his address, however, is towards a connection between inner speech and 'prelogical thinking' (thus quite distinct from Vygotsky's tying of inner speech to a development that makes of it a fully social relation of thought and language, a function of 'verbal thought'), referring this 'prelogi-cal' idea to the anthropologist Lévy-Bruhl (whom Vygotsky indeed seeks to refute on one of the very points accepted by Eisenstein[46]). In 1932, Eisenstein could express himself in ways which suggest the thought and language problematic of the contemporary inner speech discussion:

> How fascinating it is to listen to one's own train of thought, particularly in an excited state, in order to catch yourself, looking at and listening to your own mind. How you talk 'to yourself', as distinct from 'out of yourself'. The syntax of inner speech as distinct from outer speech. The quivering inner words that correspond with the visual images;[47]

In 1935, it is apparent that his version of inner speech is independent of social language and involved in a fundamental 'psychic associationism':

> Since 'inner speech' is prelogical and sensuous, [Eisenstein's earlier project] of stimulating abstract and ideological reasoning is abandoned; sensation and affect are now sufficient ... Now the spectator's reaction must be not thought but pathos, 'ecstasy' ... the very concept of montage is overhauled. Since the work of art must map the way we create felt concepts in life, montage's ability to render the dynamic flow of images makes it the sovereign formal principle.[48]

Eisenstein, moreover, sees himself quickly reproached with 'subjectivism', compared, even, to the hated Proust!

And yet ... there are flashes in Eisenstein of something quite radically different, at least in potential implication. An interview in 1928 has the following exchange:

'We have an incorrect attitude to the notion of symbol. It is wrong to
assert that the symbol is now without life. The symbolizing force is a
living one for it belongs to the essence of human reaction to sensa-
tion'./'Ah! so you're a Freudian!'/'No doubt. Cinema must take into
account the consequences of the fact that every individual symbolizes
unconsciously. It is not the achieved symbol that interests me but the
symbol in process [*Symbol im Werden,* literally "symbol in
becoming"]'.[49]

Freudian? Certainly not on the whole (in the fascinating correspondence with
Reich in 1934 Eisenstein sets out his objections to the importance accorded to
the sexual in Freud) but constantly caught up nonetheless in the concerns of
Freudian psychoanalysis (as stated previously, psychoanalysis is a presence in
Soviet Russia in the twenties). The 'symbol in process' is one—excellent—
definition of the unconscious recognized and described in Freud's work.

The symbol in process. The psychoanalysis of Freud and Lacan engages
the unconscious as a kind of inner speech, where this latter is neither 'social'
nor 'individual', still less the site of some universal symbolism (the 'achieved
symbol'), but, exactly, linguistic in a new assumption of the—complex,
heterogenous—reality of language as a site of history. For Freud, there is no
escape from language, ontogenetically or phylogenetically:

Thus for Freud symbolism was always derivative of verbality. As the
meanings of words change—both in the ontogeny of the individual and
the phylogeny of the species—so symbols accumulate in the unconscious
of the individual and the race. Symbols are vestigial residues; here Freud
[returns] to [the] promise of mastering archaic regression through the
development of language. Symbols are the vestiges of a time when
sexuality and language were themselves identified.[50]

There is no 'prelogical' in either of the senses given by Eisenstein (Lévy-
Bruhl) or Vygotsky (the infant/animal 'biological', 'natural' forms): what one
has, always, is another scene of shifts of meaning, slippages of identity,
intensities of desire, a whole articulation (the unconscious structured in and
as and like a language), a radical eccentricity of any 'subject' (in that action of
meanings, symbols in process). The thing-/word-presentation distinction
does not plunge into some realm prelanguage but into one where the
identities assumed and derived in language (the *vision* of language) fail, the
orders of the sign slide. 'Thing-presentations', the matter of the unconscious,
are symbolic articulations, signifiers full of language in every sense, 'words'
and 'things' intersecting (follow the analysis of any dream in *The Interpretation of Dreams*). Inner speech is then that history of language.

Simply, the point of all the difficulty, Freud and still less Lacan do not
carry through to the end of that eccentricity of the subject in language in that
history, block that movement in what amounts to a fetishization of 'subject'
and 'language'. (What does psychoanalysis believe in today? Subject and
language.) The real history with which psychoanalysis deals is still directly
and immediately social, not 'before' or 'elsewhere' to social processes, ideological places. There is a material history of the construction of subjectivity and
that history is also the social construction of the individual as subject, in a kind
of necessary simultaneity, like the recto and verso of a piece of paper; between

the psyche and the social, no 'fundamental dividing line' is to be drawn, not even with *lalangue* which can quickly become the separate realm of psychoanalysis, the term of its suspension of history.

It is very possible that in the long run the concept of inner speech itself will be found to be caught up in theoretical and ideological difficulties. Indeed, the inner/outer paradigm is at once not without evident problems. 'Inner' easily tends towards a simply 'subjective' account of individual experience in meaning and a consequent homogenization of the person (inner speech becomes a kind of *property* of 'the subject', 'that interior recitation which constitutes our person'[51]), in a way that is deeply conservative, indicating a realm of separation—at best, as in Vygotsky, of unofficial resistance—rather than a theory of action and transformation. Alternatively, by the very terms of the opposition set up, it suggests the possibility of a theoretical reversal, inner into outer, the 'through and through ideological' version which, quite apart from the problems of defining the relations of language and ideology and of the apparent extension of the ideological as a general equivalence for the social, seems to leave little place again for process and conflict—how to explain difference, contradiction, tensions of 'inner' and 'outer', tensions *in subjectivity*—not just between an 'inner' and an 'outer' sphere—that are crucial to any understanding of the political importance of cinema, its potential, its availability for use.

As far as the analysis of cinema and film is concerned, consideration of inner speech has so far been limited and, in fact, disappointing. Its introduction here, again in the Soviet context, dates from a 1927 essay by the formalist critic Boris Eikhenbaum entitled 'Problems of Film Stylistics', in which he emphasizes the inadequacy of the idea of film as a non-verbal art:

> Cinema demands of the viewer a certain special technique for divination, and this technique will of course become more complex as the art of film-making develops. Directors already make frequent use of symbols and metaphors, the meaning of which depends directly on current verbal metaphors. Film viewing is accompanied by a continual process of internal speech. We have already grown accustomed to a whole series of typical patterns of film language; the smallest innovation in this sphere strikes us no less forcibly than the appearance of a new word in language. To treat film as an absolutely non-verbal art is impossible. Those who defend cinema from the imitation of literature often forget that though the audible word is eliminated from film, the thought, i.e. internal speech, is nevertheless present. The study of the particularities of this film-speech is one of the most important problems in cinematic theory.[52]

Subsequent work has been largely occupied with Eikhenbaum's suggestion of the dependence of visual on verbal metaphor, with demonstrating the use of image translations of linguistic tropes.[53] Thus, for example, in *The Taking of Pelham 123,* the hopeless and corrupt mayor of New York is sick in bed for most of the time, quite unable to decide anything with regard to the subway train that has been hijacked; at one point, we cut to him just as he is having an injection in his buttocks and his deputy walks in, 'Come on, Al, pull your pants up'—the mayor, here as throughout the film, is *caught with his pants down*. These 'literalisms'—the visual translation depends on a literal fidelity to the linguistic metaphor—are the very stuff of certain forms of film comedy, the films of the Marx Brothers providing notable examples (in *At the Circus*, the literalization of *the last straw that breaks the camel's back*, done with a nice ironic twist through the agency of the *mute* Harpo). Their analysis keeps inner speech close to a simple recognition of stereotypes of thought, composition and reading as the one-to-one conversion of fixed—achieved—linguistic symbols.[54] Which is to say that we are still far from an analysis engaging, on the basis of a concept of inner speech, the process of the social and the individual through language in the presence—the reception, reading, performance—of a film. Paradoxically, moreover, the recourse to inner speech so far has tended to privilege the visual, leaving sound out of the picture (an appropriate enough metaphor); in the discussions of and from literalisms, the terms are always only the visual image and the linguistic expression. The paradox, in fact, is the symptom of the weak version of inner speech assumed: a version derived from Vološinov or Vygotsky or Freud, and however different in each case, would have to involve consideration of sound just as much as of image, indeed would not be able to assume the film in terms of any such given distinction as sound and image; the whole status of inner speech would change—no longer the point of a mechanical construction of a public unity of a film but the point of a complex investigation of the multiple existence of a film each time for a spectator at an intersection of constructions and intensities and slippages and times, of areas of activity and reality, contradictions, joins, displacements.

What is needed, still, and it is here that the status of inner speech could be thought through, the question of cinema and language taken up again today, is a theory of cinematic enunciation. Something of the framework of this, the model of film, might be laid out, initially at least, as follows.

A film is always finished, enounced; and finished, enounced, even in its enunciation which is given, fixed, repeated at every 'showing' or 'screening'. One has to think in this respect of the accomplished fact—that *fait accompli*—of film and the power of the image in that accomplishment (leading to those descriptions of film as characteristically an effacement of discourse; to the feeling of a loss of any historical sense, history constrained into the 'objective', into the form of a visibility and vision, where Marxism in its practice and its theory gives a history that is quite the reverse of 'visible'; and so on); the power which is there in the very regularity of the flow of images in time (smoothly, no resistance, a well-oiled defile for consciousness).

Yet, in that fixity, that givenness of the film, there is nevertheless, always, a present enunciation, the making of the film by the spectator ('making' here the join of the one and the other, the spectator making it as one makes a train, catching it, taken up in its movement, and as one makes, fashions something, articulating it, creating that movement): the whole enunciation in the seeing, listening to, following, reading, skipping, missing, interpreting, reinterpreting, remembering, forgetting, the film performance, from process to closure to process constantly, a veritable history of subjectivity in the symbolic divisions and unities and drifts, the symbol in becoming. Evidently, there is another enounced in this performance-enunciation of the film: all the meaning I am, that is me, all my identity, the history I have for-and-against the film and in-and-across the very institution of the viewing of the film, the institution of the regulation of the exchange, the exchange at stake in the process of cinematic enunciation. What we know predominantly are institutions of which the force and the reason is *facilitation* of that exchange; the ease, the flow, the assurance, the pacification of the passage across from film to spectator, spectator to film in orders of identity, hierarchies of meanings, simply in a stable timing, a 'bracketing time'.[55] That verbal language is banished from the institution of the enunciation—no speech as part of the performance before or during or after the film—is indicative, a part of the pacification; and thus, in opposition, importantly reinstated in contemporary—independent, avant-garde, political—attempts to produce alternative institutions, different 'viewings', new 'hearings'.

All this is to come a long way from the first semiology and its treatment of cinema and language, is to emphasize the need now to understand the structured process of film in cinema, to pose the terms for that understanding—in which language remains a constant and crucial point of reflection, a junction-problem for thinking cinema today.

This article has also appeared in Questions of Cinema, *by Stephen Heath (London: Macmillan, 1980).*

18   STEPHEN HEATH

NOTES

1. C. Metz, 'Le cinéma: langue ou langage?', in *Essais sur la signification au cinéma* (Paris: Klincksieck, 1971), pp. 39-93; trans. M. Taylor 'The Cinema: Language or Language-System?', in *Film Language* (New York & London: Oxford University Press, 1974), pp. 31-91. For an overall account of Metz' initial semiological analysis, see my 'The Work of Christian Metz', *Screen* vol. 14 no. 3 (Autumn 1973), pp. 5-28.

2. The same kind of conclusion can be found in the—relatively few—attempts to specify cinema in the terms of a Chomskian perspective according to a competence/performance model; cinema is a language without competence: 'If, in cinema, there are no "bits of films" that can be excluded, it is because there are no audio-visual combinations that are unacceptable by virtue of some formal system'. D. Château, 'Texte et discours dans le film', in *Voir, Entendre (Revue d'esthétique* no. 4, 1976), (Paris: Union Générale d'Editions, 1976), p. 128. Certainly, the Chomskian model gives in one sense a more active version of language description ('creativity', 'transformation', the 'generative' production of sentences), but it remains based on an immobilization of language, precisely the inert of the formal system—'grammaticality', the 'grammar'. Saussure's model is quite radically displaced at the same time that its ambition, the description of the linguistic system, is maintained; hence Chomsky's reference to Saussure's 'lucidity' and his stress that the competence/performance distinction 'is related to the *langue-parole* distinction of Saussure'—N. Chomsky, 'Current Issues in Linguistic Theory', in J.A. Fodor and J.J. Katz (eds.), *The Structure of Language* (Englewood Cliffs, New Jersey: Prentice-Hall, 1964), p. 52; and *Aspects of the Theory of Syntax* (Cambridge, Massachusetts: MIT Press, 1965), p. 4.

3. C. Metz, *Langage et cinéma* (Paris: Larousse, 1971), pp. 202, 111, 51, 44; trans. D.J. Umiker-Sebeok, *Language and Cinema* (The Hague-Paris: Mouton, 1974), pp. 268, 149, 69, 60.

4. F. Collin, 'Polyglo(u)ssons', *Les Cahiers du GRIF* no. 12 (June 1976), p. 8.

5. J.-L. Godard, *Deux ou trois choses que je sais d'elle* (Paris: Seuil, 1971), p. 14.

6. L. Mulvey and P. Wollen, 'Interview', *Screen* vol. 15 no. 3 (Autumn 1974), p. 128 (the formulation quoted refers in context to the final section of Mulvey and Wollen's first film, *Penthesilea*, but is then, as it were, something of an imagination of the problematic of the subsequent *Riddles of the Sphinx*).

7. S.M. Eisenstein, *Film Form* (New York: Harcourt Brace & World, 1949), p. 105.

8. Collin, p. 3.

9. C. Metz, *Le Signifiant imaginaire* (Paris: Union Générale d'Editions, 1977), p. 187.

10. J. Lacan, *Ecrits* (Paris: Seuil, 1966), p. 799; trans. A. Sheridan, *Ecrits: A Selection* (London: Tavistock, 1977), p. 298.

11. S. Freud, 'The Antithetical Meaning of Primal Words' (1910), *The Standard Edition of the Complete Psychological Works of Sigmund Freud* vol. XI (London: Hogarth, 1957), pp. 155-61.

12. J. Lacan, 'L'Etourdit', *Scilicet* no. 4 (1973), p. 45.

13. Lacan, *Ecrits*, p. 495; trans. p. 147.

14. S. Freud, 'Notes upon a Case of Obsessional Neurosis' (1909), *Standard Edition* vol. X (London: Hogarth, 1955), pp. 151-249; 'Psycho-Analytic Notes on an Autobiographical Account

of a Case of Paranoia (Dementia Paranoides)' (1911), *Standard Edition* vol. XII (London: Hogarth, 1958), pp. 1-82. Cf. Freud's letter to Jung of 1 October, 1910 ('I plan to introduce "basic language" as a serious technical term ...'), *The Freud/Jung Letters* (London: Hogarth and Routledge & Kegan Paul, 1977), p. 358.

15. J.-C. Milner, *L'Amour de la langue* (Paris: Seuil, 1978), pp. 22-3.

16. F.R. Leavis, *For Continuity* (Cambridge, U.K.: Minority Press, 1933), p. 28.

17. T. Adorno and H. Eisler, *Composing for the Films* (London: Dennis Dobson, 1947), p. 20.

18. H. Cixous, 'Entretien avec Françoise van Rossum-Guyon', *Revue des sciences humaines* no. 168 (1977), p. 488.

19. I. Diamantis, 'Recherches sur la féminité', *Ornicar? Analytica* vol. 5, p. 32. C. Rabant, in 'Entrevue avec Moustapha Safouan', *Ornicar? Analytica* no. 9 (April 1977), p. 101.

20. J. Lacan, *Le Séminaire livre XI* (Paris: Seuil, 1973), pp. 96, 108, 182; trans. A. Sheridan, *The Four Fundamental Concepts of Psycho-Analysis* (London: Hogarth, 1977), pp. 104, 118, 200.

21. S. Freud, 'The Interpretation of Dreams' (1900), *Standard Edition* vol. V (London: Hogarth, 1953), pp. 418-425.

22. S. Freud, *On Aphasia* (1891), (London: Imago, 1953), p. 73.

23. S. Freud, 'Moses and Monotheism' (1939), *Standard Edition* vol. XXIII (London: Hogarth, 1964), p. 99.

24. L. Wittgenstein, *Tractatus Logico-Philosophicus* (London: Routledge & Kegan Paul, 1961), p. 50 (4.1212).

25. Eisenstein, p. 105.

26. Freud, *On Aphasia*, pp. 91-2.

27. V.N. Vološinov, *Freudianism: A Marxist Critique* (New York: Academic Press, 1976), p. 24.

28. K. Marx and F. Engels, *The German Ideology* (London: Lawrence & Wishart, 1965), p. 42.

29. Ibid., p. 41.

30. Ibid., p. 43.

31. Ibid., p. 42.

32. Vološinov, p. 85.

33. Ibid., p. 82.

34. Ibid., p. 86.

35. Ibid., p. 89.

36. Ibid.

37. Ibid., p. 87.

38. V. Egger, *La Parole intérieure* (Paris: Librairie Germer Baillière et Cie., 1881); G. Ballet, *Le Langage intérieur* (Paris: Librairie Germer Baillière et Cie., 1886).

39. L.S. Vygotsky, *Thought and Language* (Cambridge, Massachusetts: MIT Press, 1977), p. 125.

40. Ibid., pp. 45, 145-6.

41. P.P. Blonski, *Memory and Thought* (1935), cit. A.N. Sokolov, *Inner Speech and Thought* (New York & London: Plenum Press, 1972), p. 48.

42. Ibid., cit. Sokolov, p. 49.

43. Vygotsky, pp. 20, 51.

44. Eisenstein, p. 130.

45. As reported by Annette Michelson from conversations in Moscow with V.V. Ivanov; cf. H. Denkin, 'Linguistic Models in Early Soviet Cinema', *Cinema Journal* vol. XVII no. 1 (Fall 1977), pp. 4, 13.

46. Vygotsky, pp. 71-2; cf. Eisenstein, pp. 135-6.

47. Eisenstein, p. 105.

48. D. Bordwell, 'Eisenstein's Epistemological Shift', *Screen* vol. 15 no. 4 (Winter 1974/75), p. 41.

49. Interview with Bruno Frei (1928), in S.M. Eisenstein, *Schriften* vol. 3 (Munich: Hanser, 1975), p. 260.

50. J. Forrester, 'Language, Symbol and History in Freud's Psycho-Analysis' (Cambridge, U.K.: unpublished paper, 1974), pp. 53-4. The present essay is indebted to Forrester's research at a number of points.

51. R. Barthes, *L'Empire des signes* (Geneva: Skira, 1970), p. 99.

52. B. Eikhenbaum, 'Problems of Film Stylistics' (1927), *Screen* vol. 15 no. 3 (Autumn 1974), p. 14.

53. See notably P. Willemen, 'Reflections on Eikhenbaum's Concept of Internal Speech in the Cinema', *Screen* vol. 15 no. 4 (Winter 1974/75), pp. 59-70.

54. Cf. Freud's initial consideration of symbolism in connection with conversion symptoms in hysteria, these being exactly the literalization of verbal expressions (a patient who takes something said to her as 'a slap in the face' expresses that feeling as a literal facial neuralgia); 'Studies on Hysteria' (1985), *Standard Edition* vol. II (London: Hogarth, 1955), pp. 178-81.

55. Y. Rainer, Letter, *Camera Obscura* no. 1 (1976), p. 96. 'The limitations of conventional narrative films: they cover a particular duration of time in which the protagonists transcend or are destroyed in the course of a single climax. Yes, it really is about bracketing time that I object to'.

From a Dream of Woman

Teresa de Lauretis

In one of Italo Calvino's works, a sort of historical science fiction, Marco Polo, the traveler, the trader and eternal exile, recounts to Kublai Khan, emperor of the Tartars, the cities he has seen. The book is entitled *Invisible Cities*.

> From there, after six days and seven nights, you arrive at Zobeide, the white city, well exposed to the moon, with streets wound about themselves as in a skein. They tell this tale of its foundation: men of various nations had an identical dream. They saw a woman running at night through an unknown city; she was seen from behind, with long hair, and she was naked. They dreamed of pursuing her. As they twisted and turned, each of them lost her. After the dream they set out in search of that city; they never found it, but they found one another; they decided to build a city like the one in the dream. In laying out the streets, each followed the course of his pursuit; at the spot where they had lost the fugitive's trail, they arranged spaces and walls differently from the dream, so she would be unable to escape again.
>
> This was the city of Zobeide, where they settled, waiting for that scene to be repeated one night. None of them, asleep or awake, ever saw the woman again. The city's streets were streets where they went to work every day, with no link any more to the dreamed chase. Which, for that matter, had long been forgotten.
>
> New men arrived from other lands, having had a dream like theirs, and in the city of Zobeide, they recognized something of the streets of the dream and they changed the positions of arcades and stairways to resemble more closely the path of the pursued woman and so, at the spot where she had vanished, there would remain no avenue of escape.
>
> Those who had arrived first could not understand what drew these people to Zobeide, this ugly city, this trap.[1]

Zobeide, a city continually built from a dream of woman, built to keep woman captive—the city a representation of woman, woman the ground of that

21

representation. In complex circularity ('streets wound about themselves as in a skein'), 'woman' is at once the dream's object of desire and the reason for its objectification, the source of the drive to represent and its ultimate, unattainable, aim.

Building and rebuilding the city, in a continuing movement of objectification *(Vergegenständlichung)* and alienation *(Entfremdung),* is Calvino's metaphor for human history as semiotic productivity;[2] desire provides the impulse, the drive to represent and dream the modes of representing. Of that semiotic productivity 'woman' (the dream woman) is both telos and origin; the foundation of representation is not its content; woman is absent from the city, stage of its performance ('This was the city of Zobeide, where they settled, waiting for that *scene* to be repeated *one night.* None of them, asleep or awake, ever saw the woman again').

It does not come as a surprise, to us cinema people, that in that primal city built by men there are no women; or that in Calvino's seductive parable of 'human' history woman is absent as historical subject. Like cinema, the city of Zobeide is an imaginary signifier, a language and a practice of language, a continuous movement of representations built from a dream of woman, built to keep 'woman' captive; in the discursive space of the city, as in the constructs of cinematic discourse, woman is both absent and captive: absent as theoretical subject, captive as historical subject.

One year ago, in these same rooms, several questions were asked about what we called the cinematic apparatus. It was proposed that the facts of cinema and its conditions of possibility should be posed as 'a relation of the technical and the social'—cinema as a 'social technology'. Ironically, in view of the absence/captivity of woman as subject and of the alleged feminine discomfort with technology, it became apparent that such a relation could not be effectively articulated without reference to a third term, subjectivity, or the construction of sexual difference; and that the questions of women, therefore, not only occupied a critical space within an historical materialist theory of the cinema, but directly invested its basic premise.[3]

If, as Annette Kuhn has said in the introduction to *Feminism and Materialism,* 'the posing of feminist issues constitutes an attack on existing theoretical frameworks, and can proceed only by actually transforming them', it is not because 'the woman question' could not be inserted into previously developed theories (a negative reason and a pragmatic one).[4] I would argue that women's critical intervention in social discourses at all levels, including theory, has a positive, political reason: in Western culture women are the agents, the subjects of a significant sector or tendency of social practice from which, alongside of which, contemporary critical reflection has been developing. In posing the questions of subjectivity, sub-cultural resistance, sexual difference, the body and so forth, the feminist critique has foregrounded them precisely as a new kind of political practice—the articulation of the social and the subjective. To what extent, for instance, has this feminist perspective informed the historical switch, within semiotic theory, from the consideration of the systemic, formal aspect of signification to the concern with the production of meaning for a subject?[5] This has not been examined. In fact, the relation of women's practice to the reorientation of current theoretical discourse—not only semiotics but particularly psychoanalysis and the recent theorizations of ideology—has been evaded and erased by its very incorporation into each of those discourses; in other words, those questions have been appropriated by those discourses, have been taken up in the 'appropriate' disciplines as areas of study that had always belonged to, that were always the 'domain' or the 'property' of, those disciplines. And this is why a feminist critique is both an attack on and a transformation of existing theoretical frameworks, is a critique at once from within and from without, in the same way in which women are both *in* the cinema as representation and *outside* the cinema as subjects of practice.

More and more frequently, and the theme of this conference confirms it, the nexus representation/subject/ideology is posed in terms of language, language thus becoming the site of their junction and articulation. Cinema *and* language. What relation does the *and* express? What is the nature of the copula? If indeed there is no sexual relation, as some claim, we might exclude right away the literal meaning—copula, copulation (of course, there are no literal meanings...). Classical semiology linked cinema and language in what could be called a metonymic relation: all sign systems are organized like language, which is the 'universal' sign system; and cinema is one system among others, a sector of that universal organization of signs. Recently, a theory of signifying practices based in psychoanalytic discourse has established between cinema and language something of a metaphoric relation: though realized in distinct practices and material apparati, both cinema and language are imaginary-symbolic productions of subjectivity, their differences being less relevant than their homologous functioning in/as subject processes.

I have used the words 'metonymic' and 'metaphoric' not inadvertently but as an ironic quotation, to underline the dependence on language common to the semiological and psychoanalytic reflections, a dependence which heavily tilts the balance of the relation and instates an obvious hierarchy, the subordination of cinema to language; and to suggest, further, that just as metaphor and metonymy—in the linguistic framework—continually slide ('are projected', Jakobson says[6]) one onto the other, so are those discourses mutually implicated, convergent and complicit; and insofar as they originate in a structural-linguistic model of language, they circumscribe a theoretical area of cinema as language, each representing one axis, one mode of discursive operation.

So I have set myself up to argue that the semiological and psychoanalytic discourses on cinema are, in some respect, similar; and from my rhetorical strategy (I began with a parable about woman as representation) you might correctly infer that my argument will have something to do with 'woman'. Semiotics tells us that similarity and difference are relational categories, that is, they can only be established in relation to some term of reference, which is thus assumed as the point of theoretical articulation; and indeed *that* term de-termines the parameters and the conditions of comparison. Should another term of reference be assumed, the relation and the terms of the relation would be differently articulated; the first relation would be disturbed, displaced, or shifted toward another relation; the terms, and perhaps the parameters and conditions of the comparison would change; and so would the *value* of the *and* which in our case expresses the relation of cinema to language.

My term of reference, and my point of enunciation (both of which, I must warn you, are fictions) will be the absent-captive woman in Calvino's city.[7] Not unlike the city, cinematic theory is built in history, inscribed in historically specific discourses and practices; and while those discourses have traditionally assigned to woman a position of non-subject, the latter deter-mines, grounds and supports the very concept of subject and thus the theoretical discourses which inscribe it. Like the city, then, cinematic theory cannot disengage itself from the trouble caused by 'woman', the problems she poses in *its* discursive operations.

The hypothesis of classical semiology that cinema, like language, is a formal organization of codes, specific and nonspecific, but functioning according to a logic internal to the system (cinema or film), apparently does not address me, woman, spectator. It is a scientific hypothesis and as such addresses other 'scientists' in a closed economy of discourse. In building the city, the semiologist wants to know how the stones are put together to make a wall, an arcade, a stairway; he pretends not to care why any of these is being built or for whom. However, if asked about 'woman', he would have no doubt as to what woman was and he would admit dreaming about her—during the breaks from research. Woman, he would say, is a human being, like man (semiology, after all, is a human science), but her specific function is reproduction—the reproduction of the biological species and the mainte-nance of social cohesion.

You see, the semiologist has read Lévi-Strauss as well as Saussure plus some Freud and probably Marx. He knows that the incest prohibition, the 'historical' event instituting culture and found in all human societies, requires that women be possessed and exchanged among men to ensure the social order; and that although marriage regulations, the rules of the game of exchange, vary greatly throughout world societies, they all ultimately depend on the same kinship structures, which are really quite like linguistic struc-tures. In short, for Lévi-Strauss, women are objects whose value is founded in nature ('valuables *par excellence*' as bearers of children, food gatherers, etc.); at the same time, they are signs in social communication established by men through kinship systems. Hence the double status of woman as object of exchange, bearer of economic, positive value, and woman as sign, bearer of semiotic, negative value, of difference.[8]

Lévi-Strauss' entire theory of culture as symbolic system(s) thus *depends on* his positing woman as the functional opposite of subject (man), which 'logically' excludes the possibility of women's social role as subjects and producers of culture. So it is not that in the real world women are held in the mute position of chattels; it is his theory, his conceptualization of the social, that inscribes them in a discourse where they are doubly negated as subjects: first because they are vehicles of men's communication—signs of their language, carriers of their children; secondly because women's sexuality is reduced to the 'natural' function of childbearing, that is to say, to a capacity for production like that of a machine. Desire, like symbolization, is a property of men, property in both senses of the word—something men own, possess, and something that inheres in men, like a quality. Let me shift, briefly, to Lévi-Strauss' point of enunciation.

> The emergence of symbolic thought must have required that women, like words, should be things that were exchanged. In this new case, indeed, this was the only means of overcoming the contradiction by which the same woman was seen under two incompatible aspects: on the one hand, as the object of personal desire, thus exciting sexual and proprietorial instincts; and, on the other, as the subject [sic] of the desire of others, and seen as such, i.e., as the means of binding others through alliance with them.[9]

Who speaks in this text? The syntactic subject throughout is an abstract noun, 'the emergence of symbolic thought'; the verbs are mostly passive in form and conditional in mood, as if a pure language, scientifically hypothetical, value-free and subject-less, were speaking. And yet a speaking subject, an historical subject of enunciation, has left his footprints. Consider the sentence 'the same woman was seen . . . as the object of personal desire, thus exciting sexual and proprietorial instincts'; barring a homogeneously homosexual society (from which Lévi-Strauss could not have descended), the personal desire and the sexual and proprietorial instincts must be those of men, who are then the terms of reference for desire, sexuality, property—and for the adjective 'personal', women being in this case non-persons.

This woman, seen as 'the subject of the desire of others', is of course the very same character running naked through the city's streets. But if we asked the semiologist about the dream woman he would say that she is just that—a dream, a fantasy, an escape from reality, a movie. By now, years have passed, and the semiologist has been reading Lacan and forgotten Lévi-Strauss.

The city, he begins to think, is where the unconscious speaks, where its walls, arcades and stairways signify a subject appearing and disappearing in a dialectic of difference; upon entering the city, the traveler is taken up and shifted in the symbolic order of its layout, the disposition of buildings and empty spaces through which the traveler pursues imaginary reflections, apparitions, ghosts from the past. Here and there the traveler seems to recognize a certain place, stops for a moment, sutured; but that place is already another place, unfamiliar, different. And so, moving through the city—made hundreds of years ago but always new to each entering traveler and in continuous metamorphosis like the ocean of Lem's *Solaris*—the newcomer becomes a subject.

This is an interesting city indeed, thinks the semiologist, and she continues to read, she wants to know whether the traveler, having become a resident, so to speak, a subject-in-process through the city, can do anything to change some of its blatantly oppressive aspects, for example doing away with ghettos. But she finds out that the city is ruled by an agency, The Name of The Father, which alone undergoes no metamorphosis and in fact oversees and determines in advance all urban planning.

At this point the semiotician goes back to reread Lévi-Strauss, the essay entitled 'The Effectiveness of Symbols' in *Structural Anthropology,* and realizes that Lacan's conception of language as the symbolic register is forged on the trace of Lévi-Strauss' formulation of the unconscious as the organ of the 'symbolic function'; no longer located in the psyche, the Lévi-Straussian unconscious is a structuring process, a universal articulatory mechanism of the 'human mind', the structural condition of all symbolization.[10] Similarly, the Lacanian symbolic is the structure, the law which governs the distribution-circulation of signifiers, to which the child accedes in language, becoming a subject. In shifting the focus to the subject Lacan departs from Lévi-Strauss' structuralism, but the incest prohibition and structure of exchange guaranteed by the Name of the Father are still the conditions—a structural condition—of the subject's rite of passage through culture. It is that structure which psychoanalysis holds responsible for a non-coherence or division of the subject in language and theorizes as the function of castration. Again, as for Lévi-Strauss, the point of enunciation (and term of reference) of desire, drive and symbolization is a masculine one; for, even though castration is to be understood as a metaphor and referring to the symbolic dimension, its signifier, the phallus, can only be conceived as an extrapolation from the real body.[11] It follows that signification and subject processes are essentially phallic; in other words, they are *subject* processes *insofar* as they are instituted in a fixed order of language, the symbolic, by the function of castration.

'She' doesn't understand. She doesn't understand. On the one hand, sexual difference is supposed to be a meaning-effect produced in representation; on the other, paradoxically, it turns out to be the very support of representation. Once again, as in the theory of kinship, a single formula gives two inconsistent equations: woman = representation (woman as sign, woman as the phallus), and sexual difference = value founded in nature (woman as object of exchange, woman as the real, as Truth). That this inconsistency is a fundamental contradiction of both semiology and psychoanalysis, due to their common structural heritage, is confirmed by the recent work of Christian Metz.[12]

In 'The Imaginary Signifier' Metz shifts his investigation from the semiological study of the cinematic signifier (its matter and form of expression) to the 'psychoanalytic exploration of the signifier',[13] to the cinematic 'as a *signifier effect*'.[14] The great divide, in this exploration, is the Lacanian concept of the mirror stage, which generates the ambiguous notion of 'imaginary signifier'. In this text, the term signifier has a double status which corresponds to the two sides of the inconsistency mentioned earlier, and thus covers up a gap, a solution of continuity in Metzian discourse from linguistics to psychoanalysis. In the first part of the essay, his use of the term is consonant with the Saussurian notion of signifier; he speaks in fact of signifiers as 'coupled' to signifieds, of the film script as 'manifest signified', and of the 'manifest filmic material as a whole' including signifieds and signifiers.[15] Elsewhere, however, the cinema signifier is presented as a subject-effect, inaugurated in or instituted by the ego 'as transcendental yet radically deluded subject':[16]

> At the cinema ... I am the *all-perceiving* ... a great eye and ear without which the perceived would have no one to perceive it, the *constitutive* instance, in other words, of the cinema signifier (it is I who make the film).[17]

The filmic material as 'really perceived imaginary', as already imaginary and as object, becomes significant (becomes an imaginary signifier) to a perceiving subject in language. Metz thus abandons the signified as too naive a notion of meaning (with which Saussure himself was never concerned) only to include, to subsume meaning in the signifier. The problem with this notion of meaning is that, being coextensive with the signifier as a subject-effect, meaning can only be envisaged as always already given in that fixed order which is the symbolic. In this sense Laplanche and Pontalis can say that 'the phallus is found as a meaning, as what is symbolized in the most diverse representations';[18] as the signifier of desire, the phallus must also be its meaning, in fact, the only meaning to exist in the psyche. And so, caught between the devil and the deep blue sea, Metz in the last instance goes back to the equation of cinematic code(s) and language, now called the symbolic; he speaks of the 'mirror of the screen, a symbolic apparatus'[19] and of 'inflections peculiar to the work of the symbolic such as the order of "shots" or the role of "sound off" in some cinematic sub-code';[20] he returns, that is, to a systemic and linear notion of signification as approached by linguistics. What/where is semiotics in all this, one wonders.[21]

The double status of the Metzian signifier—as matter/form of expression and as subject-effect—covers but does not bridge a gap in which sits, temporarily eluded but not exorcised, the referent, the object, reality itself (the chair in the theater 'in the end' is a chair; Sarah Bernhardt 'at any rate' is Sarah Bernhardt—not her photograph; the child sees in the mirror 'its own body', a real object henceforth, therefore, *known* to be its own image as opposed to the 'imaginary' images on the screen, and so on).[22] In the linguistic model, that gap, the substantial discontinuity between discourse and reality can neither be bridged nor its terrain mapped. On the contrary, the project of semiotic theory has been precisely such mapping: how the physical properties of bodies are socially assumed as signs, as vehicles for social meaning, and how these signs are culturally generated by codes and subject to historical modes of sign production. Lévi-Strauss retained the linguistic conceptual framework in his analysis of kinship and myth as semantic structures, and Lacan reinscribed that structuration in subject processes. This is why, finally, the psychoanalytic vision of the cinema, in spite of Metz' effort, still poses 'woman' as telos and origin of a phallic desire, as dream woman forever pursued and forever held at a distance, seen and invisible, on another scene. Object and sign, image and representation, woman is 'cinema's object of desire', the 'sole imaginary' of the film. Like the city of Zobeide, these discourses specify 'woman' in a particular social and natural order; this is the tale they tell of cinema and its foundation: '. . . men of various nations had an identical dream. They saw a woman running at night through an unknown city; she was naked, with long hair, and she was seen from behind . . .' (because, naturally, the sex of the woman is invisible).

After hearing the story once again, the semiotician thought: what this theory cannot countenance, given its phallic premise, is the possibility of a different relation of the spectator-subject to the filmic image, of different meaning-effects being produced for and producing the subject in identification and representation; in short, the possibility of other subject processes obtaining in that relation.

The importance of psychoanalysis for the study of cinema and of film is not to be denied; it has served to dislodge cinematic theory from the scientistic, even mechanistic enterprise of a structural semiology and urged upon it the instance of the subject, its construction and representations, in cinematic signification—just as the historical importance of semiology was to affirm the existence of coding rules, and thus of a socially constructed reality, there where a transcendental reality, nature, had been supposed to manifest itself. However, the hierarchical setting up of 'language' as universal model, which was the error of classical semiology, is also the structural heritage of Lacanian theory. To repeat once again, in the former the language of linguistics was the privileged model for all signification systems and their 'internal' mechanisms; in the latter the symbolic as phallic structure is taken as the primary model of subject processes. If and when either of those models is immediately, unmediatedly transferred to the cinema (generating statements like 'cinema is the language of reality' or 'cinema is the imaginary, death at work, the dream machine in Plato's cave' and so on), certain problems are voided and avoided, excluded from the theoretical discourse or disposed of within it.

For example, the problem of materiality: while the material heterogeneity of the cinema in relation to language is readily asserted, the possibility that diverse forms of semiotic productivity, different modes of sign production, may entail other subject processes has not been seriously considered. Then there is the problem of the concrete historicity of language, of cinema, and of the other apparati of representation, their uneven ratios of development, their specific modes of address, their particular relations to practice—and their combined effects in subject construction.

Many have argued for Lacan's project as a materialist theory of language, or a materialist rewriting of the idealist discourse on love from Plato on;[23] but where a dialectic is certainly the movement of the subject's passage through language, and thus of its 'personal' history, it is not obvious to me that that dialectic is a historical materialist one; in a preestablished structural order, a logic of the signifier, that is always already determined for each entering subject, the personal history ends up being written with a capital H.

As I walk, invisible and captive, through the city, I keep thinking that the questions of signification, representation and subject processes in cinema must be reformulated from a less rigid, less static view of meaning than is fixed by psychoanalytic theory—and I will return to this shortly; secondly, that a material theory of subjectivity cannot start out from a given notion of subject, but can only approach the subject asymptotically, as it were, through the apparati, the social technologies in which it is constructed. Those apparati are distinct, if not disparate, in their specificity and concrete historicity, which is why their co-participation, their combined effect in subject production, though undeniable, cannot be easily assessed. For example, while the novel, the cinema, and television are all 'family machines', they cannot simply be equated with one another; as social technologies aimed at reproducing, among other things, the institution family, they do overlap to a certain degree, but the amount of overlap or redundancy involved is offset, precisely, by their material and semiotic specificity; so that the family that watches together is really an other institution, or better, the subject produced in the family that watches tv is not the same social subject produced in families that only read novels or listen to the radio. Another example: the reworking of visual perspective codes into a narrative space in sound films[24] certainly recreates some of the subject-effects of perspectival painting, but no one would seriously think that Renaissance painting and Hollywood cinema, as social apparati, address one and the same subject in ideology.

Now, language is certainly one such social apparatus, and perhaps a universally dominant one; but before we elect it to absolute representative of subject-ive formations, we ought to ask: what language? The language of linguistics is not the language of psychoanalysis; the plain language fantasized by some literary and film critics is not the fantasmatic language of others; language we hear in the film is not the language spoken in the theater; and the language we speak outside the movie theater can not be quite the same language that was spoken on Plymouth Rock. The point is too obvious to belabor; to put it briefly, after all the work done on the forming influence of visual codes like perspective, the still and motion cameras, etc., can one really think that the various forms of mechanical reproduction of language (visual and sound), and its incorporation into practically all apparati of representation have no impact on its social and subject-ive effects? (In this respect, we should consider not only the question of internal speech in film but also, reciprocally, the possible question of an internal sight or vision in language, both of which invoke the problem of the relation of language to sensory perception, of what Freud called word-presentation and thing-presentation in the interplay of primary and secondary processes.)[25]

If cinema can be said to be 'a language' it is precisely because language *is* not; that is, language is not a unified field, outside of specific discourses like linguistics or the *Village Voice*. There are 'languages', discourses, discursive apparati that produce meanings; and there are different modes of semiotic production, ways in which labor is invested in the production of signs and meanings. The types of labor invested, and the modes of production involved, it seems to me, are directly, materially, relevant to the constitution of subjects in ideology—class subjects, race subjects, sexed subjects, and any other differential category that may have political use-value for particular situations of practice at particular historical moments.

Here again, a year ago, it was pointed out that, if language can be considered an apparatus, like cinema, producing meanings through physical means (the body, the articulatory and hearing organs, the brain), cinematic enunciation is more expensive than speech. True enough. That observation underscores once more the irreducible heterogeneity of cinema and language as signifying practices; but the single economic parameter is not sufficient to define what may be called modes of sign production. The problem is not, or not just, that cinema operates with many different matters of expression and more 'expensive', less available 'machinery' than 'natural' language; the problem is, rather, that meanings are not produced *in* a particular film but 'meanings circulate between social formation, spectator and film'.[26] The production of meanings, I rephrase, always involves not simply a specific apparatus of representation but at least several. While each can be described analytically, in its matters of expression or its social-economic conditions of production (for example, the technological or economic modalities of, say, sound cinema), what is at issue is the possibility to account for their joint hold on the spectator and, *thus*, the production of meanings for a subject and/or of a subject in meaning across a plurality of discourses. If, to put it bluntly and circuitously at the same time, the subject is where meanings are formed and meanings constitute the subject, the notion of semiotic productivity must include that of modes of production; and so 'the question of how semantic values are constructed, read and located in history' becomes a most pertinent question.[27]

You may have noticed that in the last few sentences I have carefully avoided using the term code and used, instead, the word apparatus. I do have my reasons. The notion of code, somewhat emarginated by current film theory after its heyday in semiology, has been importantly redefined in Eco's *A Theory of Semiotics*. I would like to discuss it now, in connection with what I proposed earlier: that cinematic theory must displace the questions of representation and subject construction from the procrustean bed of phallic signification; that we must seek, that is, other ways of mapping the terrain in which meanings are produced.

In the structural formulation of classical semiology, a code was construed to be a system of oppositional values (Saussure's *langue*, or Metz' code of cinematic punctuation) regardless or upstream of the meanings produced contextually in enunciation and reception; 'meanings' (Saussure's signifieds) were supposed to be subsumed in, and in a stable relationship to, the respective signifiers. So defined, a code could be envisaged and described, like a structure, independently of any communicative purpose and apart from an actual situation of signification. For Eco this is not a code but a structure, a system; whereas a code is a significant *and* communicational framework linking differential elements on the expression plane with semantic elements on the content plane or behavioral responses. In the same manner, a sign is not a fixed semiotic entity (the relatively stable union of a signifier and a signified) but a 'sign-function', the mutual and transitory correlation of two functives which he calls 'sign-vehicle' (the physical component of the sign, on the expression plane) and 'cultural unit' (a semantic unit on the content plane). What is important to note here is that the latter, the content of the sign-vehicle, is also a unit in a semantic system—not necessarily a *binary* system—of oppositional values.

Each culture, says Eco, segments the continuum of experience 'making certain units pertinent and understanding others merely as variants, "allophones" '.[28]

> When it is said that the expression /Evening star/ denotes a certain large physical 'object' of a spherical form, which travels through space some scores of millions of miles from the Earth one should in fact say that: the expression in question denotes 'a certain' corresponding *cultural unit* to which the speaker refers, and which she has accepted in the way described by the culture in which she lives, without having ever experienced the real referent. So much is this so that only the logician knows that the expression in question has the same denotatum as has the expression /Morning star/. Whoever emitted or received this latter sign-vehicle thought that there were *two different things*. And she was right in the sense that the cultural codes to which she referred provided for two different cultural units. Her social life did not develop on the basis of things but on the basis of cultural units. Or rather, for her as for us, things were only known through cultural units which the universe of communication put into circulation *in place of things*.[29]

Even within a single culture, most semantic fields disintegrate very quickly (unlike the field of colors or kinship terms which have been studied systematically precisely because, in addition to being made up of highly structured cultural units, they have been, like syntax or phonemic structure, durable systems); and most semantic fields are constantly restructured by movements of acculturation and critical revision; that is, they are subject to a process of change due to contradictions within each system and/or to the appearance of new material events outside the system. Now, if cultural units can be recognized by virtue of their opposition to one another in various semantic systems, and can be identified or isolated by the (indefinite) series of their interpretants, then they can be considered to some extent independently of the systemic or structural organizations of the sign-vehicles. This makes it possible to envisage a nonlinear semantic space constructed by the multilevel interaction of many heterogeneous sign-vehicles and cultural units—the codes being the networks of their correlations *across* the planes of content and expression. In other words, signification may involve several systems, superimposed or juxtaposed to one another; but the 'plurality of codes' that characterizes textual processes works vertically, not horizontally. What distinguishes this notion of code is that both planes, expression and content, are assumed at once in the relationship of meaning. Thus it appears to be very close to the notion of cinematic apparatus that was proposed here last year: not a technical *dispositif* (e.g., the camera) but a social technology, a *relation* of the technical *and* the social, the physical-material sign-vehicle and the cultural meaning.

For our purposes, this poses the possibility of approaching signification processes from the content plane, taking cultural units as starting points and following them along the paths and modes of their inscription in specific sign-vehicles and through particular apparati (codes) of representation. Thus, that dream woman who is both the creation and the foundation of Calvino's city is a content inscribed in the work of the text; but if we have recognized it as a *cultural* meaning, it is because that content is also inscribed, in a thousand and one ways, in other texts and discourses of our culture. The inscription is a matter of codes; it is not yet a meaning. In my tentative definition, meanings differ from Eco's cultural units, as they differ from Saussure's signifieds, because they are functions of a subject, and not simply a subject of enunciation, a producer of sign-vehicles as Eco's 'subject of semiosis' appears to be; but a subject located and dislocated in the points of intersection of the codes, constituted and displaced, so to speak, in the spaces between signs.

I have no picture of the city where that subject would live. For me, historical woman, discourse cannot cohere, perhaps must not cohere. Perhaps what matters now is that we find a way for the subject to exceed the codes, to elude representation, not to be captured. And so it may be that the subject must remain the horizon of a materialist semiotics, and of a historical materialist theory of the cinema—but a horizon may make all the difference in the world.

NOTES

1. I. Calvino, *Invisible Cities*, trans. W. Weaver (New York: Harcourt Brace Jovanovich, 1974), pp. 45-46. I have slightly changed Weaver's translation of the last two lines in order to avoid the misunderstanding made possible by his wording, 'the first to arrive'; see Calvino, *Le città invisibili* (Torino: Einaudi, 1972), p. 52.

2. T. de Lauretis, 'Semiotic Models, *Invisible Cities*', *Yale Italian Studies* vol. 2 no. 1 (Winter 1978), pp. 13-37.

3. T. de Lauretis and S. Heath (eds.), *The Cinematic Apparatus* (London: Macmillan, 1980), in particular T. de Lauretis, 'Through the Looking-Glass', pp. 187-203.

4. A. Kuhn and A. Wolpe (eds.), *Feminism and Materialism: Woman and Modes of Production* (London: Routledge & Kegan Paul, 1978), p. 3.

5. For a preliminary discussion of this 'historical switch' in the context of Italy, see T. de Lauretis, 'Semiotics, Theory and Social Practice', *Ciné-Tracts* 5 (Fall 1978), pp. 1-14.

6. R. Jakobson, 'Closing Statement: Linguistics and Poetics', in *Style in Language,* T. Sebeok (ed.), (Cambridge, Massachusetts: MIT Press, 1960), p. 368.

7. Each city in Calvino's book is named after a fictional woman. Zobeide is mentioned in *The Thousand and One Nights* as wife to the Caliph of Baghdad, Harun al-Rashid.

8. C. Lévi-Strauss, *The Elementary Structures of Kinship* (Boston, Massachusetts: Beacon Press, 1969); for a more developed criticism of his positioning of woman see E. Cowie, 'Woman as Sign', *m/f* 1 (1978), pp. 49-63 and T. de Lauretis, 'Through the Looking-Glass'.

9. Ibid., p. 496.

10. C. Lévi-Strauss, *Structural Anthropology* (Garden City, New York: Anchor Books, 1967), pp. 181-201.

11. The ambiguity in the phallus/penis relation is emphasized by J. Laplanche and J.-B. Pontalis in *Vocabulaire de la psychanalyse* (Paris: PUF, 1967); see also S. Heath, 'Difference', *Screen* vol. 19 no. 3 (Autumn 1978), pp. 50-112, and A. Wilden, 'Critique of Phallocentrism', in *System and Structure* (London: Tavistock, 1972), pp. 278-301.

12. C. Metz, *Le Signifiant imaginaire* (Paris: Union Générale d'Editions, 1977); references here are to the English translation by B. Brewster, 'The Imaginary Signifier', *Screen* vol. 16 no. 2 (Summer 1975), pp. 14-76.

13. Ibid., p. 46.

14. Ibid., p. 42.

15. Ibid., pp. 38-40.

16. Ibid., p. 54.

17. Ibid., p. 51.

18. Laplanche and Pontalis, op. cit., quoted in the translation by P. Kussell and J. Mehlman in *Yale French Studies* 48 (1972), p. 199.

19. Metz, p. 59.

20. Ibid., p. 29.

21. After stating, at the beginning of 'The Imaginary Signifier', that 'the psychoanalytic itinerary is *from the outset a semiological one*' (p. 14), Metz then singles out linguistics and psychoanalysis as sciences of the symbolic *par excellence*, 'the only two sciences whose immediate and sole object is the fact of signification as such' (p. 28), which specifically explore, respectively, the secondary and the primary processes, and 'between them . . . cover the whole field of the *signification-fact*' (p. 28). Where, then, does semiotics stand in relation to the fact of signification? What is the position, or the theoretical object, of semiotics in relation to linguistics and to psychoanalysis?

22. Metz, pp. 47-49.

23. For example, J. Brenkman, 'The Other and the One: Psychoanalysis, Reading, the *Symposium*', *Yale French Studies* 55/56 (1977), pp. 396-456.

24. S. Heath, 'Narrative Space', *Screen* vol. 17 no. 3 (Autumn 1976), pp. 68-112.

25. P. Willemen, 'Reflections on Eikhenbaum's Concept of Internal Speech in the Cinema', *Screen* vol. 15 no. 4 (Winter 1974/5), pp. 59-70.

26. S. Heath, 'Notes on Suture', *Screen* vol. 18 no. 4 (Winter 1977/8), p. 48-76.

27. P. Willemen, 'Notes on Subjectivity', *Screen* vol. 19 no. 1 (Spring 1978), p. 43.

28. U. Eco, *A Theory of Semiotics* (London: Macmillan, 1977), p. 78. This is one reason why translation presents problems and why a film can be read so differently in different cultures or viewing situations, e.g. Antonioni's controversial 'documentary' on China discussed by Eco in an interview with William Luhr in *Wide Angle* vol. 1 no. 4 (1977), pp. 64-72.

29. Ibid., pp. 65-66. The quotation has been slightly edited.

The Film's Time and the Spectator's 'Space'

Mary Ann Doane

I would like to focus attention on certain points, within the boundaries of what has been labeled the classical Hollywood text, which might be described as witticisms. The witticisms of the classical text mark the places where its language is not 'straight' but deviates—where the trope *irony* best characterizes the work of the signifying materials. My purpose is to locate a pleasure which is not that guaranteed by an imaginary signifier. This is not necessarily a pleasure which is 'proper' in any sense to the classical text but it is nevertheless, and very importantly, a potential resource of the enunciation.

The tropological work of irony is isolated here not in the interests of describing the purity of a particular rhetorical strategy but as a point of entry to a discussion of certain difficulties in the contemporary application of psychoanalysis in film theory—difficulties which revolve around problems of determination, of models of the spatialization of the subject/spectator and thus of psychical effectivity, and, more particularly, of the mechanism of identification in the cinema. The most influential account of cinematic identification is that provided by Christian Metz in his essay 'The Imaginary Signifier'.

Drawing heavily on the work of Jean-Louis Baudry, Metz there maintains that the 'primary cinematic identification' is the spectator's identification with his or her own look and is, consequently, an identification with the camera:

> ... the spectator *identifies with himself*, as a pure act of perception (as wakefulness, alertness): as condition of possibility of the perceived and hence as a kind of transcendental subject, anterior to every *there is* ...
> And it is true that as he identifies with himself as look, the spectator can do no other than identify with the camera, too, which has looked before

him at what he is now looking at and whose *post* (= framing) determines
the vanishing point.[1]

In this account, the identification with the look/camera is not unlike the
identification of the Lacanian mirror phase. Although the screen upon which
the film is projected, different from a mirror, reflects everything *but* the
subject, in both cases the subject constitutes itself, through the gaze, as a
coherent and homogeneous unity. The film viewer, according to Metz, is
positioned by the entire cinematic apparatus as the site of an organization—
the viewer lends coherence to the image ('as condition of possibility of the
perceived') and is simultaneously posited as a coherent entity ('a kind of
transcendental subject').

In this description, the image acts as the unit of analysis and the initial
look at the screen is founding. The question has thus been one of positioning,
of placing—'Where is the spectator at this moment in the unfolding of the
text?' Metz puts the spectator in the place of the camera but that place, more
importantly, presupposes a figurative space—one of homogeneity, unity, and
coherence. In the mirror stage, this unity is discovered in the security of the
reflected image of the body. In the cinema, it is guaranteed by the omnipo-
tence of the eye. The question—'Where is the spectator, how is he/she
positioned?'—is heavily dependent upon the topographical model of Freud.
The spectator of the cinema is constituted as the site of a fusion of the two
spaces of the subject: the space of consciousness and the space of the unconscious. A spatial metaphor, then, sustains this description of identification.
But perhaps the question might be posed in a different way, from a different
direction—not *where* is the subject but *when* is the subject? In pursuing this
question, I would like to shift attention from the image as unit to the scene, in
order to trace a necessary cleavage between the two looks—the look of the
camera and the look of the spectator. In the measure to which the image is
understood as belonging to, inscribed within, a scene, temporality (of both
subject and scene) is introduced.

The witticisms or ironies of the classical text cannot be understood
through recourse to spatial metaphors. For irony is a trope which operates
across time. I am not referring here to irony in its looser sense as a tone but to
its much more specific function as a trope—a trope whose significance has
been elided by the dominant concern with metaphor and metonymy as the
master tropes. Metz, for instance, expands the respective fields covered by
metonymy and metaphor until they are large enough to include the other
tropes.[2] Metaphor and irony, despite the fact that Metz defines them as
opposites (metaphor names a relation of similarity, irony one of contrast or
opposition) are grouped together under metaphor defined at a higher level as
a relation of comparability. Metz' gesture in reducing the number of pertinent
tropes repeats that which marks the history of rhetoric, leading to the gradual
restriction of its field and a diminishing of the figurative potential of language. Genette has shown how, from Dumarsais to Jakobson, this 'restricted

rhetoric' manifests a stronger and stronger predilection for sensory figures, resulting in a valorization of the spatial relation of contiguity and the relation of analogy. It is the non-sensory or 'intellectual' figures such as antiphrasis, litotes, hyperbole and irony that are eliminated. For Genette, modern rhetoric restricts 'the play of figures to their physical or sensible aspect alone'.[3] And yet, irony does not rest as easily beneath metaphor as Metz would imply. The broadest definition of irony is that of figurative language in general—in irony, as in metaphor or metonymy, 'saying' and 'meaning' do not coincide. But in the other tropes, this non-coincidence exists only so that, ultimately, the two may supplement one another. While the other tropes exist in the service of cognition, of the construction of a meaning inaccessible to 'proper' language (mythical as that may be), the effect of irony is one of negation. Irony leaves no residue of meaning but presents itself as a performance which props itself upon other tropological constructions. As Paul de Man maintains, irony constitutes itself negatively as the 'undoing' of 'tropological cognition'.[4] If irony is sustained throughout a discourse, it is 'sustained' not in the sense of building a duration, but as a repetition of an interruption. Irony interrupts the expectations of a given grammatical and rhetorical movement and, in doing so, denies the claim of tropological discourse to knowledge and truth.

The first instance of irony which I would like to isolate acts in a confrontation with the heavily codified use of the dissolve in the psychological film. The knowledge to which this kind of dissolve lays claim is a knowledge of the 'inner reality' of a character. Early in Hitchcock's *Spellbound*, it becomes evident that Dr. Constance Peterson (a young psychoanalyst played by Ingrid Bergman) is attracted to 'Dr. Edwards' (the man she believes to be the new director of Green Manors, played by Gregory Peck) despite the fact that she is portrayed initially as a frigid intellectual woman. She finally submits to this attraction in a scene in 'Dr. Edwards' room. Constance enters the room believing that she came to discuss 'Dr. Edwards' book with him but ultimately admits that she is 'amazed' at her own 'subterfuge'. Their conversation at this point is depicted through a shot/reverse shot construction in which each character successively 'frames' the other through an open doorway which separates the two of them. 'Dr. Edwards' walks through the doorway and there is a cut to a close-up of Constance. In a closer shot of 'Dr. Edwards', he moves forward toward the camera and a subjective shot from his point of view, a track in to an extreme close-up of Constance's eyes, follows. After a parallel shot of 'Dr. Edwards' eyes, this close-up is repeated. Constance slowly closes her eyes and the image dissolves to a shot of a long corridor in which doors swing open one after another to reveal a brightly lit 'exterior'. The doors then dissolve to a shot of the two kissing.

It is to the first dissolve that I would like to draw attention. The dissolve is one of the few cinematic devices which has been subjected to a kind of grammatical codification. Through habitual use in the narrative film, the dissolve has come to designate either a temporal or spatial change (or both)—hence its frequent appearance as a transition between two sequences. Within a sequence, it is specifically related to time when it introduces a memory and to space when it moves us from the outside of a building or house to a room inside. It is this spatial movement which leaves its imprint on (or rather, provides the premise for) the association of the dissolve with psychology. In order to *see* the thoughts of a character, we must make the *visible* movement from 'outside' to 'inside' the character's head and the visibility of that transgression of a certain limit is sustained by the dissolve. Whether or not the thoughts portrayed receive a temporal specification (as memory or prophecy), the 'psychological' dissolve is always supported by a spatial dislocation—from outside to inside—revealing another scene.

The dissolve in *Spellbound* bases itself, at least initially, upon this 'grammatical' intelligibility and consistency. A 'straight' reading of the sequence would lean on the traditional psychological implications of the dissolve: the device signifies a movement from outside to inside Constance's mind (and this is reinforced by the fact that she closes her eyes—we are, in effect, presented with an introverted point of view shot). Furthermore, the depiction of her inner 'thoughts' as the image of a series of opening doors suggests the initiation of a new psychological state of freedom (the movement is reversed—it is now from inside to outside and a bright light appears as the last door swings open). However, this reading of the dissolve is complicated by the fact that doors are not unmarked in the film. In fact, the signification of the doors is anchored by the opening title (superimposed, significantly, over the door of Green Manors):

> Our story deals with psychoanalysis, the method by which modern science treats the emotional problems of the sane. The analyst seeks only to induce the patient to talk about his hidden problems, to open the locked doors of his mind.

The act of opening doors is transformed into a metaphor within the textual system—a metaphor for the psychoanalytic session. The sequence just described thus constitutes a *literal* reading of the opening title, and the irony lies in the consequent equation of the psychoanalytic session and a love scene which are somewhat arbitrarily yoked together (the kiss becomes a cure—and it is the psychoanalyst who is ill). The dissolve is given a temporal specification, but the time to which it refers is a textual one (that of the opening title). Similarly, the work of spatialization performed by the dissolve is initially the conventional relocation from outer 'reality' to inner 'reality'. Yet the construction of an inner space is aborted by the immediate reversal of direction—the doors swing from inside to outside. Furthermore, the tropological status of the act of opening doors is not entirely dependent upon the opening title. The phrase 'to open a door' receives an extra-textual codification through its habitual use in verbal language. It is, in effect, a clichéd metaphor of crude psychology. The fact that the image presents not one door opening but a series of doors down a long narrow corridor situates the image as an overly obvious 'Freudian' symbol as well. The dissolve refers itself to another, heavily overdetermined text. It displaces sexuality, but does so through recourse to an obvious symbol of that sexuality, thus disrupting its own momentum.

In addition, doors are not simply invoked as metaphoric in the opening title but are a continual obsession of the film. The inside/outside dichotomy, embodied in the repetitious shots of doors in *Spellbound*, is, in fact, the dilemma of the film which attempts to be psychological: the cinema does not provide many means of signifying 'inner reality' (the dissolve and the voice-over are among the few devices appropriated for this purpose). One tends, instead, to think of the cinema as being concerned largely with surfaces—the camera cannot get 'inside' the character. The dissolve, effecting a dissolution of the body in favor of the emergence of the mind, together with the movement from outside to inside, constitutes a point at which the 'straining' of the psychological film becomes evident. But this straining is concealed by the grammatical rules which provide the spectator with a clear and unquestioned reading. In *Spellbound*, the dissolve refers the spectator back to yet another trope, the metaphor invoked in the opening title (as well as the extra-textual metaphor), and, in so doing, points to the dissolve structure's inability to support its own codified meaning. For the dissolve reveals only doors which reverse its own directional force—doors which monopolize the 'outer reality' of most of the film. The opposition inside/outside, the support of the psychological dissolve, is blurred (together with several other oppositions at work in the film: sickness/health, patient/doctor, love/reason). The grammatical 'rules' concerning the dissolve are not simply forgotten: they are pushed to their limit, interrogated, and ultimately transformed into a kind of joke about their own operation.

The knowledge of character which is conventionally ensured by the psychological dissolve is withheld from the spectator, if only momentarily. Irony thus forces a certain eccentricity of the subject with respect to the image which fails to *hold* its truth by conforming to the logic of a grammar. It is in this way that irony can, indeed, be described as Metz describes it—as the opposite of metaphor. Metaphor operates by orchestrating the elements of language in a construction of sense; irony works in the opposite direction. While Metz goes on ultimately to recombine the two tropes under the 'higher' unity of similarity, resistance to such recombination finds support in a revealing comment by Lacan in 'The Insistence of the Letter in the Unconscious':

> ... metaphor occurs at the precise point at which sense comes out of non-sense, that is, at that frontier which, as Freud discovered, when crossed the other way produces what we generally call 'wit' *(Witz)*; it is at this frontier that we can glimpse the fact that man tempts his very destiny when he derides the signifier.[5]

Irony aligns itself with the witticism because it can be located on the other side of that frontier of signification which Lacan demarcates. It is the witticism or joke as described by Freud in *Jokes and Their Relation to the*

Unconscious which the tropological work of irony most closely resembles and it is that text which provides the most accessible point of entry for an examination of the effect of irony upon the spectator. How then does Freud describe the psychical effectivity of the joke? In what does its pleasure consist?

Jokes and Their Relation to the Unconscious may at first dismay the reader because, in it, Freud repeats the familiar gesture by means of which all psychical events are traced to their 'origins' in childhood. The pleasure derived from the joke is said to be a repetition of the childish pleasure of play which escapes the constraints of reason and criticism; the essential characteristic of the joke thus being its renunciation of rational meaning, its ability to locate pleasure in pure nonsense. But this analysis of the joke-work is made more complex when Freud traces the evolution or the 'psychogenesis' of jokes through three stages: play, the jest, and the joke. Play in childhood, which foreshadows the adult's joke, is associated with a pleasure derived from repetition, recognition, and a kind of 'economy'. In play, according to Freud, children

> come across pleasurable effects, which arise from a repetition of what is similar, a rediscovery of what is familiar, similarity of sound, etc., and which are to be explained as unsuspected economies in psychical expenditure. It is not to be wondered at that these pleasurable effects encourage children in the pursuit of play and cause them to continue it without regard for the meaning of words or the coherence of sentences. *Play* with words and thoughts, motivated by certain pleasurable effects of economy, would thus be the first stage of jokes.[6]

The second stage in the evolution of the joke is the 'jest', which responds to the child's development of a critical faculty which makes pure play impossible. As the child grows older, play is 'rejected as being meaningless or absurd'.[7] The jest succeeds in overcoming this critical judgment by giving the play a façade of meaning. The meaning does not have to be new or valuable— it simply functions to make the fundamental nonsense of play permissible. The joke, as the third and final stage, continues this evasion of the obstacle posed by criticism but in a more refined way—'If what a jest says possesses substance and value, it turns into a joke'.[8] The joke, therefore, works with two necessarily contradictory aims: that of re-evoking the childish pleasure in nonsense and that of making this nonsense possible by overlaying it with a meaning. Apparently, the joke must be 'impure' in this way in order to succeed.

Yet, while the origin and end of the joke are located by Freud in the 'economy' or reduction of psychic energy which is characteristic of children's play, this is clearly not the same kind of economy or pleasure which Freud had already introduced in *The Interpretation of Dreams*. As Samuel Weber points out in a provocative rereading of *Jokes and Their Relation to the Unconscious* (a rereading to which this paper is greatly indebted), the Freudian notion of pleasure is characterized above all by the fact that it is '*conflictual* in nature, involving not absolute quanta of energy . . . but a relation of forces, a state of tension . . .'.[9] In Freud's description of the childhood play recaptured by the joke, however, pleasure is the result of a simple saving of energy. Moreover, the pleasure of play resides in its toleration of nonsense, its opposition to rational cognition. Yet that pleasure is also described as arising from 'a repetition of what is similar' and 'a rediscovery of what is familiar'—in short, a type of re-*cognition*. According to Weber, this difficulty emerges because Freud's description of the pleasure associated with the joke neglects the concept of conflict, 'in whose force field the joke is necessarily situated':

> Behind the semblance of unmediated exteriority, therefore, Freud's notion of play reveals itself to be the mirror-image of its apparent other: rational cognition. And if this is so, it is because both cognition and play, as Freud describes them, involve the solitary activity of a subject engaged in the process of developing its consciousness as self-consciousness. The cognitive pleasure of play, in this version, far from being the simple antithesis of critical reason, is its purest manifestation: its pleasure is the pleasure of consciousness. And more precisely, that of the ego in ascertaining its own *identity*.[10]

The element of conflict, so integral to the Freudian notion of pleasure, is not totally absent in Freud's description of the joke which, unlike the play of childhood of 'the comic', is a social event and can only operate successfully within a dialogical relationship established between teller and listener. The pleasure of both teller and listener is guaranteed by the laughter of the latter (who, in Freud's terminology, is actually the 'third person'—the 'second person' is the subject matter or object of the joke). It is in Freud's analysis of the type of joke paradigmatic for the evocation of pleasure—the dirty joke or smut—that the conflict which is so essential to the Freudian conception of pleasure reenters the scenario of the joke.

Smut, according to Freud, is 'originally directed towards women and may be equated with attempts at seduction'.[11] The man uses words as a means to excite the woman. Sexuality is deflected onto the play of signs. The initial purpose is actually an *exposure* of the woman—a purpose which Freud traces back to 'one of the original components of the libido', that is, 'a desire to see the organs peculiar to each sex exposed', in other words, scopophilia.[12] If the man encounters resistance on the part of the woman, the sexual drive is colored by aggressivity and the words become obscenities. This is not yet, however, a dirty joke. In order for a dirty joke to emerge in its specificity, the object of desire—the woman—must be absent and a third person (another man) must be present as witness to the joke, 'so that gradually, in place of the woman, the onlooker, now the listener, becomes the person to whom the smut is addressed . . .'.[13] The status of the woman is both that of the repressed addressee and that of the figure latent in the narrated content. Henceforth it is clear that 'where the *Witz* is concerned, the pleasure of the first person will be mediated by, and dependent on, that of the third . . .'.[14] The third person, through his laughter or its absence, makes the essential decision as to whether the joke is, in fact, a joke, whether it is successful or not. In a sense, therefore, the third person determines the status of the first—the third person confirms, through his laughter, the fact that the first is, indeed, a joke-teller, an author, an ego.[15] The structure of the joke is thus essentially narcissistic, and it is in that narcissism that the joke recapitulates the pleasure of childhood play. The joke acts as a reconfirmation of the coherence, unity, and homogeneity of the subject. And it does so in an extremely sophisticated manner—through the process of story-telling.

At the same time there is an alternative form of signifying practice which makes its appearance in *Jokes and Their Relation to the Unconscious*, and which must be distinguished from the jest and the joke as Freud describes them. The jest and the joke require a façade of meaning, however thin, in order to circumvent the censorship of the critical faculty. In fact, Freud distinguishes between the 'good joke', the 'bad joke', and the jest on the basis of the value of that meaning. Nevertheless, the primary aim of the joke, it will be recalled, is to recapture the pleasure of meaningless play: the essence of the joke lies in its ability to *avoid* meaning, to call forth its other. There is still another kind of joke, however, whose relationship to meaning is decisive. Although this type is dealt with only marginally (in a footnote added by Freud in 1912), its significance lies in a relationship between teller and listener which is fundamentally different from that of the joke proper. Freud first describes these 'jokes' as 'productions resembling jokes',[16] in other words, as the simulacra of jokes: '. . . they rouse the expectation of a joke, so that one tries to find a concealed sense behind the nonsense. But one finds none: they really are nonsense'.[17] Yet these jokes are not entirely nonsensical since they have a purpose which resides in the relationship established between teller and listener:

> These jokes are not entirely without a purpose; they are a 'take-in' [*Aufsitzer*], and give the person who tells them a certain amount of pleasure in misleading and annoying his hearer. The latter then damps down his annoyance by determining to tell them himself later on.[18]

Freud refers to this kind of joke as an *Aufsitzer* because it 'dupes' the listener, depriving him of that residue of meaning guaranteed by the joke. The listener's only choice is 'to assume his duplicity, by ceasing to listen and beginning to tell: another story, another *Aufsitzer*'.[19] Clearly, the effect of the *Aufsitzer* is quite different from that reconfirmation of the ego which can be associated with the joke proper. The laughter of the joke marks its completion as an organically unified narrative. The joke conforms to the tenets of information theory: the content or material of the joke is passed from sender to receiver and the success of the joke depends upon whether the listener 'gets' it (that is, understands it by matching, repeating the understanding of the teller). In the *Aufsitzer*, however, there is nothing to 'get'. The narrator dupes the listener by refusing to fulfill his desire for this kind of understanding. All that is 'communicated' is the desire to repeat a performance, the desire to move from the position of narratee to that of narrator.

It is here that we can leave Freud's text to return to irony—for it is in the *Aufsitzer* that we find the point of intersection of an analysis of ironical discourse with *Jokes and Their Relation to the Unconscious*. It is not *Witz* (the joke) which fully crosses that frontier Lacan mentions (the frontier which, in the case of metaphor, pinpoints the emergence of sense out of nonsense) but the *Aufsitzer*. As Freud stresses, the *Aufsitzer*, unlike the joke which is always an impure form, 'really is nonsense'. It is necessary, however, to avoid the pejorative connotations of the term nonsense; it would be better to follow Weber and replace 'nonsense' with 'sense-less'.[20] The *Aufsitzer* is indifferent to sense, to knowledge or cognition as we normally view them. It makes use of the purely formal mechanisms of producing sense without ever presenting us with the final product. We can see, by reinvoking the example of the dissolve sequence in *Spellbound*, that irony also functions in this way. The sequence utilizes the grammatical codification of the dissolve as well as a rhetorical figure already established by the film (the metaphor in which the psychoanalytic session is represented by the act of opening doors). Yet the dissolve ultimately effects a deconstruction of that grammar and that rhetorical figure—the opposition between inside and outside which supports the psychological dissolve is dismantled while the application of the metaphor's 'vehicle' (the act of opening doors) to a 'tenor' which rearranges and confuses the first (the 'tenor' is no longer the psychoanalytic session but a love scene between psychoanalyst and patient) renders the work of the metaphor absurd. The dissolve culminates, therefore, not in knowledge, meaning or sense, but in sheer performance—a performance which is that of the *Aufsitzer*. Irony is indeed analogous to the *Aufsitzer*, for it places itself at the service of something other than rational cognition. The dissolve in *Spellbound*, by offering resistance to the film's own metaphor, constitutes an 'undoing' of 'tropological cognition'.

Another example can be found in the same film—one that demonstrates even more clearly irony's alliance with the *Aufsitzer*—in a scene which leans heavily upon one of the most clichéd scenarios of Hollywood film: the walk of two lovers through a beautiful country setting. The fake 'Dr. Edwards', in the hope of temporarily getting away from the psychoanalytic institution and becoming better acquainted with Constance, extends the following invitation to her: 'We'll look at some sane trees, normal grass and clouds without complexes'. In the scene itself, these 'trees', 'grass' and 'clouds' are quite obviously the result of the technique of rear projection and it is thus the very artificiality of the 'nature' background which is marked. It is worth quoting the conversation between 'Edwards' and Constance in full since it concerns the representation and the representability of love—a theme which is a recurrent obsession of the film (and which also serves an important function in the dissolve sequence discussed earlier):

> **Constance:** I think the greatest harm done the human race has been done by the poets.

'Edwards': Poets are dull boys most of them, but not especially fiendish.

Constance: But they keep filling people's heads with delusions about love—writing about it as if it were a simple orchid or a flight of angels.

'Edwards': Which it isn't, eh?

Constance: Of course not. People fall in love, as they put it, because they respond to a certain hair color or vocal tones or mannerisms that remind them of their parents.

'Edwards': Or sometimes for no reason at all.

Constance: Oh, that's not the point. People read about love as one thing and experience it as another. Or they expect kisses to be like lyrical poems, embraces like Shakespearian dramas.

'Edwards': And when they find out differently they get sick and have to be analyzed, eh?

Constance: Very often.

Leaving aside for the moment the fact that the Freudian explanation of 'illness' is somewhat more complicated, the depiction of this conversation is not innocent of the very kind of 'literary' strategies which are being discussed. The clichés of the love scene promulgated by the cinematic institution are all present as Constance talks: the pastoral setting, the rustic turnstile, the fall of the woman and the ensuing laughter, the magnified gesture with which the woman brushes the hair out of her eyes, the close-up in which the man gives the woman an admiring look. In fact, Constance is describing precisely what the film is doing when it links the two characters within a heavily coded pastoral setting—producing (or reproducing) figures which are purely textual and which cannot be directly transferred to an extra-textual or referential realm. But the scene extends beyond the point at which Constance drops her line of reasoning; and the ironical interruption, the parabasis of this textual movement by means of which the film produces and reproduces the clichéd figures of the love scene, is effected by the final shot of the scene. When the couple reach what appears to be their destination (a 'beautiful spot'), 'Dr. Edwards', in medium shot, asks Constance whether she would prefer ham or liverwurst for lunch. There is a cut to a close-up of Constance in which she gazes dreamily at some offscreen point, brushes her hair out of her eyes, and sighs before whispering in a seductive tone, 'Liverwurst'. This is the shot on which the scene ends. The expectation at work here stems from a kind of grammatical codification governing the relationship of sound to image (one of agreement and subordination)—a codification whose work is 'duped' by the stress on the word 'Liverwurst'. Now, a reading which did not account for the ironical rupture constituted by the 'Liverwurst' shot would have to conclude that the work of the scene is directed solely toward a depiction of the way in which Constance's frigidity (manifested most explicitly in the 'cold-ness' of her analysis of love) is gradually reduced during her walk with 'Edwards'. In other words, the scene would be viewed as reduplicating the mechanism of the typical Hollywood love scene (a mechanism which ensures the reading: Constance is 'falling in love'). Yet the early work of the scene, its accumulation of figure after figure in the service of a love scenario, is 'undone' by the 'Liverwurst' shot. For perhaps the last word acceptable within the context which the close-up provides is —'Liverwurst'. And the very meaning-lessness of 'Liverwurst' in this context situates the parabasis as an *Aufsitzer*. It is not a joke in Freud's sense, for it is not integrally linked with any meaningful byproduct. The entire rhetorical apparatus of the scene implies that 'Liverwurst' must mean something, that it must, in fact, be another figure—but the spectator is actually led to a dead end of meaning. The spectator has been 'had'.

This ironical interruption cannot be isolated from the reception of the scene 'intact'. The spectator is forced retrospectively to reread the scene and what is exposed in that rereading is the desire for rationality, a rationality which the irony, as *Aufsitzer*, has subverted. Irony, as a trope which leans upon other tropes, nevertheless culminates in an 'undoing of tropological cognition'. Any consideration of the scene's positioning of its spectator must take into account what Weber calls:

> the unique position and power of the *Aufsitzer*: as the joke of (on) the joke, it brings into play not simply a partial aspect of the *Witz*, such as the suspension of rational constraints, but rather demonstrates how *the desire of a certain rationality*—and not only the inhibition of reason—is the necessary precondition of the joke. This desire, the urge to know— what Freud elsewhere calls the *Wisstrieb*—and which he relates, geneti-cally and structurally, to the desire to see, the *Schautrieb*—is the *theoretical Trieb* par excellence.[21]

One might add that 'the desire of a certain rationality' is also the necessary precondition of tropological systems. Furthermore, it is that same desire which supports 'primary cinematic identification' as Metz describes it. For the desire to know, as Weber points out, is related by Freud both genetically and structurally to the desire to see, to scopophilia. When we say 'I see', we signify 'I understand'. In primary cinematic identification, according to Metz, the spectator attains a kind of mastery of this desire to see by identifying with the 'look' of the camera and thus positing himself as the 'condition of possibility of the perceived'.[22] He *rationalizes* the image by making himself its source and this rationalization is simultaneously, and reciprocally, a rationalization of the spectator as subject: the subject constitutes itself, through the gaze, as a coherent and homogeneous unity, as an ego.

In the example of filmic irony described above, the interruption consti-tuted by the 'Liverwurst' shot, it is apparent that the image/sound structure rests upon a fundamental incoherency and is essentially unreadable. Like the *Aufsitzer*, it succeeds through its very senselessness. But again, it is not pure nonsense. Irony is not present in the absolutely unintelligible image; rather, it consists of an 'undoing' or deconstruction of sense: the mechanisms of meaning-making must be present initially in order to be dismantled. Sim-ilarly, primary cinematic identification must be present initially in the specta-tor's work of apprehending the image. Yet the 'Liverwurst' shot, through its very incoherency and unreadability (its non-sensicality), does not allow the spectator to persist under the illusion that the unified and coherent image mirrors and is simultaneously mastered by his own power as unified ego. The lack of ready meaning induces a rupture in perception; the irony undermines the unitary meaning *apparently* supported by the image. Perception can no longer be understood as an instantaneous and solitary act—the guarantee of a unified ego—and this rupture is effected *retrospectively*, as the result of a second event (which is precisely a non-event, the revelation of an absence of rationality). Filmic irony works to position the spectator elsewhere—in a place other than that constituted by the certainty and security of the unified ego and identity. At the very least this irony, like the *Aufsitzer* as Weber describes it, constitutes an assertion of the ambivalence of that ego. It manifests itself as a certain duplicity of the narration. It is Metz' 'primary cinematic identification' (the basis of his description of the cinematic signifier as 'imaginary') which is revealed as untenable by filmic irony in its work as the *Aufsitzer*, for filmic irony, if only momentarily, asserts the fundamental ambivalence of that supposed source of unified perception—the subject.

But is filmic irony simply an aberration, an exception to a more general rule dictating that the spectator of the cinema, *most of the time*, will identify with the 'look' of the camera and therefore with himself/herself as a unified subject? The preceding analysis of Freud's theory of the *Aufsitzer* and the joke seems to indicate that this is not at all the case. That analysis initiates a more far-ranging questioning of some basic presuppositions of Metz' theory. According to Metz, primary cinematic identification is the product of an instantaneous and founding positioning of the spectator as the 'look' of the camera. He supports this notion with an appeal to Lacan's description of the mirror stage as paradigmatic of the Imaginary (and hence of narcissism). The joke is also narcissistic, but its work is fundamentally different from that of the mirror stage. While the joke mimics the effect of the mirror by acting as a reconfirmation of the subject's unity, it does so not in the undivided space of a moment but by means of two events which are related *diachronically*: the telling of the joke and the explosive laughter of the listener. For Weber, this indicated that the Freudian notion of narcissistic identification differs radically from Lacan's mirror stage:

> This [the joke's reconfirmation of the subject's status as a unity] adds a new dimension to the process of narcissistic identification and the constitution of the ego; for what it indicated is that this process, far from being the result of an instantaneous and solitary *act* ... would instead have to be conceived as *the (after-)* effect of a story: that is, of a diachronic narration, directed towards and culminating in a burst of laughter, which in turn functions less as the embodiment of the instant than its effraction.[23]

Two events form the necessary condition for narcissistic identification and in this description Weber is much closer to the Freudian theories of time and causality than Metz. For Freud, the concept of 'deferred action' (*Nachträg-*

lichkeit) is indispensable for the understanding of psychical phenomena. The formation of a neurosis, for instance, cannot be traced to one traumatic event since it is the result of the interaction between two different traumas. As Jeffrey Mehlman explains, '... the very notion of *Nachträglichkeit* subverts the idea of a traumatic *event*: the "trauma" is suspended in the vibratory displacements between two temporally separate events'.[24] Freud uses the term *Nachträglichkeit* to specify the *working over* of earlier material (experiences, impressions and memory-traces) at a later date. The metaphor appropriate to this form of psychical activity is not that of 'delayed reaction' but of 'rewriting'. Freud introduces this concept of *Nachträglichkeit* very early and it continually informs his work.

> ... Freud had pointed out from the beginning that the subject revises past events at a later date *(nachträglich)*, and that it is this revision which invests them with significance and even with efficacity or pathogenic force. On December 6, 1896, he wrote to Wilhelm Fliess: 'I am working on the assumption that our psychical mechanism has come into being by a process of stratification: the material present in the form of memory-traces being subjected from time to time to a *re-arrangement* in accordance with fresh circumstances—to a *re-transcription*.'[25]

Thus Metz' application of psychoanalysis to film theory and his emphasis upon primary cinematic identification are informed by a misconception of the Freudian notion of determination. And, as Mehlman points out, this kind of misreading is itself symptomatic—'... for the reader of Freud, is not the true "trauma" the erosion of the very notion of an original, grounding event...?'[26] Metz retains the notion of 'an original grounding event' in his emphasis upon that first (and 'primary') 'look' of the spectator at the screen.

The idea that spectator-positioning is the aftereffect of a story or a diachronic narration may not at first seem to be applicable in the case of film. For Metz retains the advantage of stressing *sight*—a necessary and structuring component of the film-viewing situation. Hence his reliance upon Lacan's mirror stage, in which the child's situation prefigures that of the cinema spectator, would seem to indicate a closer adherence to the concept of cinematic specificity (though that specificity must be a kind of heterogeneity—a fact Metz tends to ignore). Furthermore, as Metz points out, not every film is a narrative: thus, if spectator-positioning is the aftereffect of a story, it cannot always be a true 'story'. Nevertheless, the important point is that positioning must be the effect of a diachronic structure and not of the synchronic moment of the gaze. The moment of the gaze constitutes only one stage in spectator-positioning—the first stage. Metz' concept of primary cinematic identification is complicit 'with a general overvaluation of perception as a datum, which is very unFreudian...'.[27] In Freud's description of the dirty joke, scopophilia is, indeed, the motivating force behind the joke, but it is not sufficient in itself to specify the joke. In order to describe the emergence of the dirty joke, Freud finds it necessary to outline *two* scenarios—one in which the woman is present and one in which she is absent.

History, *for the subject*, cannot be explained, in Freudian psychoanalysis, as a linear determinism. Yet Metz has taken up the search (always leading to disillusionment in Freud's case) for an earlier and earlier 'scene' which would *found* the spectator's relationship with the film. The scene which contemporary film theory gives us is a 'primal' scene involving a 'look' (of the camera) and an immediate identification of the spectator with that look. The spectator's organizing capability is therefore defined entirely in terms of perception. Perception provides a unit—the image—which in its unity and coherence confirms the homogeneity of the subject. This approach, in overemphasizing the status of the 'look' and the image, risks the recapitulation of a kind of materialistic monism.

But it is precisely the possibility, within the classical text or, in fact, within any film text, of the image 'dissolving', or going out of focus, which reveals the difficulties of a theory of primary cinematic identification uninflected by secondary identifications. I am not arguing here that the moments of incoherency isolated in the two scenes in *Spellbound* act in any way as proof that the film is 'radical'. The 'Liverwurst' shot, for instance, constitutes only a slight deviation in a narrative which is otherwise quite homogeneous and coherent. For it is true that in order to 'follow' the narrative, one must acknowledge the fact that the clichéd figures of the love scene have indeed 'worked'—Constance and 'Dr. Edwards' have 'fallen in love'. *Spellbound* proceeds by covering up the very thing which it enunciates. The classical text is able not only to tolerate moments of nonsense or incoherency but to exploit them because its power of containment of those moments lies not in the image or look but in an enunciation which takes place across time. It is the orchestration of the various signifying materials which produces the effect of a unified source of enunciation. The enunciation provides the second 'event' of the diachronic series which effects spectator-positioning. The unified subject/spectator of the cinema is not the precondition for the film but the aftereffect of a diachronic narration. It becomes necessary to think about the reciprocal relation between image and enunciation and its effect upon the positioning of the filmic spectator. While perception may provide the 'glimpse' of an organization, the enunciation, within which the 'look' of the camera is 'placed', solidifies that 'glimpse' as the sustained 'look' of a unified ego.

THE FILM'S TIME AND THE SPECTATOR'S 'SPACE' 49

NOTES

1. C. Metz, 'The Imaginary Signifier', *Screen* vol. 16 no. 2 (Summer 1975), pp. 51-52.

2. C. Metz, *Le Signifiant imaginaire* (Paris: Union Générale d'Editions, 1977), pp. 213-218.

3. G. Genette, *Figures III* (Paris: Seuil, 1972), p. 39.

4. P. de Man, 'The Purloined Ribbon', in *Glyph I* (Baltimore, Maryland: Johns Hopkins University Press, 1977), p. 46.

5. J. Lacan, 'The Insistence of the Letter in the Unconscious', in *Structuralism*. J. Ehrmann (ed.), trans. J. Miel (Garden City, New York: Doubleday/Anchor, 1970), p. 116. This passage occurs on p. 158 of J. Lacan, *Ecrits: A Selection*, trans. A. Sheridan (London: Tavistock, 1977).

6. S. Freud, 'Jokes and Their Relation to the Unconscious', *The Standard Edition of the Complete Psychological Works of Sigmund Freud* vol. VIII (London: Hogarth, 1960), p. 128.

7. Ibid., p. 128.

8. Ibid., p. 131.

9. S. Weber, 'The Divaricator: Remarks on Freud's Witz', in *Glyph I*, p. 19.

10. Ibid., p. 20.

11. Freud, p. 97.

12. Ibid., p. 98.

13. Ibid., p. 99.

14. Ibid., p. 21.

15. Ibid., p. 25.

16. Ibid., p. 138.

17. Ibid., p. 139.

18. Ibid.

19. Ibid., p. 18.

20. Ibid., p. 17.

21. Ibid., p. 26.

22. Metz, 'The Imaginary Signifier', p. 51.

23. Weber, p. 26.

24. J. Mehlman, 'How to Read Freud on Jokes: The Critic as *Schädchen*', *New Literary History* vol. 6 no. 2 (Winter 1975), p. 454.

25. J. Laplanche and J.-B. Pontalis, *The Language of Psycho-Analysis*, trans. D. Nicholson-Smith (New York: W.W. Norton & Co., 1973), p. 112.

26. Mehlman, p. 452.

27. G. Nowell-Smith, 'A Note on History/Discourse', *Edinburgh '76 Magazine*, p. 31.

Problematizing the Spectator's Placement in Film

Malcolm Le Grice

Since I began making films in 1965 much of my theoretical concern has been with the role and condition of the spectator. The shift towards a similar concern in Christian Metz' writing represented by the article 'The Imaginary Signifier'[1] enables (and demands) a relationship between his work and my own practice. This paper addresses some of the concepts Metz presents in that article from the position of a film practice which seeks to transform rather than exploit or simply analyze the condition of the spectator.

A major object of Metz' article is to define that which is special to the cinematic signifier. More precisely, he terms this a signifier effect (already introducing the spectator subject by implication), which he defines as 'a specific coefficient of signification (and not a signified) linked to the intrinsic workings of the cinema . . .'.

In discussing signification in general earlier, Metz quite clearly aligns himself to the awareness that signification is not 'just a consequence of social development' but becomes 'a party to the constitution of sociality itself'. Whilst quoting Lacan as a footnote, 'The order of the symbol can no longer be conceived as constituted by man, but rather as constituting him', he still makes it plain that he sees, by what he nicely calls 'the partial "uncoupling" of the laws of signification from short term historical developments', the capacity of the semiotic to function as a radical, definitional, sociality. In other words, he makes it evident that the conditions of signification are not immutable, however deeply determined.

In approaching the definition of the intrinsic condition of the cinematic signifier, Metz is forced to go by the route of the only form of cinematic practice which he knows, namely the dominant industrial fiction film. He defines the fiction film as 'film in which the cinematic signifier does not work

50

on its own account but is employed entirely to remove the traces of its own steps, to open immediately on to the transparency of a signified...'. However, this 'intention' of transparency applies in structural terms to every film which Metz might quote, including his nonfictional genres like documentary, coming as they do from a context which has an investment in maintaining the transparency of the signifier. This in part leads Metz to the notion: 'Every film is a fiction film'.

Without positing the whole avant-garde cinema, or even structural/ materialist film as some *absolute* alternative to the cinematic form which provides Metz' historical reference points, it is nonetheless a polarity within which instances can be quoted providing some embodiment of what is the implicit obverse of Metz' definition, namely 'film in which the signifier *does* work on its own account'.

When Metz says 'Attempts to "defictionalise" the spectacle, notably since Brecht, have gone further in the theatre than in the cinema...', he helps to obscure substantial cinematic developments which have aimed themselves directly at this problem. I see the predominance of the fictional in cinema as an historical problem related to the economic/social function cinema has been called upon to perform and the deep effects this has had in the development of cinematic conventions. Metz, on the other hand, unaware of films which have attempted to 'work on the signifier' and 'defictionalize the spectacle', sees it as a product of intrinsic conditions of the cinematic signifier itself which is from the outset 'fictive and "absent" '. In spite of his own earlier concept of the partial 'uncoupling' of the laws of signification, which he would evidently consider to be at play in Brechtian theater, his argument on the cinematic signifier sails very close to naturalizing it as an immutable essence of the cinematic.

In support of his argument of the intrinsic fictiveness of cinema, the concept of a special condition, or degree of 'absence', for the cinematic signifier is fundamental. He supports this contention of 'absence' in various ways—from a demonstration that a can of film does not 'contain' those 'vast landscapes' which are the subject of its images to detailed comparison with theater where the actors (here seen as synonymous with the signifiers) are really there in the real time and space of the theater. He points out emphatically that everything in film is recorded and that what is recorded is by definition absent. In both the comparison with theater and in the issue of recording, Metz' argument for a special 'absence' of the cinematic signifier is faulty. If, in the theater, the actors (or props) are considered either as the signifiers themselves, or their 'real' presence somehow resists the transparency of the theatrical signifier, this is no more than an argument of an awareness of the material reality of the signifying substance. It is parallel to those movements in painting which drew attention to the material of the painting rather than simply using that material to construct a pictorial illusion. There are more than enough films from the avant-garde cinema which draw attention to, or work with, the cinematic materials like color, light, screen, acetate, shadow, auditorium etc., to make it quite clear that an awareness of the signifying substance is as possible in cinema as in any other medium. However, even if we pass beyond this concept of the material substance of the cinematic image, and consider it in its state as a record (or recording), even if that which had been the subject of its recording is absent, its recorded trace, like a footstep in concrete, is present. Locked in this terminology, it must be argued that the cinematic image is a real image, within the specific parameters which the recording mechanism is capable of recording. The confusion occurs when the specific limits of the recorded image are read beyond those limits not as a real image, but as an image of 'the real'.

In fact, some of the specific considerations of the cinematic signifier (its 'intrinsics') might best be pursued along the lines of the problematics of the relationship between the substance of the record, the material processes of recording and that continuum out of which it is a recording—for the image is a production and inscribes its production (though these inscriptions may be effaced or attention drawn away from them).

In many respects, the cinematic signifier for Metz is the theatrical signifier at an extreme end of theatrical naturalism (where the actor is also made transparent in respect to the character—which again goes equally for props, vast landscapes or what you will), and absent in cinema because parameters of presence are assumed beyond the specifics of the cinematic image. This condition is only possible whilst film's specificity is *made* transparent in order to preserve the naturalistic theatrical signifier. However much Metz may argue the extension of perceptual registers in cinema, a factor which clearly assists transparency, these registers (better expressed as the parameters of range and resolution of the recording) remain specifiable.

The direction of this refutation shows simply that if the fictiveness, or imaginariness, of the signifier is counteracted in theater by asserting the presence of the signifier (or signifying substance), such a condition is equally open to cinema. However, this tempting elevation of the cinematic signifier to the status of its own reality, its presence, is also problematic, rebounding on the assumption that the signifier is 'present' in theater. In a film which, for example, draws attention to the screen surface, the projector beam, the intermittent mechanism or whatever 'material' aspect might be chosen, is it correct to assume that the signifier is present? At the moment that the signifier functions as a signifier, whatever the medium, it becomes transparent. Attention to the signifier in its material sense (as the signifying substance) does not escape the process of standing for that which it is not. It is incapable of standing for itself in any more than a representation of some *aspects* of its properties. Films which may be described as working on the signifier counteract transparency more by making aspects of the signifying *process* evident (tracing the path of shifts and transformations between signifying substance and signification) than by asserting the unproblematic presence of the signifier. I can see no distinction in kind to be made on this level between film and any other signifying practice. The signifier is neither unproblematically present as substance, nor absent as signification. Its absence, inevitable in certain moments of the signifying process, is not to be demonstrated on the basis of some special intrinsic condition of the cinematic medium.

To this point, Metz has looked for the special conditions of cinematic signification mainly within the medium and apparatus. More fundamentally interesting is a shift which concerns itself with the conditions of response in the spectator/subject. In order to approach this problem, Metz refers to that general science of the subject, psychoanalysis, and in particular the work done on the specular regime by Jacques Lacan.

Perhaps because of my own inadequate theoretical expression or the polemical function of much of the discourse I have been involved in, there are some misunderstandings about my attitude to psychological investigation which must be cleared up.

Much of my resistance to the dominant cinema has been expressed in terms of demanding or encouraging a more 'conscious' or self-aware spectator. I have argued against the manipulated passivity of the audience to both film and television and have sought devices in my film work to establish what I have called a speculative/reflexive mode in the spectator. The rhetoric and polemics of this enterprise have been interpreted as a denial of psychology and the unconscious. My film work and theory have rejected, on one hand, symbolist expressionism, not as a rejection of the unconscious, but as a rejection of the unconscious manipulation or exploitation of the unconscious so that it remains unconscious. On the other hand, the concept of the conscious spectator was an attempt to break the subjugation of the spectator's ego by the film and filmmaker (but more pertinently the subjugation by the multinational cinematic corporations through the agency of the film and filmmakers). Neither in any way denies the psychological or the fact of the unconscious. However, until recently, the application of psychoanalysis in cinema has been almost exclusively at the level of inter-pretation of symbolism, either a psychoanalysis of the filmmaker via the film text, or, at best, within the sociological aspect of film criticism, a form of socio-psychoanalysis. Little work was done on the more fundamental psychological mechanisms at work in the cinematic experience.

As an artist who came out of the tradition of abstract expressionism, my early reading of Freud remains an underlying frame of reference. But, except for a reading from Freud's treatise on Leonardo in the performance of my film *After Leonardo*, I have drawn less specifically on Freud in my film work than on Jean Piaget. His concept of the development of the constructions of reality in children has had a considerable influence on my theories. I do not see Piaget as a behaviorist, and though he does not address the basic psychological formations in the language of the subject, but rather in the terms of scientific observation, I see no incompatibility between his work and Freudian psychoanalysis. His work may be difficult to integrate with psychoanalysis, as it does not emerge at all from the verbal activity of its subjects, but it may be its observational basis which has recommended itself to me most as a filmmaker, and an artist in the anti-literary twentieth century tradition. From my limited reading of Lacan, I retain some reservations about the use of psychoanalytic language outside of that practice. Its language is already metaphoricized in relationship to the language of the subject, and confirmation of its theories (in the real sense of one's own experience) is difficult outside the practice. As I am not in analysis, if its concepts are to be productive to me as a filmmaker I must relate them to my experience in the cinematic.

Basically, what Metz draws on from Lacan concerns the relationship between the formation of the ego and the image—the way in which fundamental unconscious formations are embodied in the imaginary function—his main reference being to Lacan's description of the 'mirror phase'. Whether or not Metz' interpretation of Lacan is correct (taken up by Jacki Rose in her article 'The Imaginary—the Insufficient Signifier'), it leads along a path which provides a number of interesting debating points. Metz sees in the mirror phase a primary identification, the formation of the ego through the perception of the body image, this body image providing an image of completeness through which an imaginary coherence may be given to the ego. In addition, the mirror image in the presence of others (primarily assumed to be the mother) gives to the child its sense of being an other in the presence of others like itself. This likeness is used broadly to explain the basis of the capacity to identify with the other through the image of the other, a fundamental mechanism in socialization.

At once, in his discussion, Metz encounters a difficulty in relating the cinematic to the mirror phase: the fact that the spectator's body is not reflected in the film image. He overcomes this difficulty by suggesting that cinematic perception is only possible subsequent to the spectator's ego formation in the mirror phase, maintaining the analogy of cinema with the mirror by a special 'implacement', whereby 'the mirror suddenly becomes clear glass'.

In his pursuit of a mirror analogy, Metz misses what might be a productive avenue in the consideration of 'recording', namely film's capacity to 'reflect' time in the way in which the mirror reflects space. Though it is not central, it should be pointed out that in a major area of cinema, the home movie, the subject's image is 'reflected' in the scene.

Taking account of the spectator's bodily absence from the screen, Metz turns to identification with the represented characters, but because he is drawn towards his more challenging formulation of the spectator's 'placement' (my term) in the scene, he moves very quickly over the identification with character in the fiction as secondary to the primary identification afforded by the 'self-identification' of the mirror phase. This is unfortunate for a number of reasons.

It seems to me debatable that the mechanisms of identification with others are secondary and subsequent to the identification of ego with the self body-image. Many aspects of the mechanisms of identification either with others or objects in the child's stages of extreme dependency must have a very primary psychological form. Furthermore, in the form of cinema which Metz uses as his basis of reference, because of the transparency of the signifier, identification with character is paramount. His argument that there is no loss of identification during long periods in which no image of a character appears on the screen fails to take account of the fact that identification with 'others' on the screen, as in its social formation, is not simply an identification with the likeness of their bodies to our own, but an intricate concern with the consequences of their actions.

Long periods (which in fact are always short except in the area of cinema I would quote as an 'alternative') of what Metz calls 'inhuman' sequences, are always contained within structures of narrative consequence, identificatory response to them being conditioned by their context. If we are to understand the psychological mechanisms at work in the film spectator we must examine how the mechanisms of identification which form the basis of social relationships function in the identificatory response to images of others, objects, the reading of consequentiality, etc., within the cinematic. This is particularly important in a critique of cinema where the signifier is transparent, opening directly, as it were, onto the scene of the imaginary action. If the mechanisms of identification are in significant development preceding and superceding the mirror phase, they become deeply intricated with what Metz tries to differentiate as the spectator's identification with self. At the same time, even in those avant-garde films which eliminate the portrayed character or even eliminate all photo-recording, the issue of identification in the consequences of the film's transformations is raised by the investment implicit in the spectator's attention. Whatever distinctions may ultimately be drawn between the spectator's self-identification and the identification with the characters, actions and objects of the screen image, it is evident that the 'structural/materialist' films provide virtually the only frame of reference where these issues are raised in the film texts themselves (as opposed to being superimposed by an advanced theoretical stance onto film works which pay no attention to the problem).

In attempting to define the spectator's identification with self as more primary than identification with the screen's characters, Metz turns the lack of image of the spectator on the screen to profit, reasoning that the spectator's ego must therefore identify itself elsewhere.

In one paragraph, in which he talks of the 'subject's knowledge', he outlines a number of factors necessary to be *known* by the spectator in order for film to be possible. After a (metaphorical?) first person description of a knowledge of being within a cinematic space knowingly perceiving and knowing therefore 'that I am the place where this really perceived imaginary accedes to the symbolic. . .' he goes on to what is for him a key concept: 'In other words, the spectator identifies with himself, with himself as a pure act of perception . . . as a kind of transcendental subject. . .'. He sees this inevitable self-identification of the spectator as a necessary consequence of the very possibility of the cinematic perception. Fundamental here is Metz' concept of the spectator as 'the constitutive instance . . . of the cinema signifier (it is I who make the film)'. Of course it is *in* the spectator that the film experience is constituted, but, and it is crucial, to what extent does the spectator make that constitution, and to what extent is that constitution made in the spectator as the final point of the corporate production? Unconscious complicity in the constitutive process has a different status to knowledge of that process, and it must be distinguished from the necessary condition of choice in the spectator before the imaginary can approach the symbolic.

In spite of recognizing that this transcendental subject places the spectator into the illusion of deity, in spite of recognizing that the state of 'all-perceiving . . . all-powerful' is an extreme reaction of the ego to the frustration of its power, and with all his consequent attention to the 'perversion' of voyeurism in cinema, Metz does not attempt to dislodge this condition of the spectator from an intrinsics of cinema. Before we can begin to consider the specific psychological formations of the spectator in relationship to the film, the spectator as constitutive instance must be given an historical and economic description. The cinema's spectator is the unconscious agent of a corporate consumption. Whilst the film seems to be a dream of the spectator, the spectator's cinematic dream is the final point of the institutional production. As this condition is deeply embedded in the form of the cinematic institution (its modes of production and presentation), its apparatus (the machinery and techniques), its conventions of structuring (modes of editing, camera use, etc.) and in the psychology of its audience, perhaps we should avoid over-general conclusions and concentrate on details of its modes.

Metz follows his general concept of the spectator's identification with self by some consideration of identification with the camera. There is a parallel in my own film work; a period in which I attempted to address directly the problem of the spectator's physical (temporal and spatial) location within the cinema auditorium largely by minimalizing or expelling the photo-cinematic from the screen has developed since 1974 into a consideration of the spectator's relationship to the camera and cinematic recording. Metz' transition from the spectator's transcendent self-identification to identification with the camera broadly follows the argument concerning the placement of the spectator/subject in quattrocento perspective and its continuation in the development of the optical apparatus. The spectator, it is argued, by occupying the 'empty implacement' inscribed by the viewpoint of the camera, puts the spectator in the relationship to the scene previously occupied by the camera in the act of recording the image. Through the psychological arguments which express the equation between seeing and causing as a reaction of the ego to its inability to possess or control the object of its gaze, Metz interprets this empty implacement as implicitly that of an all-seeing, all-powerful 'God himself'. Whilst I accept the broad terms of the psychological argument concerning the formations in the specular regime, there is a significant sense in which the camera as a definable mechanism is capable of clarifying the limits which the apparatus imposes on the image.

The image can become specifiable in its relationship as a production through awareness of the camera and its properties as a mechanism, thus counteracting the omniscience of the point of view by giving limits to the method of access to the scene. In this way, the viewpoint becomes relatable to a causal agency, readable in a materialist sense rather than as a generalized ideal access (in effect unread through the transparency of its inscription). This point of access need no longer be interpreted as an immutable 'natural' condition before which the subject is powerless, leading in turn to the illusion of absolute power as a reaction to support the ego. It might be argued that the camera as a mechanism, like quattrocento perspective, is more intrinsically inclined toward the materialist specificity of access to (and construction of) the image, than the transcendental omniscience which Metz sees as intrinsic. Whichever way this is read, the camera and its functioning in a film constructs the image within a system of production (a motivated causality), and this is inscribed in the resultant image. It is an historical problem if this inscription is suppressed and if film practice fosters a misreading of the historical for a 'natural' or theistic causality, however much this is supported by the psychological compliance of the spectator. Where Metz talks of identification with the camera, I feel a better expression would be identification 'through' the camera.

Before the issue of identification with the camera can be approached as a theoretical or critical problem, it is necessary to consider film texts which can clarify the distinction between identification with the camera and with the narrative thread of the film construction. Except in a small line of development from the early films of Warhol, which includes work by Michael Snow, Peter Gidal, myself and a few other filmmakers, there is little to refer to where the camera identification becomes problematic within the film text itself. In these cases, certain constraints in camera movement and edited construction demand some consideration of camera implacement (both in a spatial and temporal sense). In this work, whilst there is identification through the camera with the components of scene or action, there is also an inevitable shift towards an identification *of* the camera as a spatio/temporal implacement.

In order to make use of a concept like 'identification with the camera', we must attempt to distinguish to some degree an identification with the camera as camera, as mechanism, from the components of the scene on one hand and subsumption as an agent of the narrative on the other. The camera is a mechanism, and identification with the camera incorporates identification with that mechanism and is not the same as identification through the camera with the agency which controls it. Crucial here is the distinction between identification 'of', 'with' and 'through'. If identification-with involves a transfer of the subject's ego to the condition of another object, with all its vicariousness but social necessity, in the same process identification-of involves a differentiation of the subject ego from that object. The ambivalence of the subject in the mirror phase might show us that identification 'with' and 'of' are interdependent in the process of relationship between the ego and other objects. In the process of identification-with a character, it is necessary to make some identification-of that character. In the same way, if there is to be any meaning to the concept of identification-with the camera, there must be some element of identification-of the camera. Identification-with the camera, far from being a common condition within the cinematic experience, is a difficult condition to initiate and maintain, as this involves a conceptualization of an implacement not represented directly in the scene but inscribed through its effects. In general, this identification is most frequently approached via the personification of the camera in the character point-of-view shot, or its extreme extension as the point of view of the first-person filmmaker. In both these cases, identification with the camera, as such, is lost as the identification becomes relocated in the personification, becoming again an identification with a character. In a sense, the more the identificatory process bypasses the conflict implicit between identification 'with' and 'of' and transfers itself to another object, the more we should consider this as an identification 'through'.

In most cases where we talk of identification 'with', because identification 'of' is suppressed, it constitutes identification 'through'. Whilst the most evident identification through the camera in the dominant cinema is with the components of the scene and action, it is mainly because of the continual dislocation of the viewpoint that the spectator has no alternative but to identify through the camera with the source of the narrative continuity. Some continuity in the camera implacement, which begins to differentiate the viewpoint from the scene, also begins to develop some distinction between the mechanism and the ordering authority. Without this continuity of viewpoint, as a consequence of the spectator's incapacity to locate the ordering authority, the ego is forced to adopt an 'idealist' location. The spectator's illusory identification with this unspecifiable ideal location masks that it is in fact an identification with the power of the institutional authority behind the narrative order.

Metz may point us in the right direction for the psychological theory which deals with the mechanisms of this identification, but rather than begin from the general psychoanalytic theory and look for its correspondence in the cinematic, I would prefer to look in more detail at the condition of the spectator in cinema and then suggest some relationship to psychoanalytic theory.

Metz refers us to Baudry's observations in his 'Ideological Effects of the Basic Cinematographic Apparatus',[2] that the spectator is in 'a sub-motor and super-perceptive state'. I consider that an examination of the relationship between the motor and sensory regimes in the cinematic experience is crucial. I use the term sensory here rather than specular, so as to include the auditory aspect, as, for example, the concept of identification with the camera should be extended to take in the identification with the microphone. Fundamental dissociations between the sensory and motor regimes are at work in cinema. The spectator is at rest in a seat, and not only is the more obvious motor activity—that of walking about in the space—eliminated (it is largely only effective in the initial and subsequent instances of walking to and from the cinema) but in the cinematic experience in the most obvious way the spectator is unable to enter into the action and cannot influence its outcome by intervention. The latent desire to do so is maintained through identification with those portrayed characters who seem able to do so by their actions. By identification with the characters, the spectator seems to act toward the determination of consequence. This vicarious identification is at the cost of any real implication of the spectator in the consequence of the film.

In the fundamental development of the relationship between the subject and the world, the subject becomes implicated in the sensory through the consequences of general motor engagement in the world. Thus, whatever the fundamental psychological basis of motivation, its transformation towards relative volition is molded by the developing capacities of the motor regime—motricity and motive become deeply correlated.

The effect of this 'implicatedness' in the world is inscribed in the sensory construction of the subject within which the effects of the mirror phase are a stage. In the cinematic, the question of the spectator's implication or dis-implication becomes fundamental. It is evident that the spectator's sense of implication in the narrative action itself is unavoidably vicarious and illusory, but what of the more detailed issues of the specular and auditory response?

In the same way in which motor engagement in the film's action is impossible, the less evident motor actions normally deeply intricated with the specular and auditory are also highly reduced. In the specular, the neck muscles are not called upon to swivel the head as the screen is contained within the visual field of a static head; the eye has little lateral or vertical movement to make as the pertinent aspect of the image is normally held near the center of the screen. As the image is flat, there is not even a necessity to refocus for various distances. Similarly, no motor demands are made in locating the auditory source.

For the moment, we will leave aside the auditory issue in its sense of the dissociation of the spectator's voice, and concentrate on the active component of the specular, 'the look' (for which 'the listen' might be an auditory equivalent). The look is the operation of the motor regime in the specular. In the same way in which motor and motive become generally interrelated, in the specular they are intricated through the expenditure of energy in the determination of the perception. It is evident that the greater the perceptual shift desired by the subject, the greater the motor energy required to initiate it. Perceptual changes in the world are deeply related to the economics of this expenditure. In the conventions developed by the cinema, the dis-implication of the spectator under the illusion of implication extends to the look through the dissociation of the specular and motor regimes.

The consequences of this are particularly demonstrable in the conventions of camera movement and action montage. Whatever the basis of specular desire, the initial engagement of the spectator in the cinematic rests on some correspondence between the object of that desire and the agency which initiates the film image. This engagement is maintained in the film by a continuing correspondence through the desired development and transformation. In particular, the conventions of camera movement and montage follow the desire to maintain contact with the development of the action. The camera follows movement or the cut opens on to the pertinent continuation of the action. Though the devices may include sophisticated suspensions, they only do so within the context of ultimate coordination. What is important here is in the detailed psychological effect of the continued provision of the desired object in the scene. Desiring to follow the consequential structure initiated in and by the film, when confirmed by its provision, the spectator seems to bring about the perceptual change as an act of volition. When a camera follows the action, there is sufficient correspondence with the desire of the spectator that the experience seems (unconsciously) to be one of choice exercised in the look. But, in the same way in which the spectator is unable to enter the action in the crude sense of intervening in its consequence, the spectator initiates no perceptual changes of the cinematic scene. The apparent implication of the spectator—by the apparent responsiveness of the camera movements and scene changes to the spectator's volition—produces a fundamental illusion of choice and control where none exists. If, in cinema, the sensory/motor dissociations are basic, is the dissociation of the sensory/motor from implicated volition inevitable, and in what sense can the spectator appropriate the cinematic experience?

Many of the devices which the 'structural/materialist' work has adopted might be interpreted in terms of making the fundamental dissociations evident or problematic, in this sense clarifying the relationship which exists between the film, the filmmaker and the spectator. To this end, the devices and strategies have served to expel the spectator from the text (also attempting in some respects to expel the filmmaker) rather than create an unconditional engagement. Correspondences between the film's structure and the expected desire of the spectator have been resisted. However, the various

oppositional devices have been developed together with an attempt to permit, encourage, or initiate the spectator's own symbolic activity as the basis
for appropriation of the film experience.

Both aspects, which are difficult to distinguish from each other, form the
basis of the problematics in my own current film work. My experience from
this work suggests that the point at which the two questions come together
can be approached through the relationship of the symbolic activity to the
motive in the motor aspect of the sensory/motor relationship. In the auditory
regime, the symbolic activity of the subject emerges from the aural *production,* the motor activity of the voice. We may note that not only is the
spectator's voice not produced in the cinematic, it is invariably subsumed by
the film text in the same way in which the spectator's action and perceptual
action are subsumed. In the specular the directedness of the look might be
considered as an equivalent in some respects to the voice in the auditory. We
might then suggest that the development of the symbolic in the specular is
directly related to the subject's implicatedness in the act of choice and
selection in the look. If this concept of the basis of the symbolic activity is to be
seen as a point from which the spectator's implication in the film by appropriation is to be developed, its interiority must be taken into account.

Whilst the concept of the spectator's interior voice may be readily
grasped, the concept of the operation of the look in an interior sense is more
problematic. However, in both cases, it is necessary to assume that the
spectator must *produce* an auditory and specular construction for the film
which is not directly that of the film presented—the spectator must be
expelled from the film text in order to produce the conceptual construct as an
act of the symbolic. In other words, the spectator must *become* the constitutive instance of the film in the limited sense of a relationship to the definition
of the limits of the film text. What occurs to me in this formulation is that
such a conceptual construct is not synonymous with the spectator's ego in any
whole sense. In fact, I suspect that the expulsion of the spectator from the text
counteracts the tendency of the ego to identify itself satisfactorily within the
form of the body image, via any identification it might make within the screen
image. A cinema signifier locked into the form of ego construction of the
mirror phase, as a stage in ego development which short-circuits the ego
concept into a body image, might be considered as helping to maintain a
fixation at that stage. As a consequence of such a notion, we must ask if the
pleasure involved in cinema is a regressive pleasure utilized by the cinema
institution to maintain the dis-implication of the spectator.

These notions are presented more in the spirit of a search for the
productive problematics than a rhetorical conclusion.

NOTES

1. C. Metz, 'The Imaginary Signifier', *Screen* vol. 16 no. 2 (Summer 1975), pp. 14-76; quotations throughout are from this article.

2. J.-L. Baudry, 'Ideological Effects of the Basic Cinematographic Apparatus', *Film Quarterly* vol. XXVIII no. 2 (Winter 1974/75).

Jokes and Their Relation to the Marx Brothers

Patricia Mellencamp

With the bounteous monetary rewards of 'all talking pictures' in the late nineteen twenties and early nineteen thirties,[1] 'silent pictures', or rather, movies without heard, synchronized speech, were figuratively and commercially silenced—except in certain avant-garde films and the aesthetic debate over film's status as 'art'. In typical arguments of influential critics, e.g., Rudolf Arnheim, 'film art' depended on visual exclusivity or dominance on the one hand, or an analogy to other respectable art media, particularly music, to grant legitimacy. An alternate yet interlocked strategy in this search for artistic purity was to analyze cinema's 'effects' on the other arts—cinema somehow fulfilling a cultural function of representation which then 'freed' other arts into their 'essences'. The dichotomy—silence versus sound, visual gestural body codes versus synchronized, speaking voices—was symptomatic of class and economic upheavals, with 'art' as an elite practice which should therefore be strongly differentiated from 'popular' or 'mass' cultural practices. Like hysteria, these scenarios of polarization and purity depended upon the repression of actual political conditions: the maintenance of capitalist systems of ownership and domination, whether labeled 'art' or 'popular culture'. For the Hollywood studios, the economic guarantee and cure was indeed a talking one; for art critics (recapitulating nineteenth century romanticists and early twentieth century formalists), ideal film art became a silent vision of a transcendental utopia, outside language, outside history, reifying the unique self.

Sound (more accurately language as arbitrary, unmotivated, set against the referential 'real' of the image) has continued to be a problem of silence for contemporary film theory. The diachronic intersection of the synchronic, Eisenstein's vertical montage, the aural with the visual, perhaps the ear's diagonal distance from the eye, are still largely uncharted territories, an

63

absence which illustrates Jean-Louis Comolli's iteration of 'the dominance of the visual' in Western representation.[2]

For example, in the exceedingly influential critical work, 'The Imaginary Signifier', Christian Metz locates two passions operative in the spectator/auditor: 'the desire to see ... the desire to hear (...the invoking drive, one of the four main sexual drives for Lacan.)' After discussing mechanisms of voyeurism and the spectator, Metz states: 'The same could be said, making the necessary modifications of course, about the invoking (auditory) drive, less closely studied by psychoanalysis...'.[3] The psychoanalytic mechanisms of the film auditor, as Metz correctly assesses, have not been fully articulated. Like the Hollywood major studios' massive and expensive conversion to sound production in 1927 and 1928, film theory must make 'necessary modifications' particularly in relation to psychoanalysis, a practice dependent on talk but lodged, even in its language, within sight. Luce Irigaray forcibly suggests a reason, based on cultural and sexual difference, for the paradoxical acknowledgement/denial of the importance of sound.

> Investment in the look is not privileged in women as in men. More than the other senses, the eye objectifies and masters. It sets at a distance, maintains the distance. In our culture, the predominance of the look over smell, taste, touch, hearing has brought an impoverishment of bodily relations. It has contributed to disembodying sexuality. The moment the look dominates, the body loses in materiality. It is perceived above all externally and the sexual becomes much more a matter of organs that are highly circumscribed and separable from the site of their assembly in a living whole. The male sex becomes *the* sex because it is very visible.[4]

This statement deserves lengthy elaboration and discussion in relation to cinema. Here, however, I will merely note that the spectator rather than the auditor dominates the parameters of sexual discourse, with the historically constructed female body at a dominated distance, silently bespeaking her infamous and threatening 'lack' because invisible. Furthermore, 'the moment the look dominates'—in cinema, scopophilia, the look of desire as 'identification'—is just that, a look of an instance, suggestive of Metz' cursory mention yet lack of development of the auditory drives. As Mary Ann Doane points out in relation to 'The Imaginary Signifier':

> The spectator of the cinema is constituted as the site of a fusion of two spaces of the subject: the space of consciousness and the space of the unconscious. A spatial metaphor then, sustains this description of identification. But perhaps the question might be posed in a different way, from a different direction—not where is the subject but when is the subject?[5]

This lucid critique brings sound back into the picture through temporality, through the problem of enunciation. Doane concludes: 'It becomes necessary to think about the reciprocal relation between image and enunciation and its effect upon the position of the filmic spectator'.[6] It is this 'reciprocal relation' that I would like to examine in this essay—the movement in time of narration, specifically the jokes of the Marx Brothers in relation to the process of imaging, both funneled through Freud's model of the joking process.

In the discursive complex labeled Marx Brothers films, the relations between the verbal barrage of Groucho with his leering, lecherous lover's posturing, and the nimble pantomime of Harpo in his coat of armament (magically realized literalisms) are mediated by the dialect and sound play of Chico's Italian immigrant/swindler. Permutations of language, collisions between image and sound, continually and complexly reposition or disperse the spectator/auditor within the film. (Up to this point, history repeats itself in my argument's assumption of a sexually undifferentiated audience, or more accurately, the female conscripted into the male's service and compliance.)

Harpo literalizes every metaphor, wreaking havoc (a potential Marx Brothers line comparable to 'waxing Roth' in *Horsefeathers*) on the clichés of language and the mise-en-scène; Chico puns with the sounds of speech and is incapable of keeping secrets (his impossibility with societally coded silence or censorship); while Groucho fractures all the rules of reasoning, relishing his own, Chico's and Harpo's derailment of logic and of grammar's proprietary laws. For example, 'The Password' routine from *Horsefeathers*:.

Chico: Who are you?

Groucho: I'm fine, thanks, who are you?

Chico: I'm fine, too, but you can't come in unless you give the password.

Groucho: Well, what is the password?

Chico: Aw, no! You gotta tell *me*. Hey, I tell what I do. I give you three guesses ... It's the name of a fish.

Groucho: Is it Mary?

Chico: Ha Ha! Atsa no fish!

Groucho: She isn't, well she drinks like one. Let me see ... is it sturgeon?

Chico: Ah, you crazy, sturgeon he's a doctor, cuts you open whenna you sick ... Now I give you one more chance.

Groucho: I got it! Haddock!

Chico: Atsa funny, I gotta haddock too.

Groucho: What do you take for a haddock?

Chico: Wella, sometimes I take-a aspirin, sometimes I take-a Calamel.

Groucho: Say, I'd walk a mile for a Calamel.

Chico: You mean chocolate calamel. I like that too, but you no understand English? You can't come in here unless you say swordfish! Now I give you one more guess.

Groucho: Swordfish ... I think I got it. Is it swordfish?

Chico: Hah! atsa it! You guess it!

Groucho: Pretty good, eh?

After Groucho as Professor Quincy Adams Wagstaff, the newly appointed Huxley College President (whose inaugural song is "Whatever It Is, I'm Against It"), and Chico as Baribelli (given their 'real' vaudeville names, does it matter?) enact one of their many locked-out routines. Harpo enters the frame, takes a fish from his baggy pants, inserts a sword, presents it to the speakeasy bouncer, and walks in with ceremonial aplomb while Wagstaff and Baribelli unabashedly crawl in after him. In the speakeasy, one man asks his partner to cut the cards; Harpo overhears, produces an ax, and maniacally grinning, does just that. The arbitrary nature of language, its infinite capacity for substitution, 'logically' cascades to meaning less and less; or its circulation as signifier is abruptly stopped, as Harpo produces the 'real' referent, the object signified by the signifier. For Harpo, language is never arbitrary, merely ridiculous and completely unnecessary.

In *Duck Soup* (an interesting verbal, and in the film's titles, visual metaphor), the following exchange between Chico as Chicolini, Harpo as Pinky, and Ambassador Trentino occurs:

> Trentino: Then you didn't shadow Firefly?
> Chicolini: Oh, sure, we shadow Firefly. We shadow him all day.
> Trentino: But what day was that?
> Chicolini: Shadowday! Hahaha! Atsa some joke, eh, Boss?

Chicolini is often his own best audience; Pinky appreciates the 'logic' of the scene; Trentino is outraged and frustrated, enacting, like so many other characters in the films, a prolonged 'slow burn'. Trentino asks for Firefly's record. Pinky hands him a phonograph record, which is then thrown into the air and transformed by their play into a clay pigeon, of course shot down in midair by Pinky. Words slide, objects are transformed, the skid of referent to signifier to signified becomes an avalanche stoppable by a fade to black or the film's end. In a twist, their films document the endlessness of language (whose symbolic order Harpo and Chico have never fully entered, and therefore cannot tolerate as a means of power, of authority). The sliding, language's arbitrariness, only ceases with the finality of The End. Nothing is ever gained or lost in this game of language.

As another example, a scene from *Horsefeathers:* Professor Wagstaff is rifling the top of his officious, mahogany desk, littered with nut shells which he cracks open with the telephone receiver, looking for the official University seal. Harpo brings in a live, glistening, honking seal; everyone, including the seal, climbs over the desk before the inevitable fade to black. Objects as referents (but their signifiers as well) are mutilated by 'walking over' them, documenting geometry's first school law: 'the shortest distance between two points...'. In *Duck Soup* an insert shot announces that the Fredonia Cabinet is in session. We hear the sound of a bouncing ball; a dissolve to Groucho as Rufus T. Firefly, the new Prime Minister, reveals him, again behind a large desk, playing jacks. Firefly and the Minister of War have the following exchange:

> Minister of War: Gentlemen! Gentlemen! Enough of this. How about taking up the tax?
> Firefly: How about taking up the carpet?
> Minister of War: I still insist we must take up the tax.

Firefly: He's right. You've got to take up the tacks before you take up the carpet.

The problem of what to take up now is also my difficulty: the films starring the caricatured, costumed bodies and stylized voices of the Marx Brothers and their writers (Harry Ruby, Bert Kalmar, George S. Kaufman, Morris Ryskind, and S. J. Perelman, a virtual compendium of early twentieth century comic writing); or Freud's lengthy taxonomy and analysis in *Jokes and Their Relation to the Unconscious.*[7] First I will sketch out certain problems discussed by Freud: 1) the terrain of auditory pleasure and its sources in an amalgam between unconscious and conscious process; 2) the necessity for a listener, Freud's 'third person' who completes the joking process; 3) the signal role of laughter as a discharge documenting the joke's existence *as* a joke as well as the completion of the process, the pleasure of closure and narcissistic acknowledgement; 4) the position of a woman as object, the 'second person' within the joking exchange; and 5) a brief consideration of the 'comic'. Woven through this selective explication will be examples from Marx Brothers films. Both texts are bound by late nineteenth and twentieth century social histories and institutions, including vaudeville as a family entertainment machine, and its more respectable counterpart, Broadway musical comedies and revues. I will return briefly to vaudeville, but now the problem of the tacks and the tax, a taxing dilemma.

Freud locates the joke's work and its sources of pleasure in relation to 1) the technique (an envelope, a container); 2) the play of words and sounds; and 3) the lifting of inhibitions—in a join, or a brief, *mutual,* disparately timed slippage into the unconscious, between the first person maker and the third person listener. Jokes *work* by 'consciously giving free play to unconscious modes of thought'[8] which have, through acculturation, been rejected as faulty. The joke is directed and, more importantly, defined by its work; it is a process and is temporal in its passage, finally dependent on intelligibility. Jokes have both a retroactive and an anticipatory narrative movement in time, posing in miniature the 'when' of the subject.

This social process involves the same mechanisms (condensation and displacement) at work in dreams, which are an individual, subjective process. Although condensation and displacement are interrelated as 'process', condensation involves the play with words and sounds, 'tacks' and 'tax', or later in *Duck Soup*:

Minister of Finance: Something must be done. War would mean a prohibitive increase in our taxes.
Chicolini: Hey, I got an uncle lives in Taxes.
Minister of Finance: No, I'm talking about taxes, money, dollars.
Chicolini: Dollas! Thatsa where my uncle lives. Dollas, Taxes.

This during a trial for treason, with Firefly as Chicolini's attorney who tries to outriddle him.

Displacement, 'a diversion of the train of thought',[9] (carpet and tacks to tax) is dependent on knowledge of language and logical reasoning. Both techniques secure pleasure from regression *and* the lack of criticism. This pleasure circulates through the third person, the auditor in the movie theater, rather than through the characters within the film—who react with bewilderment or outrage toward the Brothers' antics. The spectator/auditor does not pass through the usual relay of character look or word, but is directly in collusion with the stars.

At this point, a detour or update of Freud through Lacan is relevant to the question of language—the elaboration of the science of linguistics within psychoanalysis. Specifically, Lacan defines condensation as 'the structure of the superimposition of signifiers which is the field of metaphor'. Displacement is described as 'closer to the idea of that veering off of meaning that we see in metonymy',[10] a means of circumventing censorship, or 'the power to bypass obstacles of social censure'.[11] In relation to *Jokes and Their Relation*...

> We see then, that metaphor occurs at the precise point at which sense comes out of non-sense, that is, at that frontier which, as Freud discovered, when crossed the other way produces what we generally call 'wit' *(Witz);* it is at this frontier that we can glimpse the fact that man tempts his very destiny when he derides the signifier.[12]

Jokes, operating through the figures of metaphor and metonymy, are a derision of the signifier, a risky endeavor for the subject, particularly given Lacan's conclusion in the same essay: 'For the symptom is a metaphor ... as desire is a metonymy'. 'Metaphor [is linked] to the question of being and metonymy to its lack'.[13] These questions of being, lack, desire indicate that jokes are clearly not simple. Perhaps they can be viewed as miniature histories of the subject's constant entry into and construction by language. But, to 'return' to Freud.

Freud's metaphor of the joke technique as an 'envelope' for the ideas, as a 'container' of speech, partially explains the momentary slip into the unconscious—the concealment enabling the hearer's delight in getting it and the jokester's pleasure in making it: 'The thought seeks to wrap itself in a joke because in that way it recommends itself to our attention ... This wrapping bribes our powers of criticism and confuses them'.[14] Technique 'gets our attention' as well as 'safeguards against the objections raised by criticism'.[15] Both censorship and analysis of language and other sign systems of protocol are circumvented in a double move: the rules of the jokes' games are also the butt of the joke as well as the source of pleasure.

The Marx Brothers' play trammels the authority of language used by social and political institutions. Chico's immigrant peddler with his fractured Italian dialect, the only character with a 'legitimate' job, at which he rarely works and can instantly transform into a con game, suggests the potential depth of the protest, the gentle subversion of the US' founding legend: a country of immigrants without class or race division, of unlimited opportunity through hard work in capitalism. The swindle and the non-sequitur are equally employed as emblems and mockeries of that economic/social system. Groucho continually mocks the phrases and clichés of corporate executives in his many 'take a letter' interruptions, as well as police jargon, e.g., 'Pull over. I want to see your marriage license'. The attack escalates from the destructive phsyical 'play' of Harpo, through the sound games of Chico to Groucho's assault on marriage and money. Groucho endlessly tries to marry Margaret Dumont for her money and to get paid for this unsavory act. In the opening sequence of *Duck Soup* he says: 'Will you marry me? Did he leave you any money? Answer the second question first'.

As I have stated, the Marx Brothers are the first person; the audience in the theater, the third person. The objects of their jokes, the second person, are not only women—Dumont and 'starlets'—but the opera, symphony, universities, governments and society parties. Inevitably, Groucho, relentlessly pursued by Chico and Harpo (whose sanity he needs and whose mayhem he joins with wise and joyful resignation), is brought into the narrative to save crumbling institutions faced with economic crises: the insanity of the insane saving the asylum. In a telling and captivating metaphor, Metz describes the ritual of 'going to the movies':

> ... going to the cinema is one licit activity with its place in the admissible pastimes of the day ... and yet that place is a 'hole' in the social cloth, a 'loophole' opening onto something slightly more crazy, slightly less approved than what one does the rest of the time.[16]

J. Cheever Loophole, an attorney in *At the Circus*, would certainly agree, with asides about certain perverse 'pastimes'. Imagine Groucho as a semiotics teacher (or for that matter a reader of this paper) and replace the contract scene in *A Night at the Opera*:

> Groucho: The party of the first part shall be known in this contract as the party of the first part.
> Chico: Well, it sounds a little better this time.
> Groucho: Well, it grows on you. Would you like to hear it once more?
> Chico: Just the first part.
> Groucho: What do you mean, the ... the party of the first part?
> Chico: No, the first part of the party of the first part. ...

with sign, signifier, signified and we might conclude with:

> Chico: I no like-a the second party, either.
> Groucho: Well, you shoulda come to the first party, we didn't get home 'til around four in the morning ...

By this point, the legal contract has been shredded, as well as 'legal' language.

The reaction of authority representatives, 'something of a high category (respectability) in juxtaposition with something of a very concrete and even low kind' is always indignation, never laughter.[17] They don't perceive the split between 'the thought contained and the technique', the tension that enables the discharge of laughter. Unlike the spectator/auditor in the theater who is in cahoots with the Brothers' antics and stories, they take the laws of language and decorum literally and don't momentarily slip into the unconscious. They are not bribed, as are we, by the joking process.

The term 'bribe' reappears in Freud's description of tendentious jokes: 'obscene jokes, serving the purpose of exposure', 'hostile jokes, serving the purpose of aggressiveness and satire', and 'cynical jokes', usually attacking marriage and dealing with 'the personal claim for sexual freedom, the pleasure of lifting inhibitions by bringing into prominence sexual facts and relations by speech'.[18] Freud puts women in their historical place, as object, dispossessed of language—the very speech necessary for making a joke, and, reciprocally, understanding it. Predicated on his desire to see women's sex, to have sex (usually more accessible with less educated women), the male joker goes wild:

> When the first person finds his libidinal impulse inhibited by the woman, he develops a hostile trend against that second person and calls on the originally interfering third person as his ally, who, as listener, has now been bribed by the effortless satisfaction of his own libido . . . These jokes make possible the satisfaction of an instinct in the face of an obstacle . . . The obstacle is . . . nothing other than women's incapacity to tolerate undisguised sexuality, an incapacity correspondingly increased with a rise in education and social level . . . in her absence her influence still has an intimidating effect on the men. . .[19]

(This reads suspiciously like a working premise for Woody Allen's *Manhattan*.) The initial pleasure of the visual (as well as its threat), displaced onto a verbal triangulation (the voyeur now the *écouteur*) in a spoken ménage-à-trois, enlists the third person, the audience, against the enemy: female sexuality. The 'technique' opens up sources of male pleasure/displeasure that have become inaccessible. The 'he' of language's control is an 'us', the auditor as the original spectator, absent from the screen but present in the theater. Thus the verbal pleasure of joking production, consumption and discharge must circulate through an 'unconscious' defined and demarked as 'male'. To an uncanny degree, Freud's marriage broker jokes replicate the Marx Brothers' repetitive attack against marriage, depicted as a female institution for male entrapment. In *Animal Crackers* Groucho says: 'Why, you're one of the most beautiful women I've ever seen, and that's not saying much'. And, later in the film:

> Groucho: Well, what do you say, girls? Are we all going to get married? All of us?
>
> Girls: All of us? But that's bigamy.
>
> Groucho: Yes, and it's big of me, too. It's big of all of us. Let's be big for a change. I'm sick of these conventional marriages. One woman and one man was good enough for your grandmother, but who wants to marry your grandmother? Nobody, not even your grandfather.

At the risk of belaboring the obvious, a few more examples from the films. The last shot before the closing title of *Horsefeathers* is of the three Brothers dressed in top hats and tails, marrying the 'college widow'. They all say 'I do', and then jump all over her and each other. When Firefly first meets Mrs. Teasdale in *Duck Soup*, he orates: 'Say, you cover a lot of ground yourself. You'd better beat it. I hear they're going to tear you down and put up an office building where you're standing'. The ending of this film literally depicts woman as the enemy. Trentino, the duplicitous ambassador has been captured and is pinioned in the door. The brothers pelt his head with fruit. From the corner of the room, Mrs. Teasdale begins to sing that by now extremely irritating (constantly played but never completed) national anthem, "Hail Fredonia". The fruit attack is shifted to her. Fade. The End. At least all women are treated equally; no hierarchy of age, beauty or fashion exists. Although marriage is the critical institution of assault, it is true that all authority and most institutions, including male power figures, are targets for derision.

Freud's definition of the joking process (as distinguished, for example, from the comic) *depends* on its telling. 'The psychical process of constructing a joke seems not to be completed when the joke occurs'.[20] The process is temporal, over time; the *need* to tell is connected with the laughter produced. The critical function of laughter from the third person, absent from the pro-filmic event, is performed by the spectator/auditor who 'laughs his quota off'.[21] Pleasure paid for with laughter signals the joke's completion.

> A joke is thus a double-dealing rascal who serves two masters at once (the Janus-like, two-way-facing character of jokes) ... Everything in jokes that is aimed at gaining pleasure is calculated with an eye to the third person, as though there were internal and insurmountable obstacles to it in the first person. And this gives us a full impression of how indispensable this third person is for the completion of the joking process.[22]

This rascal joke thus serves two masters: the male teller (or original looker) and the male auditor, a direct relay doubly marked by Groucho's straight-faced verbal asides and his direct looks at the camera which break the closed circuit of looks, acknowledging the presence of an audience, its conspiracy in the film's manipulations. For example, in *Horsefeathers* Groucho walks up to the camera and says: 'I've got to stay here. But there's no reason you folks can't go to the lobby 'til this thing blows over'. The necessity of laughter from within the theater both suggests that comedy is not closed, completed, but is timed for and with a live audience, and dramatizes the desire for auditory pleasure. (By necessity, this pleasure is limited, or different, for women—the absent second person, yet, at the same time, the reason for the tendentious joke. Margaret Dumont's characters as the second person of Groucho's jokes could hardly be figures of identification for female spectators who can only be objects, never subjects of the joke. To laugh within this system means to slip into a male seat and laugh at self as other. For example, again in the initial encounter between Firefly and Mrs. Teasdale in *Duck Soup*:

> **Firefly:** Not that I care, but where is your husband?
> **Teasdale:** He's dead.

Firefly: I'll bet he's just using that as an excuse.

Teasdale: I was with him 'til the very end.

Firefly: No wonder he passed away.

Teasdale: I held him in my arms and kissed him.

Firefly: Oh I see. Then it was murder.

The differences for males and females of auditory, as well as visual, pleasure are theoretical areas that need to be carefully examined and historically scrutinized.) Certain conventions of their films, e.g., gaps on the sound track waiting to be filled with laughter, the episodic structure and visual pauses, historically allude to vaudeville performances—the 'origins' of the Brothers and countless other comedians not preserved in films. In one sense, the Brothers' films are histories of vaudeville routines: the three of them climbing over couches, desks, beds and each other; Harpo handing his leg and pocket to anyone; their very names resonant of all the Bippos, Knockos; the schoolroom routine in *Horsefeathers* directly derived from Gus Edwards; the mirror scene in *Duck Soup* as a recreation of hundreds of vaudeville turns; to say nothing about the puns, the jokes, and their history in language denying notions of authorship, of ownership.

Irving Thalberg took this need for the third person quite literally, sending the Marx Brothers and their writers on the road. Sketches from *A Night At the Opera*, their first MGM film and the only one supervised by Thalberg, were tried out for eight weeks. They performed five times per day, six days a week, in 50-minute shows: 12:30, 3:00, 5:00, 7:30 and 9:30 PM, with constant rewriting. Each gag was meticulously timed with the live audiences, times which were subsequently included in the film's performance and editing.[23] The presence of a laughing audience, inscribed in the film, 1) concluded the joke's narrative and 2) signaled the pleasure of subverting language as power, as law. Roland Barthes exulted about this film:

> What a textural treasure, *A Night At the Opera!* If some critical demonstration requires an allegory in which the wild mechanics of the text-on-a-spree explodes, the film will provide it for me ... each of these episodes is the emblem of the logical subversions performed by the text.[24]

Important is Barthes' use of the term, 'episodes': the films as endless (until The End is arbitrarily declared by a title) strings of episodic jokes reminiscent of vaudeville sketches, the mixture of performance genres resembling Lacan's description of the signifying chain: 'rings of a necklace that is a ring in another necklace made of rings'.[25]

The remainder of Barthes' comment resembles Lacan's homology (mentioned earlier) between the unconscious process of condensation and the linguistic figure of metaphor: '...the structure of the superimposition of the signifiers, which metaphor takes as its field...'.[26]

> ... and if these emblems are perfect, it is ultimately because they are comic, laughter being what, by a last reversal, releases demonstration from its demonstrative attribute. What liberates metaphor, symbol,

emblem from poetic mania, what manifests its power of subversion, is
the preposterous . . . The logical future of metaphor would therefore be
the gag.[27]

Whether or not the gag is metaphor's 'logical' future, the path of the films is
clearly not that of 'rational' logic. The texts are on a spree, the visual
competing with the verbal as well as with the authorized positions of speech,
particularly its question-answer decorous structure. In another text, Barthes
asks then answers his question:

> Where is speech? In locution? In listening? In the *returns* of the one and
> the other? The problem is not to abolish the distinction in functions . . .
> but to protect the instability and giddying whirl of the positions of
> speech.[28]

The 'instability' of positions of speech operates *between* the Brothers, with
other characters in the films, and with the film's audience. Antagonists—
women, crooks, professors, ambassadors—are interrupted or insulted.
Groucho never really listens. He answers his own questions and questions his
own answers (in fact 'answer' might better be described as 'non-sequitur'),
while impatiently waiting for other characters to finish their lines or for the
cessation of laughter. Rufus T. Firefly anticipates Ambassador Trentino's
response to an offer of international friendship and thus peace with the
following:

> Mrs. Teasdale, you did a noble deed. I'd be unworthy of the high trust
> that's been placed in me if I didn't do everything within my power to
> keep our beloved Fredonia at peace with the world. I'll be only too happy
> to meet Ambassador Trentino and offer him, on behalf of my country,
> the right hand of good fellowship. And I feel sure that he will accept this
> gesture in the spirit in which it is offered . . . But suppose he doesn't? A
> fine thing that'll be! I hold out my hand and he refuses to accept it! That'll
> add a lot to my prestige, won't it? Me, the head of a country, snubbed by a
> foreign ambassador! Who does he think he is that he can come here and
> make a sap out of me in front of all my people. Think of it! I hold out my
> hand and that hyena refuses to accept! Why, the cheap, four-flushing
> swine! He'll never get away with it, I tell you . . . He'll never get away
> with it![29]

After one of the film's many musical fanfares, Trentino enters; Firefly slaps
his face with gloves, thereby initiating a film war that summarizes and
collapses all wars and their costumes. In *Duck Soup* the insult is both the crux
of the plot and the cause of war, comically illustrating that 'speech is irrevers-
ible', 'a word cannot be retracted. . .'.[30] Groucho never retracts; he just adds
insult to insult, only stopped by the actions and reasonable illogic of Chico and
Harpo or a fade to black. The authority implicit in language as law is reversed.
As Firefly sings in his inaugural song:

> These are the laws of my administration.
> No one's allowed to smoke . . .
> Or tell a dirty joke.
> And whistling is forbidden.
> If chewing gum is chewed

The chewer is pursued,
And in the hoose-gow hidden.
If any form of pleasure is exhibited,
Report to me and it will be prohibited.
I'll put my foot down,
So shall it be
This is the land of the free.

And, then, the chorus: 'If you think this country's bad off now, just wait till I get through with it'. It's back to grade school for everyone, and one has to wonder whether there is really any difference between governments' behavior and rules of protocol and second grade restrictions. Law is law, at any age, at any time. Language is always arbitrary, a potential means of power cleverly disguised as 'truth' or 'science' or 'law'.

Barthes' solution of 'instability' is protected not only in 'the giddying whirl of the positions of speech' but also in the shifting perceptual processes of looking and listening. Auditory pleasure competes with, plays with, visual pleasure in a torrent of cascading jokes and routines often impossible to catch up with. In *Duck Soup* the noisy breaking and entering scene, including Harpo's battle with a stubborn and infernal safe (actually a radio) that refuses to stop playing "Stars and Stripes Forever", is followed by the absolute, ghostly silence of the Groucho and Harpo mirror scene.

More complexly, the relation between jokes and the comic shifts our positions within the texts, away from listening to looking, then back again. We see Harpo's mayhem; Chico sees; the victim sees too late, if at all. This system of looks further solidifies our collusion with the Brothers against respectability, against systems which we so arduously learned. Freud's distinction between the processes of joking and the comic particularly dramatizes our relation to Harpo (and to a degree, Chico), often described as a child (but what an evil one)—although he was 40 years old when *Coconuts* was released in 1929. Only two people are necessary for the comic, which is found not made, as is the joke. To the comic, to Harpo who perversely refuses to use symbolic language, we respond as to 'the naive' in which 'someone completely disregards an inhibition because it is not present in him'.[31] This is in contrast with the operation of the joking process which depends on the maker and listener possessing the same inhibitions. In the comic, our pleasure comes from 'empathy'. The malicious and angelic 'innocence' of Harpo would be an interesting case study of the complex nature of the stages and processes of identification.

The process of the joke plays with the interchange of the comic; the verbal collides with or reinforces the visual; the spectator/auditor is complexly repositioned within the films. Yet there are, in addition, moments of perceptual respite, although these sequences frequently contain disconcerting social pronouncements, e.g., the quoted inaugural song, "All God's Chillun Got Guns", also in *Duck Soup*, and "Lydia", in *At The Circus*. These spectacles often parody the musical forms they seemingly replicate—yet the 'split' or tension or slip of Freud doesn't occur for either the spectator/auditor in the movie theater or within the film. Harpo's solos and Chico's shooting of the piano, both playing familiar songs and typically 'shot' in each film the same way, are restful interludes amidst the visual and verbal bombardment of other sequences. In these performances, the 'envelope' and the substance are not at odds for the spectator/auditor. No matter how subversive the lyrics might be, the characters within the film and the audience of the film are nonplussed, in union with the Brothers. Apparently, the wrapping of words in familiar melodies is a 'technique' of greater containment than the joke's, as Andy Kaufman's 'sing-along' routines so contemporarily illustrate

The fact that the spectacles in the films are lulls, with theater and onscreen audience perceptions unified, also separates the workings of these films from the genre labeled 'musical comedy', whose structure they resemble. In musical comedies, the spectacles are usually excessive moments of perceptual/motor discrepancy between performer and immobile audience.[32] Musical spectacles in the Marx Brothers' films follow a comparable pattern, with a critical difference, suggesting that the complexity of the process of opening the joking envelope by slipping into the unconscious and thereby lifting inhibitions (usually 'lifted' in musicals by the erotic spectacles of bodies, dancing, swimming, singing) has granted discharge to such a degree that there is nothing left to invest/discharge. During the performance numbers, the spectator/auditor can only recharge, an interesting reversal of subject process.

As I have mentioned, interruption is the pattern of the narrative movement of the films. The opening sequence of *Duck Soup* in which "Hail Fredonia" is begun three times to announce the arrival of Firefly encapsulates this structure. In a comparable displacement (Firefly slides down a fireman's pole and joins the film audience ceremoniously awaiting his arrival), the Brothers turn against the narrative, particularly in the Paramount films (1929-1935). They torment its 'rules' of construction and convention, breaking and entering the narrative as well as houses, constantly shattering any imposed cause-effect logic. Herein, for me, lies the disruptive potential of their films, which explode convention systems, go on a spree, and stand as 'emblems of the logical subversions performed by the Text'. Unlike the films of Keaton's characters who accomplished the impossible in deft, easy moves, they create complex machinations to achieve simple ends, including their very entrance into a scene. (The many fanfared entrances are tactics of delay; they never really leave a scene.) In *Monkey Business* (1931), it's not enough that they sneak on board ship and hide in the hold (a bit which returns, as do most of them, in, for example, *A Night At the Opera*). They sing rousing choruses of "Sweet Adeline" and send insulting notes to the Captain. When 'sneaking' off the ship, disguised as themselves yet declaring that they are all Maurice Chevalier, they imitate Chevalier's voice. In *At the Circus*, Harpo puts on his shoes *before* they enter the strongman's room; Chico says 'sh',

Harpo's Pavlovian cue for chaos. As in *Duck Soup*, 'sh', is followed by loud noise and discovery; disguise piled upon disguise, then discovery. In the breaking and entering sequence in *Duck Soup*, all three brothers do Groucho imitations, with Chico's voice and dialect, and Harpo's hair signaling difference. Harpo disguises himself as Harpo, in reverse, the back of his head; during the battle, Groucho, with an urn over his head, asks for help. Harpo responds and paints a face of 'Groucho' on the urn. The plethora of Marx Brothers' 'stuff' perpetuates the signs of the caricature, suggesting that anyone can look like a Marx Brother. Given the particularity of Groucho's vocal patterning, Chico's dialect, and Harpo's taxi-cab horn and whistle, anyone can sound like a Marx Brother. To a degree, the films' pleasures are derived from recognition of the familiar. And, in relation to other concurrent films, their texts were on a spree. Yet, the logic, the expectations and conventions created within each film and between the films are rigidly codified. Thus, on the one hand, the Marx Brothers were always the same, in any social situation, in any medium, this sameness resulting in social or textural derailment; and, in every film, in every medium, this sameness granting the comfortable pleasure of recognition and predictability.

With their move to MGM in 1935 (historically a time of standardization of the economics and conventions of the classical, sound film), the process of explaining or containing the Brothers began. Increasingly they were held within a narrative of a youthful couple needing help to marry. Harpo became a charade character who couldn't speak rather than a perverse brat who refused to use words. Chico became a nice guy worrying about the couple. In *At the Circus* even Groucho helped Miss Julie solve her marital and economic problems. With this 'reduction', according to Freud, of their roles to benefactors of marriage-bound ingenues, the Brothers' anarchy began to disperse, much as for Freud the joke disappears when its technique is 'reduced'. To be classically narrativized is to be sanitized, even for males, but particularly for clowns who, unfortunately, belonged *At the Circus*. Their comedy depended on their being out of place or in a place of potential disgrace.

NOTES

1. For historical elaboration see Douglas Gomery's doctoral dissertation, *The Coming of Sound to the American Cinema* (University of Wisconsin, Madison, 1975).

2. For recent elaboration of Comolli's work in English, see *The Cinematic Apparatus*, T. de Lauretis and S. Heath (eds.), (London: Macmillan, 1980).

3. C. Metz, 'The Imaginary Signifier', *Screen* vol. 16 no. 2 (Summer 1975), p. 61.

4. M.-F. Hans and G. Lapouge (eds.), *Les Femmes, la pornographie, l'erotisme* (Paris: Seuil 1978), p. 50. (Quoted by Stephen Heath in lecture at the Center for Twentieth Century Studies, 1979.)

5. M. A. Doane, 'The Film's Time and the Spectator's Space', (see this Monograph, p. 36).

6. Ibid., p. 48.

7. S. Freud, *Jokes and Their Relation to the Unconscious* (New York: W. W. Norton & Co., 1960).

8. Ibid., p. 204.

9. Ibid., p. 51.

10. J. Lacan, 'The Insistence of the Letter in the Unconscious', in *Structuralism*, J. Ehrmann (ed.), (Garden City, New York: Doubleday/Anchor, 1970), p. 119.

11. Ibid., p. 117.

12. Ibid., p. 116.

13. Ibid., p. 137.

14. Freud, p. 132.

15. Ibid., p. 130.

16. Metz, p. 65.

17. Freud, p. 85. It should be noted at this point that this pattern is directly reversed in the musical spectacles. University professors, cabinet ministers and society matrons become a singing/dancing backup chorus for the center-framed stars.

18. Ibid., p. 97.

19. Ibid., p. 101.

20. Ibid., p. 144.

21. Ibid., p. 149.

22. Ibid., p. 155.

23. J. Adamson, *Groucho, Harpo, Chico and Sometimes Zeppo* (New York: Simon & Schuster, 1973), p. 277.

24. R. Barthes, *Roland Barthes*, trans. R. Howard (New York: Hill & Wang, 1977), p. 80.

25. Lacan, p. 110.

26. Ibid., p. 119.

27. Barthes, p. 81.

28. R. Barthes, 'Writers, Intellectuals, Teachers', in *Image-Music-Text*, S. Heath (ed.), (London: Fontana/Collins, 1977), pp. 205-206.

29. This section, like the previous quotations, was transcribed from my audio tapes. Scripts are, however, available.

30. Barthes, p. 190.

31. Freud, p. 185.

32. My formulations of the musical comedy as a genre, its operation and conventions, is in *Ciné-Tracts* vol. 1 no. 2 (Summer 1977) as 'Spectacle and Spectator'.

Approaching Japanese Film

Noël Burch

In the introduction to his *Analyse structurale de la syntaxe du Japonais moderne*, Bernard Saint-Jacques has this to say about the difficulties encountered by linguists in their efforts to describe Japanese linguistic functions:

> Traditional methods are clearly inadequate for such a description. For, indeed, they take as their initial postulate that they can satisfactorily be described within the frameworks and categories offered by the grammars of European languages. As E. H. Jordan has quite rightly pointed out: 'The syntax of the spoken (Japanese) dialect, insofar as it has been described by both Japanese and Western scholars, is striking in its resemblance to the traditional descriptions of English and Latin syntax'. Clearly such descriptions can offer only very meagre information regarding the functioning or the particular structure of a language such as Japanese. In this connection, the linguist Tokieda points out the incomprehension of Japanese syntax systems stems precisely from its having been formulated in accordance with the patterns of English or Dutch grammar.[1]

Reading over this passage, I am struck by its relevance to my own decision, some eight years ago, to undertake a major study of Japanese film history. A comprehensive exhibition of Japanese films from all periods at the Paris Cinémathèque had made it clear to me that the descriptions of Japanese film history in general and of this or that significant film text in particular which were then available to Western readers were totally inadequate to their task, and that this was precisely for the reasons invoked by Saint-Jacques in connection with linguistic descriptions: they were predicated on the notion that the frameworks and structures of the Western cinema institution were intangible, that they were valid for all cultures, that to 'understand' or evaluate the films of Japan, a reading mastery of the codes of world cinema need only be completed by a crash course in the mysteries of Japanese 'culture'. The fact that the reading of Japanese culture that accompanied these pioneer attempts to acquaint Western readers with the cinema of Japan ultimately suffered from the same occidento-centrism inevitably compounded what already appeared to me eight years ago as an intellectual felony. The work which I have since had occasion to do on Japanese cinema has only strengthened this conviction.

At the end of his study of Japanese syntax, Saint-Jacques suggests, somewhat provocatively, that, from the point of view of structural analysis, Japanese may be unique among human languages, unclassifiable in terms of one or other of the great linguistic families; a suggestion made on the basis of the sum of structural idiosyncrasies revealed by his and other synchronic studies, as well as by the bulk of diachronic ones. These, it seems, all tend towards the conclusion formulated as follows by a Japanese linguist (Professor Izui of Tokyo):

> It is quite difficult to prove any definite affinity of Japanese according to the strict rules of comparative linguistics. Scholars both in Japan and abroad have already made every effort to arrive at a definite solution; still, we have had no really convincing solution up to now. Japanese remains, as before, a language without any definite assignable genealogy.

Such statements parallel the conclusions I have reached in my own work regarding the profound uniqueness, the profound *otherness*, of what I have called 'the classical Japanese cinema'.

It is the recognition that this otherness can only be read by me—by us—in terms of some category or other of Western thought that is indeed inscribed in the title of my book, *To the Distant Observer*.[2] Just as Saint-Jacques and other modern linguists have turned away from the culturally biased patterns of Indo-European languages to the more neutral and open possibilities of language analysis offered by structural linguistics, so too I have tried to enlist concepts forged in a number of contemporary disciplines in the hope of bringing to the surface dimensions of the Japanese cinema which appear to me capable of contributing to the 'distancing' or 'deconstruction' of our own cinema institution as it is constituted as a mode of representation. It soon became apparent, to me, that is, that an understanding of the otherness of the classical Japanese cinema could be of great help in furthering our understanding of the mode of representation which has been at the center of the Western cinema institution for over 50 years—that the demonstrable existence of a specifically non-Western mode of cinematic representation could make possible considerable strides towards the demonstration that our own Institutional Mode of Representation (hereafter IMR) can only in a very limited sense be regarded as 'natural', as inherent in the technology of the camera, that it is, in fact, historically and culturally overdetermined to a degree and in ways that have only recently begun to be suspected.

One of the main features of my book, then, is that the experience of the

Japanese cinema is unique. I have, I feel, adduced fairly cogent reasons in favor of such a thesis, but I will confess that until I have been able to devote the necessary time and money to viewing films made over a comparable period of time in other non-Western countries—and we know that in China, India and Egypt, at least, film production thrived at a very early date—I cannot be entirely categorical in my assertion that the Japanese film of the nineteen thirties provides the only large-scale example of a cinematic mode of representation derived not from the basic requisites of the IMR, but from the signifying practices of a particular non-Western culture. Jay Leyda's study of Chinese cinema—*Dianying* or *Electric Shadows*[3]—would seem to bear out this assumption, as do the few hints that have been available to me concerning the early production of other non-Western countries, but the main thrust of my argumentation has been inferred from external evidence. Japan is the only major country of non-Western culture never to have known the rigors of colonial rule in any form until 1945, and which in fact, at the time of her most characteristic film production, was fast becoming an imperial power in her own right. In China, and as far as I can ascertain in India and Egypt, the colonial powers—particularly England and Germany—provided both the technical know-how and personnel, as well as the financial backing, for all the films produced during that crucial period which witnessed in Europe and the USA the development of the IMR (I am referring to a period which extends from approximately 1908 to 1929). In Japan, this was absolutely not the case. There, through the half-century that had followed the opening of the country and the restoration of the Emperor Meiji, the general policy of the ruling class had been to send home all Western advisers as soon as the technology which they had to teach had been learnt by the Japanese themselves. We must remember that the decision to open Japan to Western influence after three centuries of conservational seclusion had not been simply bowing down to Perry's display of gunboat diplomacy. It had been consciously aimed as well at enabling Japan to avert the fate which had already befallen so much of Asia in that period of rampant Western imperialism. The avowed goal of the forced industrialization and 'modernization' of the country was to enable Japan to resist Western economic and military expansionism by beating the West at its own game.

Now, the technology that the West had to impart to Japan during the first few years following the invention of the Cinématographe was simple indeed. Once the Western technicians had disclosed the secrets of operating that really elementary piece of machinery, along with those of manufacturing and processing film stock, which can scarcely have taxed the resources of a chemical industry that was already quite advanced, they could be asked to leave. This was what happened after only a very few years, so that the Japanese were forming their own cameramen, for example, decades before this became possible in China. To my mind, this state of affairs is by far the most important single factor to be taken into account in attempting to explain why the Japanese cinema, seemingly alone among those of the non-Western world, evolved along lines which were fundamentally Japanese for 50 years—at least until the second 'opening' of the country which came through the defeat of fascist militarism in 1945 and the ensuing years of American occupation 'democratization' in accordance with the Western bourgeois model.

This, then, schematically, may be said to account for the 'passive' side of the question, so to speak, for the absence of an imposed Western model whose premise was felt elsewhere in the East so strongly (for example, although China as a whole was never actually colonized in the manner of, say, India, film production there was concentrated in cities like Shanghai and Hong Kong, where the great capitalist nations controlled commerce and industry in the purest colonial tradition).

What now of the 'active' side of the question? How did the Japanese ultimately come to draw upon their cultural traditions—upon their arts and language and indeed upon their very social structure—to forge this uniquely non-Western cinema, non-Western in terms not only of its thematic substance—in this respect, of course, even those nations that suffered most directly under colonial rule produced non-Western films from the very start—but non-Western at the level of representation itself?

My answers to this question—undoubtedly incomplete—fill a volume of over 100,000 words and within the framework of this paper I can only sketch in the main features of my argumentation. I shall also attempt—and this perhaps will be slightly more relevant to the overall theme of this conference—to raise one further issue which in fact is not coped with in the book at all.

Accepted histories of film often state or imply that Western cinema—the cinema of France, England and the United States, and later that of Denmark and Italy—in order to 'grow up', in order to 'develop its own language', had to leave behind its theatrical origins, generally regarded—and I do not think I am overstating the case—as the Original Sin of the movie industry. At the same time, we all know that when cinema really did 'come of age' as an entertainment industry, that is to say after the introduction of lip-synch sound, the dominant form for many years, which is still very much with us today, was canned theater. Of course, the paradox here is only apparent, since the theater which cinema was called upon to 'outgrow' was absolutely not the same as that which was the ultimate object of emulation for the galaxy of innovations which led from Hepworth to the *Jazz Singer* via Griffith, the Ince brothers, etc. At one end of the process we have the popular theater of the nineteenth century, the circus, the vaudeville stage and the music hall. At the other we have the bourgeois theater as it had achieved perfection on Broadway, Drury Lane and the Boulevards of Paris at just about the time of Louis Lumière's invention.

This pattern of development, the analysis of which is central to a work I am now doing with Jorge Dana on the genealogy of the IMR, was made spectacularly graphic to me during a short survey of early Danish cinema recently organized by Dr. Barry Salt at the National Film Theatre in London. In the habitual terms of the linear view of film history—postulating a teleological 'progress' from Lumière to, say, Sam Peckinpah—the films made by Urban Gad and his contemporaries after 1907 were literally light-years ahead of anything being made at that time in any other country. And the reasons why are obvious. Responsible for these films were men and women (Asta Nielsen's role at that early period is considerable) who came from the bourgeois theater, who were familiar with a repertoire that included Ibsen, Bjoernsen and Shaw, and who brought with them a thematic and technical sophistication which makes Griffith, for example, appear clearly for what he was: an ambitious young man from a backwoods area of a backwoods nation, whose cultural pretentions were certainly as high as could be expected given the context of the American film industry, but whose work remained essentially rooted in certain popular forms of representation—notably the vaudeville playlet and nineteenth century melodrama. All of Griffith's work until at least 1920 occupies a position of complete ambivalence; it was 'progressive'— in the linear sense—for only a few short years and never attained the middle-class sophistication which DeMille began bringing to the American film during World War I, but which had already been achieved a hundredfold by the Danish cinema—in films which seem mostly to have been banned or boycotted in the USA, so strong were their representations of sexual passion. By their very modernity, of both subject and treatment, these Danish films illuminate spectacularly one major aspect of the fundamental otherness of our primitive cinema, grounded so strongly in what Georges Sadoul has called the urban folklore of the proletarian masses.

Now, it is my conviction that just as the Japanese cinema at its most characteristic offers us a tool for relativizing, for situating historically the mode of representation that has dominated world cinema for over half a century, so too does our own primitive cinema, in part because of its privileged relationships with the performing, graphic and narrative arts associated with nineteenth century popular culture. I am further convinced that certain aspects of the complex and contradictory developments that took place in Western cinema between 1896 and 1929 must be understood in terms of class relationships, in terms of the gradual *embourgeoisement* of cinema that was constitutive of the emergence of the IMR. This process took place in part through the conscious efforts of the entrepreneurs to interest 'the better classes' in a form of entertainment which for over 30 years in France, and for at least 20 in the USA, was enjoyed almost solely by the most exploited sections of the urban working class. It also took place through the less conscious efforts of directors, writers, technicians and actors seeking specific cinema forms capable of translating to the screen the fundamental representational strategies of the novel, drama and painting that corresponded with the world view of the bourgeoisie.

Now I do not need to tell my present audience that between the basic strategies of classical Western art and those of Eastern art in general, and of Japanese art in particular, there exists a wide gulf, in fact a set of fundamental antinomies. And needless to say, one of the main theses of my book is that it is the existence and continued popularity of a whole series of traditional performing, narrative and graphic arts which ultimately provided a model for the emergence, in the late twenties and thirties, of what I have come to regard as a filmic equivalent of the tenth century poetry or the eighteenth century drama and prints of Japan.

Before however briefly sketching some aspects of this filiation, I should say a word about the cultural implications of class relationships in Japan, for here too we have a fundamental difference with the situation of cultural alienation through class barriers which I have just alluded to in the West. It was Earle Ernst, in his remarkable book on kabuki,[4] who called my attention to the fact that in Tokugawa Japan—the Japan of the late sixteenth to early nineteenth centuries—economic and cultural seclusion and the social structures peculiar to the Japanese version of feudalism produced an extraordinary unanimity of taste: however fierce the oppression of the poor and helpless by the rich and powerful, the entire society shared exactly the same tastes in theater, verse, dress, house furnishings, etc. And by the end of the nineteenth century, when kabuki and doll theater audiences, for example, were shrinking to coterie status, a cinema which in many important aspects derived directly or indirectly from them was to replace those art forms in the role of what we must term *inter-class entertainment,* in the sense that we could certainly describe Elizabethan theater as such, in a sense which has totally disappeared from Western theater since the mid nineteenth century, and in a sense which, I believe, our cinema and television achieved only very partially and very briefly.

The habitual description of early Japanese cinema, by both Western and Japanese observers, adopting as it does the ideologically determined categories used to describe the early cinema of the West, also tells of a long, dreary period of 'theatricality' when Japanese films had an 'old-fashioned look' whose dull perpetuation through the twenties was alleviated only by a few 'Western-style' films produced by a handful of forward-looking heroes. According to this view, Japanese cinema does not 'come of age' until at least two decades after Western cinema, in the mid thirties, a coming of age which is of course symbolized by the gradual elimination of such impedimenta of the traditional arts as the *oyama* or female impersonator—and it is interesting to note the important role of the female impersonator in the primitive cinema of the West as well—the elimination above all of the despised *benshi,* or lecturer, that fierce enemy of any possible progress in the Japanese film industry—progress here being equated, of course, with Westernization. The author of a recent so-called history of Japanese cinema entitles the chapter dealing with what was no doubt an important period of transition: 'Good-bye *benshi,* hello beauty'. I shall attempt to locate the seat of this cultural-neurotic attitude later on.

In every way, the *benshi* is the Japanese equivalent of the lecturer heard in the nickelodeons of America and in the fairground cinemas of France and England prior to around 1910, and whose role in Western film history is still far from documented. However, in the Japanese cinema, he was merely one of a whole set of 'distancing' functions derived from the Japanese traditional arts and which appear in one form or another in most of the silent films made before 1930. Needless to say, I, for one, do not consider that period as a desert at all, but rather as a time of incubation.

However, before elaborating on this concept, I must emphasize here that anything I or anyone else may have to say about the first 35 years of Japanese cinema must be tempered with considerable modesty. Still today, less than half a dozen films made prior to 1920 survive complete, and of the twenties' production, I doubt that 30 films have been found. Considering that we are in fact dealing with a potential corpus of thousands of films—Japan has always been one of the most prolific industries in the world, turning out hundreds of films per year—one has to admit that the sampling is small indeed. Of course, there are a good many scraps and fragments left from the twenties, and we must not despair of unearthing more complete films now that scholarship in these matters, which has long lain in shameful neglect, is starting to develop in Japan. Since my last visit there, five years ago, many films of considerable importance from the thirties, and a few from the twenties, have been rediscovered. But when one realizes that the first major volume in a Western language devoted to the history of the Japanese cinema was written in complete ignorance of many essential films (some of them described from hearsay without this handicap being acknowledged) one realizes how strong was the need for a more rigorous approach in these matters.

Now, I have called the first 30 years of Japanese cinema a period of incubation. Of prime importance in this respect is the perduration, practically until the end of the nineteen twenties, of a kind of 'primitive mode of representation'—comparable by and large with that of late Méliès or Feuillade—or perhaps even more precisely with that form which in the United States seems to have achieved a brief stability around 1905 in, for example, Billy Bitzer's forgotten masterpiece, *Kentucky Feud.* The perduration of this 'primitive mode', in which distant frontality and the centripetal long shot remain absolutely predominant, can be perceived too as the backbone of that decisive *bulwark* which Japanese traditional culture—bodied forth in both audience tastes and filmmakers' working habits—set up against the otherwise all-pervasive mode of representation produced by the history of the occidental institution.

I further maintain that the supreme achievements associated in the nineteen thirties with the names of Ozu and Mizoguchi, and also with those of such lesser known figures as Ishida Tamizo and Shimizu Miroshi, were to a large extent the direct consequence of this period of 'conservational' incubation.

Now, I must confess that during my two stays in Japan the theses I am outlining (very sketchily) here met with very little sympathy among critics or filmmakers there. The fact is that Japan has no native theoretical tradition comparable to that of, say, France or Germany. Consequently, any critical apparatus tends to have been taken over wholesale from what is often the most archaic thinking of the West—in accordance with a pattern of imperialism well-known in Africa and the Middle East, for example. Japanese Marxism, in particular, appears not to have evolved beyond the pragmatic humanism of, say, Jean Jaurès, when it has not become inextricably entangled with remnants of the *bushido* code (I am thinking of certain bloody aberrations of the so-called New Left). Consequently, dominant thinking in Japan concerning the national cinema tends to see the pre-nineteen thirties as, indeed, a period of medieval darkness and the socially conscious films of the postwar years as a unique Golden Age. This type of attitude among leftist critics of the older generation—albeit the only serious voices raised in Japan during the twenties and thirties—has led to such aberrations as Iwasaki Akira's offhanded dismissal as melodramatic trash of what is in my view one of Mizoguchi's finest films, *The Story of the Last Crysanthemums*, or to the wholesale condemnation, by Imamura Taihei, of the work of Ozu.

I was, however, fortunate enough to meet one young scholar—Iwamoto Kenji—whose work runs parallel to and confirms my own. This, I will not deny, was of considerable solace during my period of field work, so complacently ensconced is such a large share of the Japanese intellectual establishment in what we of the West can only see as a militant philistinism.

When I met Iwamoto Kenji in 1973, he had just written an essay entitled 'The Benshi and Montage', the main thrust of which was that the entire Japanese tradition of narrative and representation, as it was crystallized in the *benshi*, was such that Japanese directors and technicians of the twenties and thirties (perhaps, Iwamoto suggests, of later periods also, though I cannot follow him there) never felt the need for the linearization provided by occidental editing, for the production of the quasi-linguistic chain which is in fact common to Griffith and Eisenstein and which is so fundamentally characteristic of our Institution.

Here indeed is, I feel, the crux of the situation. Among the pertinent traits that Jorge Dana and I have defined as basically constitutive of the IMR, the linearization of iconographic signifiers through the editing process occupies a privileged place.

Even in the rare, sophisticated instance when the primitive tableau shot was organized in such a way as to 'guide' the eye through the succession of events within the frame, even when a lecturer was present in the theater to give these primitive gestures towards linearization a helping hand, the panoramic coexistence of dozens of iconographic signifiers, the lack of any photographic means of isolating each pictorial event successively, all contributed to the fundamental nonlinearity of the primitive image. And the fact that the modern spectator so often has the greatest difficulty reading these images at all is, to my mind, conclusive evidence of the alterity in this respect of the primitive cinema. Who today can claim to have deciphered at first viewing the opening shot of the Biograph film *Tom Tom the Piper's Son*, familiar I expect to most of us through Ken Jacob's masterful rehandling? And who among us has spotted at first or subsequent viewing the 'Mickey Finn' which a traitorous hoodlum slips into Lilian Gish's drink in the dance-hall scene in *Musketeers of Pig Alley*, a film made as late as 1912 (and this detail, among many others, attests, as I have suggested, that Griffith remained a semi-primitive long after the Danes had 'invented', so to speak, Blake Edwards and Louis Malle)?

Is there justification in thinking that after ten years of moviegoing, the culturally underprivileged mass audiences of France, America and England—entirely unaccustomed as they were to the centered, directive compositions of academic painting and the bourgeois stage (but no doubt familiar with the churning activity of the circus, the fairground and the minstrel show)—actually had some kind of 'expanded' perception—if only in the sense that the audience of that time had to be constantly 'on its toes'?

Hypotheses about audience reactions experienced 75 years ago are foolhardy to say the least, especially when the experience that concerns us was that of a class which had absolutely no possibility of expressing itself in print. However, we do know that in the United States, at least, moviegoers from among the 'better class of people', whose collective moviegoing experience began far later and was no doubt far less intensive, actually did complain that they were unable to follow the sequence of events in the films that they were being shown around 1907, and were actually demanding the presence of lecturers in the cinemas to help them out. How did the inarticulate masses feel about this problem? We will, of course, never really know. Still, it is significant that the lecturer disappears totally from the American film around 1912 and from the French and English cinema a little later, precisely at a time when decisive strides were being taken away from the primitive tableau and towards the linearization of the signifier.

In contrast to the fate of the Western lecturer, his Japanese cousin, the *benshi*, does not disappear until the very end of Japanese silent film production in 1937, and is revived in a slightly modified form in the years following World War II when the shortage of films led distributors to bring out silent 'classics' with the addition of a sung narration. It is also interesting to note that there still exist in Japan many amateur *benshi*—and even a few professionals—who exercise their talents when silent films are shown in museums or to film societies.

The very idea of a lecturer speaking in the hall during a screening, commenting on the film, getting in the way of our plunge into that imaginary world, is fundamentally inimical to the Western filmgoer's habits. Which is why any mention of the *benshi* in characteristic Western studies on the subject will be couched at best in terms of condescending curiosity towards an exotic practice, at worst in terms of ironic contempt. Most modern-minded Japanese themselves consider the *benshi* to be one of those quaintly shameful corners of a past which, on the whole, they would just as soon forget—along with *tanka* verse, the *bushido* code and, of course, militarism and its historical corollary, the 1945 defeat.

As Iwamoto Kenji quite convincingly demonstrates, however, it is impossible to separate the long life of the *benshi* from the positive develop-ment of the Japanese film, up to and including the prewar masterpieces of Mizoguchi and Ozu. I would add that it is just as impossible to separate that growth from the female impersonators, traditional stage makeup and other 'primitive', i.e., traditional, factors that did not disappear until the nineteen twenties. The *benshi*, however, is without a doubt the essential factor in this galaxy of conservational traits, and even in this hurried overview, he deserves some special attention.

What exactly was the *benshi's* function? At bottom, he was there to read the images for their narrative content, he was *reading off the diegesis*. He removed the burden of the narrative from the picture on the screen in much the same way as the *gidayu-bushi*, the singing narrator of the traditional doll-theater, removed the narrative burden from the 'action' of the puppets and puppeteers on the stage. Practically devoid of titles as they were, most silent Japanese films before 1925 and even after, can scarcely be said to contain the signs of their narrative at all. Today, indeed, they are all but incomprehensible when viewed on their own. The function of the image is entirely different from that chain of pictorial events which rapidly became codified within the Western institution. I feel that we may speak rather of a field of signs whose function is to reiterate certain stereotyped poses, gestures and compositions. The meanings produced by the image are fundamentally redundant and ultimately one feels that the function of the image is one of confirmation rather than adumbration.

These are only a few of the considerations which have led Iwamoto and myself to the conclusion that Western editing was fundamentally irrelevant to the project of the Japanese cinema for several decades; that Japanese directors, though perfectly familiar with the development of editing in the films of the West, many of which were imported promptly from Europe and America, were simply not interested in making use of it (at least not at all as it was used in Europe or in the USA); that Japanese audiences, although they apparently were able to enjoy foreign films, with a little help from the *benshi*, nevertheless seemed to find Western editing structures unwelcome in native films—as witness the commercial failure of the handful of neo-Western films made in Tokyo around 1920. And I feel that it was this long indifference to Western editing, in other words to the foundations of the IMR, that ultimately made possible the rise of the classical cinema of the thirties.

Despite the fact that several papers presented at this conference showed that concern for the classical era of the Japanese film is growing in film studies in the country—and of course, I am delighted to witness this development—I am quite certain that the chief reproach likely to be leveled at my book will be that I underestimate the importance of Japanese postwar cinema and especially the later films of Ozu and Mizoguchi, and that conversely I claim for the nineteen thirties a place apart which most Japanese and Western commentators to date have preferred to reserve for the forties and fifties, or perhaps even the sixties. This debate involves, I think, crucial issues—it is not merely a confrontation of tastes, though it is true that my personal aesthetic preferences go to the films of the thirties and of these masters in particular. However, if I see a decisive morphological difference between the prewar and postwar models of the Japanese cinema, it is based upon an overall analysis of the nature of the Western institution and on a redefinition of its pertinent traits.

To illustrate the way in which this 'primitivism' of the twenties and before may be seen to have served as an incubator for a specifically Japanese mode of representation that burgeoned forth in so many films of the thirties, I will confine myself principally to two examples: the use of the long shot and the long take in the films of Mizoguchi and the approach to eyeline matching in the films of Ozu.

First, however, I must insist on what I regard as one of the book's major theses: in no way do these masters' works, however accomplished, however ultimately unrivaled, constitute a fundamentally exceptional moment in the history of the Japanese cinema of that period in the way that the films of, say, Bresson or Tati are quite unique in Western production in the forties, fifties and sixties. Indeed, one of my most solid reasons for maintaining that this 'golden age' of the Japanese cinema is a late manifestation of secular traditions in the arts of Japan is that the relationship which the work of these masters bore to that of a great many of their contemporaries is absolutely comparable to that which the verse of the Heian poet Ki no Tsuroyaki bore to the very similar poems written by thousands of courtiers during his lifetime, or the painted screens of the Muromachi master Sotatsu to the very comparable work of his contemporaries in that field. Within the larger framework of Japanese cultural history, prior that is to the opening of the country and the first full-scale contacts with the West and with Western concepts, both the notion and the reality of the artist-genius, that godlike hero, is totally unknown. The distinction between originality and plagiarism was meaningless, since neither of these concepts seems even to have been recognized. For reasons having to do with social and geopolitical structure as well as religion, there is absolutely no place in the Japanese mythos for the image of the artist as rebel, as defying the canons of his age, as a hero whose gifts stand out *in opposition* to the academy—think of our artistic giants: Cezanne, Beethoven, Proust. . . . In the Japanese tradition even the greatest artists have always been part of the academy.

In the Japanese cinema there have, of course, been instances of the idiosyncratic creator: Kinugasa in the twenties, Kurosawa in the fifties are the most outstanding. Their major achievements—*Page of Madness, Ikiru*—can be related only marginally to the mainstream of the traditional cinema. As for Oshima and his contemporaries, they of course have carried the image of the idiosyncratic, 'mad' creator to extremes, while remaining paradoxically related more profoundly perhaps than either Kurosawa or Kinugasa to very ancient traditions. However, this is somewhat outside my subject today. What I am saying is that Ozu, Mizoguchi, Shimizu, Naruse, Ishida, Yamanaka, Tasaka and most of the other important filmmakers of the thirties belong to that traditional mainstream, that their work is closely related to that of hundreds of filmmakers, some forgotten, some remembered, but whose essentially collective effort contributed decisively to the work of the masters, work which in turn was also a part of that collective effort. Tasaka Tomotaka is no master in the sense implied here, that is, his work never crystallized tradition in any exceptionally coherent way. Yet, in a film made in 1928 called *Town of Love and Hate*, he makes systematic use of the cutaway scenic shot (which I have called pillow-shot), prefiguring Ozu's own use of this suspension of the diegetic flow by some four or five years. I am not of course trying to say that he 'invented' the pillow-shot; in my opinion the concept is not useful in a context where all the elements are so overdetermined. I am simply saying that Ozu did not invent it either, and that it is simply by developing it in a certain way that he achieves a relative singularity within the collective effort. In short, the auteur theory has to undergo some very serious revamping before it can cope with this period of Japanese cinema.

In a similar way, Mizoguchi undeniably carried to unprecedented heights of beauty and discipline the single-take scene and the systematization of camera distance. However, even random soundings show that similar attitudes were extremely common, that the persistent reluctance among many directors to adopt Western procedures which characterized this period paved the way for the major traits of Mizoguchi's mature style, from *The Gion Sisters* of 1936 to *The Love of Actress Sumako* of 1947. And if I insist on a fundamental distinction being drawn between Mizoguchi's prewar masterpieces and the handsome, internationally acclaimed films made during and after the American Occupation, it is in part due precisely to the modification of the mode of functioning of the wide-angle long take. In a film such as *The Story of the Last Crysanthemums*, each composition has a kind of rigid autonomy, the 'montage' effect of the moving camera is akin to the succession of static long shots which composed the tableau films of old. In *Story of a Woman by Saikaku*, (known in the West as *The Life Of Oharu*), on the other hand, the successive tableaux have been melted together in a sophisticated, somewhat mannered flow of signification, not unrelated to the films of, say, William Wyler, whose most famed achievements of that period—*The Best Years of Our Lives, The Heiress*—are known to have stimulated Mizoguchi's emulative instincts.

In this connection, it is important to note that both Mizoguchi and Ozu, insofar as can be judged from the very inadequate evidence now at our disposal, developed during their early careers (prior, that is, to 1930) a very advanced mastery of the Western mode of representation. The fairly rapid changes in their respective approaches that took place in the early and mid thirties clearly correspond to a deliberate choice. I have suggested in my book that this choice was not merely personal, that it was in part determined by political and ideological developments in Japan, by the new emphasis placed on traditional values in connection with the rise of militarist ideology, the rejection of Western values associated with the development of a Pan-Asian imperialism. I certainly expect this hypothesis to be attacked as well, since it is always difficult to ascribe work which one admires to reactionary forces, at least I take it to be so for anyone of the Left. The debate should be an interesting one.

In any case, however, my main thesis about that 'choice' on the part of directors like Ozu and Mizoguchi, is that it could never have been made without the period of incubation, the conservational attitude of most other directors throughout the twenties. I am also prepared to admit, of course, that in their case, at least, familiarity with Western ways no doubt contributed to their capacity to make that choice as clearly as they did. It is this no doubt that sets them apart from directors who, probably unable to pose the terms of the problem at all, never did choose and produced bastard forms which can hardly interest us at all today except perhaps anthropologically. One of the best examples of this complex filiation with the Western mode can be found in the issue of eyeline matching in the Ozu films of the thirties.

The related issues of eyeline matching and the reverse field figure are in my view crucial to an understanding of the IMR. This is not the place to set forth in detail the work that Jorge Dana and I are presently engaged upon, but briefly I shall say this: the true reverse field figure (i.e., successive shots of two actors facing each other in the imaginary space of the diegesis, facing the camera in pro-filmic space—and, eventually, speaking to each other through the silent signs of the intertitle or the actual sound of the optical track) is, in our view, the keystone of the IMR; indeed, it was the last component to fall into place, before the advent of synch sound. We feel there is good reason to assert that it was not until well over a quarter of a century after Lumière's *Workers Leaving a Factory* that it became current usage to show successive front-angle shots of characters looking at each other, speaking to each other, with consistently matching eyelines and with their gazes passing close enough to the camera to directly implicate the spectator in that symbolically pregnant exchange. It may seem surprising that it should have taken so long for this figure to acquire its full status within the procedures of production. (The continuity girl, whose task it was to guarantee such elements of continuity as the eyeline match, did not appear in the studios until the late twenties.)

This apparent delay is closely related to the fascinating history of the taboo against looking at the camera. Until 1906, in the West, looking at the camera was absolutely the rule, there was hardly a film in which this did not occur (and the primitive striptease film with the delegated male voyeur hidden behind the screen on the edge of the frame whilst the stripping bride throws burning glances at the audience is wonderfully rich in signification here). It may well be observed that this habit of glancing at camera came from the variety and melodrama stage, where the aside, one of the 'presentational' impedimenta of the pre-bourgeois theater, still thrived within a system which did not posit the radical exteriority of audience viewpoint so characteristic of the serious bourgeois theater (from which the illusion-breaking aside had by now been completely expelled). However, as was clearly seen by far-sighted commentators (especially some writing in the American trade papers), the glance at the camera was even more harmful to the *illusion comique* than any stage aside, no doubt because of the intensity of the illusion itself, produced by the very special mimesis of photography, but also because the camera lens is in fact a point in pro-filmic space, as opposed to the broad 'sea of gazes' of the theater audience, and a look at the camera calls upon the individual spectator by name, as it were. By 1910, at least one American company (Selig) included among the lists of Dos and Don'ts handed out to the actors it hired a strict ban against looking at the camera for asides, or at the director for instructions or approval. This taboo soon became so strong that in a film made as late as 1919, by one of the otherwise most sophisticated directors of the period—in Maurice Tourneur's *The Bluebird*—the reverse field figure had still not progressed beyond the stage of opposing side angles; moreover, when, at the end of the film, one of the children addresses the audience in a moralizing farewell, he looks off camera by at least 30 degrees.

The principle of eyeline-direction matching, closely related with the whole issue of the spectator's monovalent orientation to diegetic space through a rationalization of editing découpage, was already in evidence before the true reverse field figure came into general use. But it was the association of the possibility of close to camera eyeline exchange with the concept of the monovalent orientation to space that put the finishing and absolutely decisive touch on that all-encompassing, imaginary space into which we enter when we are watching a movie to become an invisible, omniscient voyeur, at the very center of the face-to-face exchange.

In Japan in the twenties, the issues of matching in general and eyeline matching in particular were being coped with, if at all, by only those few filmmakers trying to introduce the Western mode. The still predominant traditional film very seldom had recourse to continuity editing more advanced than the concertina (cut-in, cut-back) and an occasional pair of opposing angles. These were used sparingly, sometimes arbitrarily, sometimes as the very special signifier of a specially dramatic event—so undomesticated were these and other procedures such as cutaway close-up, over-shoulder shot, etc. Consequently, in the Japanese cinema as a whole at this period—we are still talking about the twenties—eyeline matching—insofar as it appears at all, of course—seems about as often 'wrong' as it is 'right'. This of course was also the case in the Western cinema, until about 1925 or so, though the balance began to lean heavily towards correct matches as the scriptgirl's presence made itself felt. So it was, too, with the films of Ozu prior to 1933, at least as far as we can judge from the films that have survived. However, after 1933, (the turning point, I believe, is a film called *Woman of Tokyo*), Ozu begins systematically setting up all of the reverse fields—which make up at least half the running time of any of his films—in such a way that eyelines never 'meet' at the surface of the screen in the accepted way. The only exceptions to this rule are far too few and random to be anything but fortuitous. And in fact we know that at one point in Ozu's later career, his editor challenged the way the master set up these shots and Ozu actually agreed to experiment with shooting a scene both ways: the right way—as indicated in the Hollywood manuals available in Japan—and the wrong way, Ozu's way. After the projection of the edited rushes, Ozu's only comment was 'There is no difference', and he went blithely on having only incorrect eyeline matches in his films.

Now of course many explications of this phenomenon, generally having to do with some ideology of the incommunicable, have been set forth by various writers, Western and Japanese. Some of these are outlined in my book, along with my own attempt to analyze the role of this seminal choice in Ozu's complex systemics and its relationship to his approach to the cinematic image as picture plane. Here I can only stress my conviction that through this refusal to accept an absolutely fundamental *value* of the Western cinema—enveloping diegetic space as guaranteed by the rationalized eyeline match—Ozu is turning his back on something essentially occidental and accepting a perception of time and space which we may call 'typically Japanese', but which is also found in many aspects of Chinese and other non-Western cultures as well, a *topological* perception as opposed to the linear models offered by the classical model of representation still dominant among the peoples whose culture issues from the Greco-Christian tradition. This particular aspect of Ozu's systemics is not quite unique to him. In the important films which he made between 1933 and 1936, and especially in his masterpiece *Wife Be Like a Rose*, Naruse Mikio also systematically mismatches eyeline. To my knowledge, no other Japanese director has done so, but my contention here is that only in the Japanese context of that period could anyone have done so.

It is at this point, of course, that we touch on perhaps the most sensitive issue at stake in any intercultural confrontation.

If I have one serious reservation to formulate at this stage concerning *To the Distant Observer*, it is in connection with statements such as the one I have just made. In dealing with people as obviously different from us as the Japanese, in dealing with artifacts as obviously different from our own as certain products of Japanese culture, any observer conscious of the lie of universal humanism, conscious of the historical and political implications of occidento-centrism, will quite naturally, I think, be inclined to 'twist the stick in the other direction', as a French expression goes.

And perhaps to twist it too far.

Because in the opposite direction lies the danger of culturalism, of the cult of the *Weltanschauung*, the temptation to derive the totality of cultural behavior from some secret center of activity, much as Humboldt in the nineteenth century imagined that he had discovered the essence of the world view of this or that European people in the outward traits of their respective languages. There is also the parallel danger of taking too literally the Sapir hypothesis and imagining that the system of representation—or the language—which one has been able to describe as indeed decisively different from our own, is actually isomorphic with the literal experiences of men and women in a real society; we have only to think of Benjamin Whorf's conclusion from certain grammatical particularities of the Hopi language that Hopi Indians actually perceive existence as an eternal present.

In my own case, I fear that my attempts to detect the signs—rather than the source—of a fundamentally nonmetaphysical, nonlogocentric approach to representation, of a cultural indifference to the cult of the analog, in the double experience of phonetic and nonphonetic writing in Japan, come dangerously close to the kind of aberration which the often remarkably perceptive Whorf inclined to founder upon. Perhaps it is for this reason that I made no attempts in this book to explore the parallels—and clearly they are many—between the structures of the spoken Japanese language and the approach to narrative and spatial organization characteristic of the traditional cinema of the thirties. That the Japanese language organizes temporal and spatial concepts according to patterns very different from ours is almost a truism. That it does not present the appearance of syntactical linearity that characterizes the major languages of the West is equally obvious. Bernard Saint-Jacques shows how Japanese syntax involves an almost complete mobility of autonomous syntagma, and one could point to a similar structure in the haiku tale, notably those of Saikaku.

The system which I have detected at work in the culture, society and cinema of Japan is an invention all my own—or rather, it is an invention of a certain manifestation, at the place I call me, of modern European culture, informed by Marxism, structural linguistics, psychoanalysis ... This system, which I call Japan—and here I take my cue from Roland Barthes, whose seminal essay, *l'Empire des Signes*, has informed my work all the way—this system was, and still is, I am quite sure, related in many complex ways to the real Japan, to the experience of real people whose only language is Japanese, whose only horizon is the Home Islands. Naturally, at the scale of real History, their experience is no more central than 'my' system. And neither does there exist anywhere, no more in the Japanese language than in Zen Buddhism or in Shinto or emperor worship or flower arranging, any Japanese essence which, through concentric circles of causation, would enable us to 'explain' Japan. If my book seems at times to sacrifice to this illusion, and I'm afraid it may ... well, some revision is no doubt in order if ever a second edition is to appear.

My hope, however, is that readers, and especially scholarly readers, will be encouraged to strike out in very different directions, to explore the problems which I raise, and some which I probably do not—with regard to both Japanese and Western film culture—in terms of their contradictory reality, rather than striking out in a search for some transcendental center. In particular, and for example, I am quite sure that just as the institutional linearization of the iconographic signifier through editing was overdetermined by the linearity of Indo-European languages—or perhaps I should say the illusion of their linearity as reflected in the Saussurian model—so too the ambivalent use of certain visual signifiers—dissolves, swishpans—in certain sword play films of twenties and thirties could be better understood through serious comparative studies of Japanese syntax. It is studies of this kind which I hope will be stimulated by this book, rather than hopeless quests for the *Weltanschauung*. However, as I have seen from the experience of *Theory of Film Practice*,[5] it is often the erroneous side of uneven, contradictory research that has immediate impact. Let us hope that in this respect history will not repeat itself.

NOTES

1. B. Saint-Jacques, *Analyse structurale de la syntaxe du Japonais moderne* (Paris: 1966).

2. N. Burch, *To the Distant Observer: Form and Meaning in the Japanese Cinema* (Berkeley, California: University of California Press, 1979).

3. J. Leyda, *Dianying/Electric Shadows: An Account of Films and the Film Audience in China* (Cambridge, Massachusetts: MIT Press, 1979).

4. E. Ernst, *The Kabuki Theatre* (New York: Oxford University Press, 1956).

5. N. Burch, *Theory of Film Practice* (London: Secker & Warburg, 1973).

Kabuki, Cinema and Mizoguchi Kenji

Don Kirihara

The purpose of this paper is to examine where kabuki and cinema intersect, not in terms of theme, production techniques, or adaptations of texts, but as alternate modes of representation. It will not be an exhaustive examination of the origins, development, and expressive qualities of the kabuki theater, but will examine specifically the tensions between the two modes, theater and cinema, as expressed in a film, *The Story of the Last Chrysanthemums (Zangiku Monogatari)* and in the stylistics of Mizoguchi Kenji. In doing so I hope to raise questions about representations arising from a concept of 'a' culture or 'a' society, which for this paper will be a concept focusing on the islands of Japan.

First some introductory comments about kabuki will have to be made.[1] It was after a 1928 tour of the Soviet Union by a kabuki troupe that Eisenstein commented about that theater's 'monistic ensemble'.[2] That is, a kabuki performance seen as a collection of elements of equal significance, utilizing the actor (in his dances and gestures), utilizing the sets (such as scenery removed or set in place layer by layer during the performance), and utilizing various sounds (the recitations of the actor, the percussive beats of clapping wood blocks, or the songs of an offstage singer or chorus, accompanied by a single samisen or a large orchestra). This leads to the often-observed quality of 'spectacle' in kabuki, of a multi-sense bombardment of effects, but it is important to underline that one sense is not bombarded at the expense of another. For example, music accompanies every scene of the traditional kabuki play. In dialogue plays the accompaniment is from the *geza*, or offstage ensemble. The actor does not match his movements to the rhythm of the music. His steps do not match the drum pattern and his lines do not conform to the samisen melodies. Even in dance plays synchronization between music and movement is often avoided—a dance movement will carry on beyond the end of the melody, for example.³ The elements of the performance coexist; one is not given priority over another, one does not exist solely to reinforce another.

At each point of the performance, then, the process is complex. Furthermore, the performance, the process, unfolds on three levels. First there is the broad style of the play, which may range from a simple pantomime where the actors display themselves and assume a group tableau, to the exaggerated rough style of *aragoto*, of which it is said the actor must assume the virility and self-confidence of a sixteen-year-old.⁴ The second level is that of performance techniques utilized by the play. These techniques range from those of staging, such as the use of a revolving stage and trapdoors, to acting techniques, the most standard of which is *mie*, where the actor freezes into a dynamic pose at a specific moment of the play, halting the action of the play momentarily at that emotional high point. At the third level, the level of the individual actor's interpretation, those techniques are varied to create an identity for the actor. Actors built their reputations upon their interpretations of roles, and a genre of kabuki writing concentrates on how particular actors played famous scenes in ways different from other actors. Thus, the particular play does not—cannot—remain timeless, but must change with every actor's interpretation. This seems like an obvious, simplistic point to make in regard to any theater, but there is a tendency to think of kabuki as a theatrical form frozen in the eighteenth or mid nineteenth century, like an interminable *mie* pose, with its repeated performances merely unchanging exercises, or classical anachronisms. Kabuki underwent changes into the twentieth century not only in terms of acting style but also in terms of theater design, organization and duration of performances, management of theaters, and its role in the education of a modernizing Japan.⁵

As may be inferred from the above, the style of a kabuki play is not necessarily tied closely to the exposition of a narrative. A *mie* halts the action of the play, marks the emotional high points. In the words of one critic, the audience comes to the kabuki to see a succession of striking images.⁶ One modern kabuki theater schedules programs of famous parts of plays, lifted from their narrative context, staged and appreciated as isolated moments. The lack of narrative domination dates back to the seventeenth century origins of kabuki when the players—female and male prostitutes—danced in a manner best suited to exhibit their sexual attractiveness. It was not until after the government had banned women and young men from the kabuki stage that plays longer than one act developed.⁷ Performance techniques and the individual actor reinforce this notion of placing the narrative as an equal element of the performance. For example, actors peform crucial scenes not facing each other, but facing the audience to better display their facial expressions. Also, an actor will often insert his own name in a long recitation, interrupting the narrative to introduce himself or another actor to the audience before continuing with the story.

The element of display in kabuki can also be seen in the position of the spectator relative to the performance. The auditorium is constructed to place the spectator in close proximity to some part of the stage. The stage is wider than the Western proscenium theater stage and the seating depth is not as great, making the auditorium generally wider. In addition, an extension of the stage called the *hanamichi* runs through the house from stage right to an entrance at the rear of the auditorium. This raised runway is often used for entrances and exits of actors as well as for an acting platform in the audience. The *hanamichi* brings the performance closer to some of the audience and also provides the opportunity to set up competing areas of interest between the runway and the stage. It was common before the twentieth century to have a second *hanamichi* set up on the opposite side of the auditorium to exploit this element of the spectacle even further—the performance would take place *across* some of the audience on three platforms. Theater seating allowed the spectator free movement to observe the performance, for most of the audience sat on floor mats in the auditorium. It was not until the turn of this century that theater owners, influenced by the West, set up seats fixed to face the stage.

The spectator's closeness to the actor—as more than one writer puts it, 'close enough to touch'—again emphasizes the origins of kabuki as a sexual exhibition. The fascination with the *onnagata* may be related to this need for proximity. The *onnagata*—the male actor who plays women's roles in kabuki—is often presented as indicative of kabuki's concern for technique. A woman, the argument goes, cannot master the subtleties of the *onnagata*'s acting techniques, and the audience has come to accept and appreciate the separation of the actor and the role that he plays. Yet much of the original pleasure of kabuki was derived from the eroticism of a man playing women's roles, and vice versa. Okuni, the supposed originator of kabuki, first performed her dances on a river bed, and woodcuts often depict her on stage in the guise of a samurai. The display of this sexual tension seems to underlie the development of poses and of the audience's need to have the actor approach. The performance is contained by the stage in one sense—the stage and *hanamichi* are raised platforms, and the actors do not descend literally into the seats of the audience. But in another sense the kabuki performance tests the boundaries of that stage not by directing audience attention to one 'wall' but by utilizing the space of the auditorium and by moving the performance around that space. A Western notion of the proscenium—of containment—is not antithetical to kabuki staging, but seems to be operating on different representational principles.

The Story of the Last Chrysanthemums, briefly, concerns a famous kabuki family—the Onoe family—during the eighteen eighties. The adopted son of the family, Kiku, is an inadequate actor who wishes to marry the family nursemaid. The father refuses to give his consent and, when the son balks, the father orders him out of the house. Five years of training in small theaters follow for Kiku and the maid, Otoku, who is instrumental in his improvement. Kiku is allowed to show his improvement to the family on the condition (unknown to him) that Otoku leaves him. Kiku succeeds and goes back to Tokyo while Otoku becomes ill. At the end of the film, the couple is briefly reunited before Otoku dies. The film was released by Shochiku on October 10, 1939.

The film has a running time of about 150 minutes and contains 144 shots, including two intertitles, for an average shot length of approximately one minute. By Hollywood averages of the time, this seems incredibly long—a Hollywood film of this period had an average shot length of about ten seconds.[8] There are three kabuki presentations interspersed in the film. The first opens the film, before any of the above story elements are related. The second is Kiku's 'test' of acting competence. The third occurs after Kiku returns to his family and before his final reunion with Otoku. Those three sequences contain 48 of the film's 144 shots, with an average shot length of about 18 seconds. The kabuki sequences, then, use much more editing than sequences in the rest of the film and are closer to the Hollywood average for shot length. Furthermore, an examination of the sequences indicates the use of techniques like match-on-action and shot scale which are used in Hollywood continuity editing.

We are confronted, then, with a stylistic separation into two distinct locations—the onstage and offstage sequences. The temptation would be to divide the film into two sub-films; one sub-film showing the onstage kabuki performance using 'Western' continuity cutting to counterpoint the non-Western, noncontinuous theater performance; the other sub-film showing the offstage intrigue with Mizoguchi's long takes in classical Japanese tradition—in other words, to see the kabuki sequences as privileged stylistic moments.

But we might also see in the distinction between onstage and offstage the opportunity to make a systematic comparison of modes of representation. The stage performance, dropped into the film, creates a tension between film and theater; between the representation (the film as we, the audience, view it) and the mode being represented; between the art—theater—and the medium—film. Each of the three onstage sequences is represented in a different manner; each of them acknowledges the art being represented as well as the representation itself.

Before studying the onstage sequences, the assumptions being used about shot scale must be elaborated.[9] In the Hollywood conception of space, a relational pattern was set up: a long shot (the objects small within the frame) was used to establish the overall spatial relations between the objects, a medium shot used to see more clearly the objects interacting, and a close-up saved for viewing detail or facial expression pertinent to the narrative. If in breaking down the scene into many short shots the spatial relations of the objects changed, then a reestablishing long shot could be shown to restore the spatial relations and go on with the narrative. In this depiction of space, the centered object became more important, for the purpose of going from a long shot to a closer shot to a close-up of a detail was to 'center-in' to the important object. The object thus had to be centered in the frame, made to appear as recognizable as possible through lighting and positioning; and if the object was a person, turned face toward the camera.

In the first kabuki sequence, this notion of overlapping shot scales is respected. The second shot of the onstage sequence establishes the relations of the players on the stage. A closer shot reveals one of the actors preening. A long shot reestablishes the spatial relations as the actors perform. A closer shot reveals more detail of their performance and the final shot, an extreme long shot, coincides with the end of the performance—the curtain is drawn. The time of the performance is continuous, and the space, due to the overlapping of detail from shot to shot, is continuous, even though the performance is broken into six separate camera setups. Also, a kind of proscenium is respected: once into the sequence, offstage activity is not shown, nor is the audience shown. An argument might be made that this representation of the performance attempts to become the performance—that the strategy of centering-in to the pertinent details replaces overall staging of the theatrical text.

But there are problems in seeing this sequence as following Hollywood representational principles. The sequence's position in the narrative gives it the status of evidence—Kiku is a bad actor. The sequence thus works on two levels, that of the theater performance (the two ghosts of the first shot, the action of the three players on the riverbank set) and that of the film (the fact that Kiku is introduced—singled out—by his entrance through the door and by the shot of his preening). This tension is underlined by the backstage scenes which bracket the sequence. The actor whom we see go on stage from his dressing room and the actor who returns to the dressing room is the same actor, but obviously in a radically different costume. The quick change *(haya-gawari)* has been made during the performance but that fact is concealed because it is made during the time of the shot of Kiku preening. Our attention has been directed to a moment important for the film narrative but misdirected away from an element of kabuki spectacle—the actor playing multiple roles. Mizoguchi manipulates the technique of overlapping shot scale in a way which calls attention to that technique as well as to the theatrical representation.

The tension between modes of representation in film and theater as it is introduced in this sequence might be seen in the concept of 'unique perspective'.[10] In the theater, that is, in a live-action performance, there are as many places to view the performance as there are seats. The viewpoint remains the subject's viewpoint from a particular place in the auditorium and the play is not directed at each subject in the same way. In the film, however, it is necessary for the performance to identify with the camera. In Brecht's words, 'we only see what one eye, the camera, saw'.[11] Overlapping shot scale takes advantage of unique perspective, centering-in on detail in an irresistible manner. Brecht saw unique perspective as 'monstrous weakness' in film compared to the theater. Mizoguchi manipulates it with the misdirection of the first kabuki sequence and manipulates it in a different way in the second kabuki sequence.

The second sequence depicts Kiku's test of whether he is good enough to return to the family. The first shot of the sequence is an extreme long shot of the stage, but differences from the first kabuki sequence are immediately apparent. First, it is taken from an oblique high angle which reveals both the stage and the *hanamichi*. The layers of the performance which take place perpendicular to the camera in the first sequence are not represented in the same way in this sequence. Second, the audience is visible in the foreground. This is important in the narrative context of the sequence—as Kiku's test, the measure of his success will be reflected in the kabuki audience watching, the film's audience watching, and the family members watching *offstage*. For it is not only the space of the auditorium which is revealed, but also the space of the offstage watchers. Thus some actors watch from a position identified as stage left; Otoku watches from an unidentified position backstage; three other actors watch from the *agemaku*, the curtained entrance at the rear of the *hanamichi*. There are a number of cues which a film spectator can read which make this shot the point/object of the *agemaku* actors' point/glance.[12] The shot is taken from approximately eye level, between the shoulders of the actors at either side of the frame, which matches the spatial relations of the previous shot, and the *hanamichi* itself is visible in the foreground. It seems to be an example of continuity point-of-view editing. But what Mizoguchi does after this challenges that structure. He cuts from the long shot of the stage to Otoku looking, then cuts back to the same shot of the stage from the *agemaku* actors' position, rather than cutting to a shot from Otoku's position. Mizoguchi repeats this two more times, cutting to actors who have been established at stage left and back to the *agemaku* actors' position, then back to the *agemaku* actors and repeating their 'view' for the fourth time. The shot structure is thus:

MLS	three actors watch from *agemaku*
LS	stage from *agemaku*
MS	Otoku watching
LS	stage from *agemaku*
MLS	actors watch from stage left
LS	stage from *agemaku*
MLS	three actors watch from *agemaku*
LS	stage from *agemaku*

One point/object is shared by three points/glances; one perspective is shared by three viewers. It is a problematic unique perspective, for not only does it call to attention the ubiquitous place which is produced by the camera versus one position from which the theater performance could be viewed, but it also makes that position by itself a difficult one—a crowded one—to inhabit. The activity of watching, of the viewers in the text and their position in relation to the object being viewed, as well as the representation of that viewing, the problematic unique perspective, is called into question in this sequence.

The third kabuki sequence, a lion dance which takes place after Kiku returns to the family, develops some of the tensions between film and theater presented in the earlier sequences. Like the first sequence, the camera is positioned perpendicular to the stage at first. Backstage viewpoints are not developed as they were in the second kabuki sequence, and overlapping shot scale and match-on-action are used over 11 shots to present the performance without a temporal break. But across those 11 shots, Mizoguchi does not always center-in to the pertinent detail. After showing the three principal actors reciting their lines in medium shot, the shot scale spirals out to a long shot—a reestablishing shot—of the stage, and then to an extreme long shot, with the stage but a band across the center of the frame and the actors tiny figures. Later he pulls back even more so that the stage becomes even smaller, more remote. In terms of shot scale it functions too well as a reestablishing shot—the spatial relations are on the screen, but the film audience's ability to make out those relations is frustrated. It is not an economic use of the frame. In terms of the position of the spectator it is frustrating also, for the intimacy between actor and audience often cited in kabuki, the closeness of the audience to the display, is manipulated. In this respect, it is significant that Mizoguchi does not finish the sequence with an extreme long shot of the stage as sort of an homage to the theater form, an overview of the spectacle. Instead, for the last shot, he changes camera positions to an oblique angle which takes in the *hanamichi* in the foreground and the action on that plane, and the action on the stage in the background. At no other time in the kabuki sequences does he show simultaneous acting on these two planes in the frame. It is taken from a cinematically economic angle, that is, utilizing foreground and background in contrast to other shots in the sequence. The privileged position from which it views the performance is thus fore-grounded, calling to account its unique perspective and the economy of its cinematic practice.

The tension between film and theater is presented in the offstage sequences as well in various ways. In one sequence where Kiku is in a country theater the location of the kabuki performance is deconstructed with a high-angle shot showing the empty theater's stage, *hanamichi*, and audience pits. A reference is made to a stage technique in the first kabuki sequence when a backdrop collapses, but instead of a visual spectacle within the performance, the falling scenery here merely signals the dismantling of the stage by workmen.

But in other sequences Mizoguchi's stylistics call attention to unique perspective. At first this seems paradoxical; the use of long takes represents events in a temporal and spatial continuum, for by not cutting the camera maintains the theater-like premise of a single spectator's position. Sometimes the action will remain centered in the frame and a kind of proscenium will be set up where pertinent narrative events will not be presented outside of the borders of the frame. Mizoguchi's long takes frustrate the proscenium in several ways. The object is often concealed from the camera by barriers. An example would be the sequence of the celebrants after the first kabuki performance. They are shown, not clearly, but with an intervening fence between the celebrants and the camera so that they are only visible through the slats of the fence. Mizoguchi underscores the difficulty in making out the people in the frame by tracking, in the same shot, to Kiku, who has entered the house and is standing in the darkness, an unrecognizable silhouette.

People often obstruct each other from the camera, as in the train sequence in which Kiku returns to his family. The camera is not positioned perpendicular to the axis of conversation, but *along* the axis, resulting in speaking faces which are partially blocked from view or figures which are turned completely away from the camera. Even in conversations done in profile the speakers will sometimes deny the camera their faces. The sequence where Kiku meets Otoku at a temple ends with both figures turned away from the camera.

Camera-subject distance in this sequence and in other sequences also works to deny the recognizability of the object. Throughout the film the camera maintains such a distance from the characters that it is often difficult to make out the details of their faces. The extreme long shot of the stage in the kabuki sequence mentioned before is one example; but in another sequence where Otoku has separated from Kiku, the consistency of long camera-object distance takes on a special irony. A friend says to Otoku, 'Since we met— you've completely changed', and Otoku answers, 'Really? Yes I have. I'm sure I have'. There is a question in the narrative whether her supportive role toward Kiku has changed at all, but such a change is literally difficult to see due to the fact that through the film her figure has been kept at such a distance from the camera.

Mizoguchi is most daring in his undermining of a principle of recognizability in the long take in shots where he leaves the narrative focal point completely. For example, when Otoku is fired by Kikugoro's wife, while the two women are discussing the reasons for the dismissal, the camera pans and tracks away from them, showing the new nursemaid walking the baby and some women in another room listening. The narrative focal point in this scene is the exchange between the two women, but Mizoguchi moves the camera away from the narrative information being related to the audience within the film receiving that information. It is a situation analogous to that of the kabuki performance, with an event shown along with the spectators of that event. However, in this case Mizoguchi does not use point-of-view editing structures to pose problems of multiple positions and unique perspective, but instead uses a single take and a single position to pose those problems, for when the camera pans back to return to the end of the women's conversation, they are in a different configuration.

To take another example, in the long take when Kiku is banished from the house by his father, Kiku, his mother and brother adjourn to another room where they argue over Kiku's insistence that he be allowed to marry Otoku. The father enters frame left and orders Kiku out, then leaves the frame. There is a pause, then Kiku gets up, sits again facing offscreen left and begs for his father's permission. Kiku then gets up and exits the frame. The camera does *not* follow him as he asks his father again for permission to marry. The action of the final request, the refusal, and Kiku's departure is all done offscreen, while the camera remains fixed on the mother and the brother—the audience. The film audience, the position to which all the action must supposedly identify, has been denied the spectacle of the dismissal. A tension is created between the premise of a single spectator position and the cinematic practices used by Mizoguchi to frustrate that position.

A final example of this frustration is seen in the tracking shot of Otoku and Kiku when they first meet and buy the wind chime for the baby. Not only is it a shot of long duration, shot from a long camera-to-subject distance, but it is also a shot with the camera and subject movement so choreographed that the subjects' backs are to the camera at key moments in the exposition.

The camera tracks right as they walk, staying slightly behind them and not seeing their faces; then they stop to buy a wind chime and the camera stops also, still slightly behind them; it is only when they stop as Otoku tells him, 'As your father says, your art is your very life. Without it even Kikugoro VI is no different from anybody else', that the camera *continues* to track right, pulling abreast of them and showing their faces in profile. The choreography is repeated later when Otoku meets Kiku in Osaka. Again, the tracking movement of the camera follows the walking subjects, always seeing their backs until that moment when Kiku stops and says, 'I'm just no good'. The camera *then* pulls abreast of the two characters and their faces can be seen.

In conclusion, I would argue that what Mizoguchi's stylistics have led to is a questioning of the representational basis of cinema. The 'classicism' often cited in his style seems mediated by tensions with Hollywood codes (shot scale and the visibility of objects) and by tensions with the basis of so-called classical Japanese modes of representation (kabuki's position of the spectator).

NOTES

1. Several sources were helpful for this paper: F. Bowers, *Japanese Theatre* (New York: Hermitage House, 1952); E. Ernst, *The Kabuki Theatre* (New York: Oxford University Press, 1956); A. C. Scott, *The Kabuki Theatre of Japan* (New York: Macmillan, 1955); J. R. Brandon, 'Form in Kabuki Acting', and D. H. Shively, 'The Social Environment of Tokugawa Kabuki', both in *Studies in Kabuki*, J. R. Brandon (ed.), (Honolulu: University Press of Hawaii, 1977).

2. S. M. Eisenstein, *Film Form* (New York: Harcourt, Brace & World, 1949), p. 20.

3. Brandon, pp. 106-107.

4. Ibid., pp. 66-71.

5. T. Koji, 'The Kabuki, the Shimpa, the Shingeki', in *Japanese Music and Drama in the Meiji Era*, T. Komiya (ed.), trans. D. Keene (Tokyo: Toyo Bunko, 1956), pp. 177-328.

6. Ernst, p. 76.

7. Bowers, p. 50.

8. B. Salt, 'Film Style and Technology in the Forties', *Film Quarterly* vol. XXXI no. 1 (Fall 1977), p. 47.

9. E. Branigan, 'The Space of *Equinox Flower*', *Screen* vol. 17 no. 2 (Summer 1976), p. 75.

10. B. Brewster, 'The Fundamental Reproach (Brecht)', *Ciné-Tracts* vol. 1 no. 2 (Summer 1977), p. 48.

11. Ibid., p. 45.

12. E. Branigan, 'Formal Permutations of the Point-of-View Shot', *Screen* vol. 16 no. 3 (Fall 1975), pp. 54-64.

Mizoguchi and the Evolution of Film Language

David Bordwell

The Western avant-garde has long used the Oriental sign as a wedge to be driven between ourselves and Occidental representation. After Debussy saw Annanite opera at the 1889 World Exposition, he praised its percussive directness and by contrast belittled Wagnerian music-drama. In 1928, kabuki performances in Moscow introduced Eisenstein to a spectacle very different from that of Western naturalism. Three years later, Artaud saw in Balinese dance 'a new physical language, based upon signs and no longer upon words'.[1] For Brecht, the Chinese actor Mei Lan-fang demonstrated how an Oriental tradition could offer an alternative to the identification procedures characteristic of Western theater. More recently, Roland Barthes and the *Tel quel* group have found in the East an alternative economy of the sign. What is at issue here is how an analysis of non-Western representation can take on a critical edge. It is not a matter of asserting that the Oriental sign is simply, and irrevocably, other, but rather of analyzing that otherness and using the analysis to illuminate our habitual thinking.

The nineteen thirties work of Kenji Mizoguchi is very useful for this critical purpose because his work enables us to rethink how we construct the history of film style. If my title makes reference to André Bazin's celebrated essay, 'The Evolution of the Language of Cinema',[2] it is because Bazin's work has exercised a great power over our conception of film history.[3] A thorough investigation of Bazin's position would have to examine films produced within those two national cinemas that his essay pointedly excludes: the Soviet Union after 1928 and Japan.[4] In the space of this essay, I can only indicate how Mizoguchi's surviving films from the nineteen thirties can usefully challenge the assumptions of Bazin's account of deep focus.

What has made Bazin's essay a landmark is its three-phase account of the history of découpage. Phase one is the primitive cinema, which Bazin characterizes as that which represents a scene in a single shot and with considerable depth. The primitive filmmaker presents a spatial and temporal continuum, but the viewer's eye is undirected. What usurps the primitive style is that of classical découpage, or continuity editing.[5] Now the filmmaker channels the spectator's attention by breaking the scene into shots. The third historical phase is that of sophisticated deep focus, introduced by Renoir, Welles, and Wyler. This style combines the spatial and the temporal unity of the primitive scene with a density of narrative significance based upon classical découpage. The scheme yields not a simple additive chronology but a dialectical evolution: thesis (primitive cinema), antithesis (classical découpage), synthesis (deep focus). Bazin thus treats découpage as a representational system, or as he calls it, a language. Like verbal language, a film style transmits a given significance: the narrative information contained in a scene.

The crucial point in Bazin's analysis of Hollywood deep focus is that because the director knows how classical editing would break the scene down, s/he can choose to make this breakdown implicit within the single shot. 'Dramatic effects for which we had formerly relied upon montage were created out of the movement of the actors within a fixed frame'.[6] This passage indicates the centrality of the performer in this style. Bazin insists that Welles and Wyler both make the actor the basis of the mise-en-scène, using him or her to determine decor, lighting, and costume.[7]

Certain other qualities of the deep-focus style must be inferred from Bazin's examples and illustrations. For one thing, he assumes that the shot's foreground plane will often be a close-up or a medium shot of an actor or object. His specimen of primitive deep focus perfectly exemplifies this (fig. 1), as does the principal example—Susan's suicide attempt—from *Citizen Kane* (1941). Secondly, Bazin assumes that the actors position themselves frontally, facing us; this assures that expression and gesture are noticeable. Thirdly, Bazin assumes what we can call uniform spacing. Actors, objects, and decor will be composed so as not to block one another. The precision of the Welles or Wyler shot issues in large part from the way in which faces and setting are fitted tidily together so as to click into place from only one point of view, as in fig. 2 (from *The Magnificent Ambersons*, 1942) or fig. 3 (from *The Little Foxes*, 1941).

All these factors—the enlarged foreground plane, frontality, and even spacing—might yield only perceptual confusion if they were not controlled by one more element: the actor's glance. The deep-focus shot provides the syntactic equivalent of the edited scene not only by jamming all relevant narrative components into the frame but also by guiding the passage of our attention from one component to another. Figure movement is important here, as Bazin points out, but his examples also rely upon the actor's glance. The glance operates in almost all the examples already cited, but Bazin's most extensive treatment of it emerges from his account of the scene in Butch's tavern in *The Best Years of Our Lives* (1946). Bazin claims that the action is constructed on two planes—a secondary action occurs in the foreground, at the piano, while the significant action is secreted in the tiny rectangle of the phone booth in the background (fig. 4). Bazin praises Wyler's cleverness in inverting the scale of narrative values, but he notices that this composition alternates with close shots of Al watching the booth (fig. 5). Lest we be distracted by the action at the piano, a close-up of Al's glance relays our attention back to the principal action in the distance. For Bazin, the direction of glances 'constitutes always, in Wyler, the skeleton of the mise-en-scène'.[8] In the sum, we can say that an unimpeded *visibility* is the aim of the deep-focus style:

> Since the audience is constantly confronted on the screen by the whole cast of actors against the setting, it is essential that the space they occupy in relation to one another bring clearly into relief the dramatic arrangement of the scene.[9]

Implicitly and explicitly, then, Bazin offers a detailed account of the Hollywood deep-focus style of the early nineteen forties. The nineteen thirties work of Mizoguchi is relevant to this account not because 'he did it first', but because he proposed a contrary approach to deep space in the cinema.[10] Mizoguchi was familiar enough with Holywood découpage to grasp not only its devices but its principles. Bazin assumes that deep focus assimilates the principles of continuity editing:

> The fixed shot of *Citizen Kane* could be conceived only after the era of montage; Griffith's analysis had to reveal clearly the anatomy of presentation before Welles or Wyler, with a cameraman of Gregg Toland's class, could remodel the unity of the image much as a sculptor might do.[11]

Yet Mizoguchi challenges the logic of Hollywood 'language' not through work on montage but at one remove, through an alternative system of depth.

More specifically, Mizoguchi challenges the centrality of the actor. The result is a refusal of the visibility underpinning the Hollywood deep-focus style. First, Mizoguchi's deep space will not necessarily make the foreground plane a close-up; the scene is often filmed in long shot, whereby architecture dwarfs the figures (fig. 6). In *White Threads of the Waterfall* (1933), the heroine kneels before the man she loves, her bowing head vanishing below the table at which he sits. Sometimes the foreground will be a busy geometrical pattern that thwarts our viewing the actor (figs. 7–8). At first glance, we might be tempted to compare such compositions to those of American pictorialist directors like Maurice Tourneur or Josef von Sternberg. But unlike these directors' shots, Mizoguchi's geometrical compositions will not usually give way to closer, clearer views of the characters; Mizoguchi's long takes seldom yield any other vantage point on the action. At the same time, Mizoguchi's deep-space long shots reject frontality. Gestures and expressions cannot be seen because actors turn their backs to us. Mizoguchi's camera will often stand at a point exactly opposite that which Welles or Wyler would have chosen. Compare a shot from *Naniwa Elegy* (1936), or one from *O-sen*

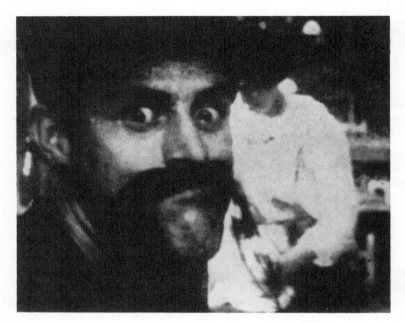

FIGURE 1. *Onésime* (a frame from the *Onésime* series, Jean Durand, c. 1912)

FIGURE 2. *The Magnificent Ambersons* (1942)

FIGURE 3. *The Little Foxes* (1941)

FIGURE 4. *The Best Years of Our Lives* (1946)

FIGURE 5. *The Best Years of Our Lives*

FIGURE 6. *O-sen of the Paper Cranes* (1934)

FIGURE 7. *Story of the Last Crysanthemums* (1939)

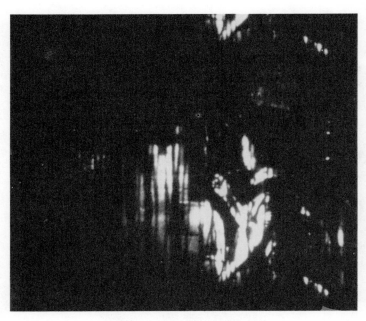

FIGURE 8. *Oyuki the Virgin* (1935)

FIGURE 9. *Naniwa Elegy* (1936)

FIGURE 10. *O-sen of the Paper Cranes*

FIGURE 11. *The Little Foxes*

FIGURE 12. *The Little Foxes*

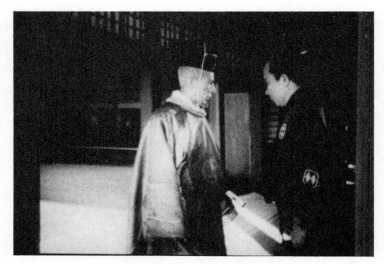

FIGURE 13. *Genroku Chushingura* (1941)

FIGURE 14. *O-sen of the Paper Cranes*

FIGURE 15. *Genroku Chushingura*

of the Paper Cranes (1934) (figs. 9–10) with shots from *The Little Foxes* (figs. 11–12). Welles and Wyler swivel their characters toward that one spot from which the grouping is intelligible; for Mizoguchi, that spot is distant from us, and the characters shrink from the camera.

If frontality becomes problematic, so does even spacing. One Mizoguchi character will block our view of another. In the train car in *The Story of the Last Chrysanthemums* (1939), a major character's reactions are concealed because the camera is at the 'wrong' spot and his friend's body blocks his. Sometimes we may not even know that a character is present in the scene, as at the beginning of *Genroku Chushingura* (1941-1942), when Lord Kira criticizes Lord Asano (fig. 13); only after Kira and his subordinate move away is Asano revealed in the background, previously blocked by the subordinate's body. Perhaps most important is the effect of Mizoguchi's scenography on the characters' glances. No longer does the look expose the skeleton of the mise-en-scène. We cannot infer a conventional breakdown of the action if we cannot follow the trajectories of the glances. Again and again, the lack of visibility in Mizoguchi's staging impedes our identification of what the characters are looking at (for instance, figs. 6, 8, 10). In a shot like fig. 14, with the daughter prostrate in the foreground and the father sobbing in the background, the absence of glances makes us uncertain about what is more important. In sum, the narrative visibility created by the American deep-focus style is questioned by Mizoguchi's films. If Welles and Wyler absorb the principles of classical découpage into the single shot, Mizoguchi's single shots criticize that style at one remove by refusing to let us pick out the components of a classically edited sequence.

Mizoguchi's films thus pose several difficulties for Bazin's account of the evolution of film 'language'. Most obviously, the films precede the work of Welles and Wyler by several years. Bazin assumes that these directors understood the principles of continuity editing and transliterated them into the deep-focus shot. Mizoguchi breaks this neat dialectic by skipping a step: it is as if he understood the principles of continuity editing, extrapolated how they *could* be transliterated into the deep-focus shot, and negated that procedure before it was manifested historically. *O-sen of the Paper Cranes*, *Oyuki the Virgin* (1935), *Naniwa Elegy, Sisters of Gion* (1936), *The Story of the Last Chrysanthemums*, and *Genroku Chushingura* challenge the deep-focus style in advance. For such reasons, the history of film style cannot be taken as a smooth evolutionary progress. We must construct that history as a series of ruptures of norms, of uneven and contrary work, of partial and precarious syntheses.

Mizoguchi's nineteen thirties films also bring out certain problems in Bazin's most basic assumptions about 'film language'. Bazin's account presupposes that découpage is a unified representation of narrative, a means of expressing the story and bringing out its significance. Mizoguchi's work shows how a film style can impede attention, frustrate knowledge, and pose perceptual problems; his films demonstrate that cinematic representation can be split from narrative structure, bringing cinematic structure forward. In this, of course, the films share the radical negativity which avant-garde thinkers have been eager to assign to the Oriental sign. For such as Eisenstein and Artaud, the Oriental spectacle is important because it puts verbal language into question.

What must be avoided, though, is the tendency to think of that spectacle as wholly negative, without unitary movements. Noël Burch's *To the Distant Observer*, for example, suggests some of the problems of positing the Japanese cinema as chiefly an art of refusal. Burch draws upon his avant-garde predecessors, especially as reworked by Barthes, in order to assign a critical role to the films of Ozu, Mizoguchi, and others. Ozu 'deconstructs' reverse-shot and eyeline-match editing, while Mizoguchi uses the long shot and the long take to distance the audience from the narrative action. When it comes to demonstrating the systematic nature of this refusal, however, Burch finds few principles (flatness and decentering of the image, for example) and must borrow concepts from other arts: the pillow-shot (to describe Ozu's transitional, empty spaces), or the scroll-shot, (to describe Mizoguchi's lateral camera movements). Despite Burch's energetic polemic for the importance of the cinema of the nineteen thirties, he seldom goes beyond the cataloguing of transgressive devices, and he does not address how those devices function systematically and positively within the films. We are left chiefly with a sense of norms violated; but does the Oriental sign say—or, rather, do—anything more?[12]

I see three fruitful lines of inquiry. One has already been proposed by the avant-garde tradition itself. For the Western avant-garde, Oriental art dramatized how the sign could visibly split the medium of representation from the idea represented. Once the signifier has become highly conventionalized, it not only abolishes reference but also draws away from conceptual significance. This signifier no longer seems naturally tied to a signfied. Brecht is the most cogent on this point: the Chinese actor does not feel or express emotions; he exhibits them as signs, identifying them precisely.[13] The actor is divided, showing simultaneously how vivacious the young girl appears and how the young girl appears vivacious.[14] Without stressing this *double jeu*, Artaud and Eisenstein suggest that in Oriental theater, the signified is assumed to be an external entity to which representation offers several equally arbitrary routes of access. Eisenstein's monistic ensemble presupposes just this absolute externality of the signified: 'Whatever notes I can't take with my voice I'll show with my hands!'[15] For Artaud, there is no emotion inside which will burst forth on the actor's face, only 'muscular facial expressions, applied to the features like masks'.[16] For Western thinkers, the fixed meanings presented by the Oriental spectacle allow it to invest its energy in producing vivid signifiers that flaunt their distinct substances, shapes, and patterns. In this sense, the Oriental sign is read as signifying virtually nothing, creating what Barthes calls *un vide de parole,* not a sign of silence but a silent sign.[17]

In analyzing the cinema, this approach would focus on the overall perceptual organization of film style. Study of the work of Ozu reveals such organizational principles in his scenography: 360° space sliced into 45° segments, a chain of dominants and overtones governing the editing, and minute graphic matching from shot to shot.[18] Similarly, with Mizoguchi one could begin with his insistence upon architectural space and show how depth composition and camera movement function to subordinate the human figure to a total composition. In a general way, what Ozu does by cutting away to adjacent objects Mizoguchi does within his deep-space compositions. In particular, one can notice Mizoguchi's very sophisticated use of Japanese graphic traditions. Burch would claim that a shot like fig. 6 creates an ambiguity of surface and depth, but the issue needs to be seen as involving the various *ways* in which depth can be represented. By reducing the concept of depth representation to the device of linear perspective, Burch assumes that when the latter is absent, so is the former.[19] Yet the so-called Japanese corner illusion, or angular-isometric perspective, articulates depth by means that, from a Western attitude, stress features of the image itself: placement in the frame (what is lower is closer to us) and an inverse perspective whereby parallel lines converge toward the picture plane rather than away from it.[20] Mizoguchi's penchant for high camera angles, short focal-length lenses, and sharp diagonals may be seen as a way of using cinema to transform the cubical space of angular-isometric perspective. This is depth, but of an unusual kind. The use of such traditions is most evident in *Genroku Chushingura*, where such shots as fig. 15 cite the narrative painting tradition of the Genroku and Edo eras.[21] Mizoguchi's negation of the performer as the central carrier of narrative meaning would need to be analyzed as a further work upon and against such pictorial traditions.

If analysis of the perceptual principles of the 'play of the signifier' offers one line of inquiry, another is suggested by the work of Brecht. Now this calls for caution. It is not simply a matter of valorizing Eastern spectacle in the name of its radical alienating powers. Burch, for example, claims that the traditional Oriental stage possesses 'an objective Brechtianism' and throughout his book implies that Japanese film style is analogous to the alienation effects which Brecht discerned in Oriental theater.[22] Yet we should remember that Brecht considerably qualified his claims for the political significance of the Oriental sign's estrangement-effects:

> Such devices were certainly a barrier to empathy, and yet this technique owed more, not less, to hypnotic suggestion than do those by which empathy is achieved. The social aims of these old devices were entirely different from our own ... The old A-effects quite remove the object represented from the spectator's grasp, turning it into something that cannot be altered ... The new alienations are only designed to free socially-conditioned phenomena from that stamp of familiarity which protects them against our grasp today.[23]

If we are to use Brecht to open up Mizoguchi's style, we must determine the style's concrete social functions.

One of Brecht's goals was to break the spectator's identification with the individual character by compelling us to see a situation as socially determined. The concept of the social gestus, for instance, responds to the need to demonstrate how an action embodies not simply psychological activity but historical significance. A gestus must 'contain a social relationship, like exploitation or cooperation'.[24] From this angle, we could analyze Mizoguchi's nineteen thirties films as functioning to reduce characters' psychological activity and to throw into question the determination of human action. Mizoguchi's refusal to let us see the characters' expressions, gestures, and glances forces us to read the scene as staging a relationship between agents with defined social roles. A frame from a Wyler or a Welles film can 'say' only *Leo is afraid that his theft will be discovered* (fig. 12) or *Al is worried that Fred will not break with his daughter* (fig. 4–5). What Mizoguchi shots yield is closer to *A woman is bargained for* (fig. 10), *An aristocrat insults a samurai* (fig. 13), or *A woman tells her lover that she has been another man's mistress* (fig. 9). (Given Mizoguchi's reputation for social criticism, the desire to dramatize social relations is plausible.) This line of inquiry suggests that the Japanese cinema of the nineteen thirties offers an instance of the Oriental sign's capacity for political functions.[25]

It would, however, be un-Brechtian to isolate such political functions from concrete historical circumstances. Mizoguchi's use of the social gestus can be seen as caused by particular factors, some direct and others more oblique. For example, the reticent mise-en-scène constitutes a fairly direct response to censorship. During the nineteen twenties and nineteen thirties Japan had one of the most stringent censorship codes in the world, and Mizoguchi ran afoul of it several times. Returning again and again to the subject of exploited women—geisha, mistresses, war victims, prostitutes— Mizoguchi's films challenge a censorship that banned depiction of adultery, nudity, 'glaring eroticism of any kind', and 'scenes of the interior of brothels, whether licensed or not'.[26] One historical effect of Mizoguchi's long shots and reversals of frontality may have been the downplaying of the immediately sensational aspects of his subjects. (Hence the frequent conflict between a highly melodramatic script situation and a detached staging of the action.) It is also possible that Mizoguchi's long take was employed to create a durational continuum which was difficult for a censor to tamper with.

More indirectly, the socialist goals of Brecht's epic theater should not lead us to expect that the social gestus in Japanese cinema automatically serves leftist ends. For example, in a nineteen thirties context Mizoguchi's social criticism is ambivalent. The films' attack upon the sexual and economic exploitation of women and upon the machination of urban capitalism was common to both left-wing and right-wing factions of the period. Films like *Naniwa Elegy* and *Sisters of Gion*, both released in the year of an aborted right-wing coup, could be read as conservative indictments of Japan's current decadence. The ambiguities of Mizoguchi's mise-en-scène then may be said to create a hesitation about how to interpret the social significance of the represented gestus. I must stress that such matters as censorship and social issues cannot wholly explain how the style works, but such historical factors can help us specify the style's political functions.

The analysis of perceptual form and of political effect will need to take into account a third line of inquiry. In 1874, long before Eisenstein or Artaud or Brecht encountered the Oriental spectacle, Japanese swarmed into Asa-kusa, the entertainment district of Tokyo, to see an invention imported from Europe. The stereopticon peepshow captivated them with its scenes of Western life. 'It is like touring the world at a glance', wrote the essayist Hattori Bushō, 'and should broaden men's knowledge while delighting their eyes'.[27] The anecdote reminds us that since at least the nineteenth century there has been no purely Oriental sign. Japanese art quickly assimilated Western representational conventions, as we see in the woodblock artist Hiroshige's use of foreshortening in his *100 Famous Views of Edo* and in the European-influenced Shingeki theater. Similarly, the Japanese cinema cannot be closed off in pristine isolation from Western film practice. Almost throughout its history, the Japanese cinema has been dependent upon the West for machinery, personnel, films and raw stock; it modeled its produc-tion practices on those of Hollywood; it took American film style as the norm.[28] Thus, picking up a third line of inquiry, we can see the nineteen thirties work of Ozu and Mizoguchi as a mixed mode, not simple repudiation but complex assimilation. Western film 'language', so economically traced by Bazin, constitutes one force in an overall pattern of variegated stylistic work. For example, some of Mizoguchi's nineteen thirties films *(Oyuki the Virgin, Naniwa Elegy)* can be analyzed as struggles between Western-style découp-age (with even some Wellesian deep-focus touches) and the more opaque, problematic style I have already described. From this standpoint, the use of Japanese pictorial devices in *The Story of the Last Chrysanthemums* and *Genroku Chushingura* constitutes not straightforward transmission of a graphic tradition (as, say, Burch suggests) but sophisticated, sometimes ironic, *citation*. Relying upon Western film style as a background, Mizogu-chi's mise-en-scène often functions explicitly to connote 'Japaneseness'— tradition, archaic values, contemplative calm.

For this reason, both the analysis of perceptual form and the reckoning of political effects must acknowledge the importance of Japan's encounter with the West. For Bushō at the 1874 Asakusa peepshow, Western images yielded an estranging vision. The picture flagrantly altered scale ('The Palace of Paris is taller than the clouds'). It displayed an alarming fixity ('The black men who paddle boats remain stuck for all eternity . . .'). The picture showed but one side of objects ('Only half the body is exposed and we cannot see the behind'). And the image was both present and absent ('Though face to face, we cannot kiss the lips').[29] Japanese pictures, of course, also possessed all these traits, but the Western encounter brought home to one distant observer some basic qualities of images as such. Just as Oriental spectacle permitted our avant-garde to hold Western traditions at arm's length, so Occidental representation may have yielded Japanese filmmakers a fresh vision of their native conventions, enabling them to frame 'Japaneseness' as one term in a complex system. What our avant-garde did not notice, we must: for us and for the Japanese, the modern Oriental sign can signify Orientalism itself.

NOTES

1. A. Artaud, *The Theatre and Its Double,* trans. M.C. Richards (New York: Grove Press, 1958), p. 54.

2. A. Bazin, 'L'évolution du langage cinématographique', in *Qu'est ce que le cinéma?* vol. I (Paris: Editions du Cerf, 1969), pp. 131-148. This essay is compiled from three earlier articles: 'Pour en finir avec profondeur de champ', *Cahiers du cinéma* no. 1 (April 1951), pp. 17-23; 'Montage', in *Twenty Years of Cinema in Venice* (Rome: Edizion dell'Ataneo, 1952), pp. 359-377; and 'Découpage et son évolution', *L'âge nouveau* no. 93 (July 1955), pp. 54-71. The essay is available in translation in *What is Cinema?* vol. I, trans. and ed. H. Gray (Berkeley, California: University of California Press, 1967), pp. 23-40.

3. So persuasive is this scheme that it informs the work of Bazin's critics. Noël Burch's recent work rejects Bazin's description and evaluation of the primitive cinema, but Bazin's periodization and his categories of analysis (depth/flatness, single take/edited scene, etc.) still govern Burch's work. Similarly Jean-Louis Comolli's extensive critique of the idealist bases of Bazin's dialectic does not question the historical givens which it deploys (primitive deep space as distinct from edited shallow space, for instance). Comolli proposes a different sort of explanation for the changes which Bazin observes, but he accepts Bazin's description of the changes. See N. Burch, *To the Distant Observer: Form and Meaning in the Japanese Cinema* (Berkeley, California: University of California Press, 1979), pp. 63-65; and J.-L. Comolli, 'Technique et idéologie: caméra, perspective, profondeur de champ', *Cahiers du cinéma* no. 229 (May 1971), pp. 16-18; no. 235-236 (Dec. 1971-Jan. 1972), pp. 95-98; and no. 241 (Sept.-Oct. 1972), pp. 23-24.

4. Although I cannot argue the point extensively here, it is evident that the later silent work of Sergei Eisenstein and the FEKS group breaks the neat unity of Bazin's account: films like *Old and New* (1928) and *The New Babylon* (1928) are committed to an extreme fragmentation of the pro-filmic event but nonetheless use deep-focus compositions extensively, and for purposes which Bazin does not envisage.

5. This is not to say that Bazin conceives classical continuity as being without its own dialectic, since he suggests a struggle in the nineteen twenties among various editing styles. See 'L'évolution', pp. 132-134.

6. Bazin, 'L'évolution', p. 141.

7. 'Welles, as a man of the theatre, constructs his mise-en-scène on the basis of the actor' (A. Bazin, in *Orson Welles: A Critical View,* trans. J. Rosenbaum [New York: Harper & Row, 1978], p. 68). 'Wyler's "direction," in the strict sense, is thus wholly concentrated upon the actor' (Bazin, 'William Wyler, ou le janseniste de la mise-en-scène', *Qu'est-ce que le cinéma* vol. I, p. 165). Similar remarks can be found in Bazin's very early essay, 'La technique de *Citizen Kane'*, *Les temps modernes* vol. II no. 17 (1947), pp. 946-947.

8. Bazin, 'William Wyler', p. 168.

9. Bazin, 'Montage', p. 373.

10. Y. Yoda, 'Souvenirs sur Mizoguchi', *Cahiers du cinéma* no. 172 (November 1965), p. 48. Mizoguchi's scenarist Yoda here discusses the employment of wide-angle lenses in *The Story of the Last Chrysanthemums* (1939), but certain shots of *Oyuki the Virgin* suggest that Mizoguchi was using them at least as early as 1935.

11. Bazin, 'Montage', p. 373.

12. Much of what follows has grown out of the discussion at the Japanese Cinema panel. I am grateful to Noël Burch, Dudley Andrew, and especially Thomas Elsaesser for their constructive questions. Noël Carroll and Edward Branigan's suggestions have improved an earlier draft of this paper.

13. B. Brecht, 'Alienation Effects in Chinese Acting', in Brecht on Theatre, trans. and ed. J. Willett (New York: Hill & Wang, 1964), p. 94.

14. B. Brecht, 'A propos du théâtre chinois', in Ecrits sur le théâtre vol. I, trans. J. Tailleur et al. (Paris: L'arche, 1972), p. 412.

15. S. M. Eisenstein, Film Form, trans. and ed. J. Leyda (New York: Meridian, 1957), p. 23.

16. Artaud, p. 58.

17. R. Barthes, L'empire des signes (Geneva: Skira, 1970), p. 12.

18. See K. Thompson and D. Bordwell, 'Space and Narrative in the Films of Ozu', Screen vol. 17 no. 2 (Summer 1976), pp. 74-105; K. Thompson, 'Notes on the Spatial System of Ozu's Early Films', Wide Angle vol. 1 no. 4, (1977), pp. 8-17.

19. Burch, To the Distant Observer, pp. 91-92, 117.

20. For a good account of the corner illusion, see D. L. Weismann, The Visual Arts as Human Experience (Englewood Cliffs, New Jersey: Prentice-Hall, 1974), pp. 184-188.

21. A complete analysis would have to reckon into account the functions of Mizoguchi's camera movements in transforming this traditional space into a more three-dimensional one. The use of the crane in Genroku Chushingura is particularly important here.

22. Burch, pp. 17, 290.

23. Brecht, 'A Short Organum for the Theatre', in Brecht on Theatre, p. 192.

24. F. Ewen, Bertolt Brecht: His Life, His Art, and His Times (New York: Citadel Press, 1969), p. 228.

25. B. Brecht, Journal de travail 1938-1955, trans. P. Ivernel (Paris: L'arche, 1976), p. 314. In this journal, Brecht records some remarks to the effect that in Japanese films reflection takes precedence over action.

26. T. Seno, 'Cinema Censorship in Japan', Contemporary Japan vol. VI no. 1 (June 1937), p. 93.

27. H. Bushō, 'The Western Peepshow', in Modern Japanese Literature, D. Keene (ed.), (New York: Grove Press, 1960), p. 35.

28. D. Bordwell, 'Our Dream-Cinema: Western Historiography and the Japanese Film', Film Reader 4 (1979), pp. 45-62; 'To the Distant Observer', Wide Angle vol. 3 no. 4 (1980), pp. 70-73.

29. Bushō, p. 35.

Discourse/Figure: The Inscription of the Subject in Surrealist Film

Laura Oswald

As Gerard Genette has so cogently suggested,[1] the notion of a 'pure metaphor', a metaphor without metonymical motivation, may be a misnomer. This is especially apparent in light of current reevaluations of metaphor and metonymy as mental processes rather than tropes, in the realms of semiology, psychoanalysis, and philosophy.[2] This insight, which has been reiterated by Paul Ricoeur in the context of a discursive theory of metaphor,[3] and by Christian Metz, with reference to the Freudian notions of displacement and condensation in dream formation,[4] has far-reaching implications for the film theorist. In fact, the analysis of the work of metonymy in the cinema is perhaps the most important theoretical issue to be pursued these days, since it raises questions as to the implication of the spectator in the film text, the articulation of the self-reflexive mode in the film discourse, and the inscription of ideology in the cinematic signifier. Due to the time limit I shall limit myself to discussion of the implication of the spectator in the film through metonymical operations in the discourse.

A case in point is the surrealist film metaphor, a metaphor which at first view is so farfetched that one feels compelled to deny it any logical, contextual motivation at all. This position is maintained by Linda Williams in a recent article, 'The Prologue to *Un Chien Andalou*: A Surrealist Film Metaphor', where the author maintains that the association of 'moon' and 'eye' in the opening sequence of *Un Chien Andalou* is a 'pure metaphor', an association based solely on the 'formal similarity' of the two images.[5] This incorrect observation about the metaphor moon/eye in this sequence is based primarily on the author's refusal to admit the work of metonymical operations in motivating this association, a refusal stemming from the methodological

118

mistake of isolating the figure from the surrounding syntagm in which it operates.

This snag in the methodology is based on several important misconceptions of a theoretical nature. First is the assumption that the 'more usual' figure is read 'as mere embellishment' of the diegetic term, such that there exists a hierarchy of the proper or diegetic sense over the figurative sense (the latter conceived as a deviation from the proper sense). Implicit in this position is the denial of the generative function of the figure in its ordinary manifestations, i.e., its ability to motivate the diegesis. Next is the assumption that the surrealist metaphor proceeds according to the reversal of the properties of the more usual metaphor: it is not motivated metonymically by the context; it thus constitutes a rupture with the diegesis; and finally, the surrealist metaphor is capable of generating the diegesis because of its very reversal of the hierarchy of the terms of the more usual metaphor. Finally, in order to justify the 'rupture' theory, which denies the surrealist metaphor any logical relation to the context, Williams resorts to the problematic hypothesis of 'nonreferential' figures, figures lacking a connotative function.

In the course of debating these theoretical issues, I intend to demystify the special status given currently to the metaphor in its surrealist and other avant-garde manifestations,[6] by demonstrating that the mental operations governing the reading of the figure and its relation to the discourse transcend genres and aesthetic sensibilities. What is true of the ordinary figure is true of the surrealist figure and vice versa.

Looking closely at *Un Chien Andalou*, one observes that the series of discontinuous units of the diegesis is given continuity through the technical operations governing metonymical associations in the cinema—movement within the frame, fades from one shot to the next, and other formal references, such as the direction of views from one shot to the next—on the level of the signifier. That is, rather than unfolding according to the gradual 'rupture' of 'our tendency to infer the syntagmatic connection of shots in the discourse as having a parallel connection in the diegesis', the film orchestrates a constant oscillation between an experience of continuity and one of discontinuity and fragmentation. This dynamic of the film emerges from the interference of the metonymy in the metaphor in the structure of *Un Chien Andalou*.

Without metonymical motivation, the association of two terms of a figure would function at best as an expression of conflict on the level of form. Such a rupture would not constitute a metaphor, but an ellipsis,[7] and is a formal strategy one associates with the constructivist sensibility.

The implication of the subject in the film form and the analysis of the act of reading in terms of textual operations has been advanced by some theorists, notably Christian Metz, in the context of an encounter of the rhetorical and psychoanalytical discourses. In this regard, the parallel between the couple metaphor/metonymy on the level of textual operations, and the couple condensation/displacement on the level of psychological operations in the subject, based on the opposition association by similarity/association by contiguity that governs the production of figuration in both systems, is crucial.[8] In *Un Chien Andalou*, reversals of cause and effect, reversals of values such as good, beautiful, and lovable into bad, ugly, and horrible, are metonymical operations that dominate the structuring of signification in this film, and motivate psychological displacements in the spectator. It is the work of psychological displacement that motivates the logical, contiguous association of disparate elements throughout this film, in the same way that it functions in the dream to shift the center of attention from one point in the dream thought to another, contiguously related point in the dream text, according to Freudian theory.[9]

For Freud, there are no condensations, or associations by similarity, in the dream that are not motivated by displacements, and an application of this observation to the reading of film texts would lead to the inference that all metaphorical associations are motivated by metonymical ones. Even if we were to isolate the association moon/eye from the context in which it emerges in *Un Chien Andalou* and were to assume, for the sake of argument, that the association of these two terms is based solely on the formal similarity of the two shots, we would see that it is the metonymical operation that serves to put into relief the formal properties of the two images, permitting their association by similarity. This insight is inspired by the following observation of Freud's in *The Interpretation of Dreams*:

> When a common element between two persons is represented in a dream it is usually a hint for us to look for another, concealed common element whose representation has been made impossible by the censorship. A *displacement in regard to the common element* has been made in order, as it were, to facilitate its representation. The fact that the composite figure appears in the dream with an indifferent common element leads us to conclude that there is another far from indifferent common element present in the dream-thoughts.[10]

For the metaphor from *Un Chien Andalou* in question, the displaced common element would be the formal properties shared by the two images, and the composite figure would be the metaphor-in-syntagm moon/eye. The displacement of interest from the substance to the form, to use the distinction of Hjelmslev,[11] permits the association by similarity of the two shots.[12] We intend to show, however, that a series of metonymies in the text leading up to this figure motivates the association moon/eye, so that the association by similarity is only of secondary importance.

The really powerful feature of the surrealist sensibility is the psychological effect of the metonymical operation to draw the subject into the diegesis, almost in spite of him/herself, in spite of the awareness of 'ruptures' in the text. Failure to see the metonymical connection in this metaphor from *Un Chien Andalou* prohibits such considerations of the spectator in the text. This oversight stems from a fundamentally incorrect methodological assumption of a 'hierarchy' of the terms of a metaphor. This assumption is rooted in the

tropical tradition of metaphorical analysis, where belief in the primacy of the
proper sense over the figurative sense forbids the more dynamic concept of
figures as operations, where it is the movement between the terms of the
figure in the imagination that constitutes the poetic experience. This latter
concept of the figure is called by Genette the 'active rapport between the
signifier and the signified', a rapport that constitutes the 'poetic state of
language'.[13] In light of Genette's work on metaphor, not to mention that of
I.A. Richards,[14] one is reluctant to view the more usual metaphor as a
deviation from a dominant proper sense, rather than as that movement
between two signs that generates the diegesis and vehicles discursive commentary upon it.

This work of the metonymy in the metaphor is more easily illustrated in
highly diegetically determined figuration, much as that in Eisenstein's
October, than in the surrealist example. In the sequence in which Kerensky
sets up his provisional government in the luxurious Winter Palace, a series of
figures links the Kerensky government to the czarist regime, and ultimately
motivates the next phase of the narration. The first figure is composed of a
series of quick, alternating shots of a mechanical peacock spreading its tail
feathers, and of Kerensky. Next is the series of shots of luxurious crystal and a
statuette of Napoleon juxtaposed alternately with Kerensky.

These two comparisons are motivated by metonymies of spatial contiguity, determined by the relation of the physical proximity of Kerensky to the
terms of the associations in the diegesis. This creates, as Genette would say,
the 'resemblance by contagion' of the terms of the metaphors. Moreover, in a
retroactive process, it is only in the moment when these metonymical
relations are transformed into metaphors that the physical proximity of
Kerensky to the luxury around him takes on meaning. The metaphor generates the ideological discourse by establishing the identification of Kerensky
with those elements of the czar's milieu.

Nothing could be more wrong-minded than to perceive the relation of
the terms of this figuration in a hierarchy of the diegesis over the figure.
Rather than merely embellishing the diegetic terms, these comparisons are
vehicles for establishing Kerensky's ideological position and generate the
next phase of the diegesis, the events of October. Clearly in this example the
metaphor generates the diegesis and discursive commentary on it.

This relation of the figure to the diegesis is no different for the surrealist
metaphor. The disparity between the two terms of the surrealist metaphor
may hinder our finding any natural, i.e., lexical motivation for their association. This does not preclude the possibility of finding contextual motivation
for the figure, however, since, as Paul Ricoeur has demonstrated, 'the metaphorical sense is not lexical, but is a value created by the context'.[15] The
context serves to reduce the *écart* or disparity between the two terms of the
metaphor, surrealist or otherwise. In the metaphor moon/eye from *Un
Chien Andalou* the context creates a new criterion of pertinence along which
the discourse and the figure, the diegetic and the extra-diegetic, can meet.

Rather than being based solely on the 'formal similarity' of the two signifiers, the metaphor moon/eye is motivated by the metonymical relation of viewer to viewed, and the subsequent transformation of the viewer, the active term of the opposition, into viewed, the essentially passive term in the syntagm, building up to the cuts from moon to woman to eye. It is the work of metonymy in this metaphor that generates the relations of power—the relations of active/passive, pursuer/pursued, sadist/masochist—that structures the diegesis.

The man's look upward and the cut to the moon create a relation of spatial contiguity in the diegesis, based on the relation of viewer to viewed. It is this same inference or understanding of the direction of the man's view when the shot cuts to the woman that creates the parallel between the moon, the passive object of the man's view, and the woman, a viewer transformed by the man's view into an instance of 'viewed'.

The parallel construction of these two cuts: man looking up (at) moon, man looking up (at) woman, creates a new basis for the association of moon with eye in the subsequent shots. The association woman-a viewer being viewed/moon-a viewed/eye-organ of vision being stripped of its capacity to view, motivates a comparison of moon to eye based on the transformation of the active term in the viewer/viewed opposition into a passive term.

Moreover, our reading of the extreme close-up of the eye as belonging to the woman in the medium close-up is not only based on the similarity of the two shots (a hand with a razor passing from right to left) nor even on their functional similarity (instances of viewers being transformed into instances of viewed), but is based on the metonymical association of whole to part inscribed in the signifier. Our inference as to the spatial and therefore 'real' contiguity connecting a medium close-up with an extreme close-up of a diegetically similar shot is deeply rooted in cinematic convention, and this convention overrides our awareness of the dissimilarity of the shots of the woman and the eye. This convention, or code, comprising a synecdoche in the signifier, motivates our association of a face in shot 10, and a part of a face, the eye, in shot 12. Furthermore, it motivates the illusion of contiguity in the diegesis between the beginning of a gesture—hand with razor moving across face in shot 10, and the 'completion' of that gesture in shot 12. Throughout this film the displacement of signifiers, such as the hand with the razor, from one context to another creates mental links between those contexts in the spectator. This creates an oscillation between the continuous and the discontinuous, between the code and the uncodifiable, in this film, and is a typical feature of the surrealist sensibility.

As far as the present analysis is concerned, the formal similarity of the shot of the moon, based on the foregrounding of the geometric pattern of the circle with the line moving from right to left through it, only serves to assist the comparison of the moon and the woman, the viewer being viewed, being objectified, based on the common element 'viewed'. The disparity between

these terms is finally not felt as a rupture or a non-sense, since the metonymical operation motivates the movement between these two terms in the
spectator's imagination, a movement that generates the discursive intentions
of the diegesis.

The metaphor mouth/wound from *Le Sang d'un Poète* is another
example of a surrealist metaphor which is not only motivated by a metonymy
in the signifier, but whose metonymical underpinnings cause it to generate a
discourse on the experience of the creative act. In an early episode of that film,
entitled: 'The wounded hand, or the scars of the poet', a living mouth is
displaced from a portrait on a canvas to the hand of the artist, and then to the
face of a female statue, by means of superimposition. The initial displacement
of the mouth from the canvas to the hand of the artist motivates the
metaphor already suggested in the subtitle about wounds, between mouth and
wound, by purely technical means. However, what begins as a simple metaphor based on the formal similarity of the two terms—lips covering an
opening—becomes complicated as one refers metonymically back to the
whole bodies from which the two terms have been isolated.

The mouth is that of a woman, the hand that of a man. The sexualization
of the metaphor mouth/wound implicit in the condensation female/male in
one figure gives rise to the association by metonymical displacement of the
mouth with the female genitals and the wound with the castrated male
genitals. The metonymy in the metaphor mouth/wound motivates the condensation of these various terms into an androgenous figure threatened by
phantasms of castration, penetration, and annihilation.

By its very nature the metonymy inscribes in the text an absent signifier.
The relation of this absence to the spectator is an even more important
feature of the metonymical operation than its role in generating the diegesis.
Moreover, failure to see the work of metonymy in the surrealist metaphor
prohibits the analysis of the subject's inscription in the film text. In *Un Chien
Andalou,* the comparison of woman to man then moon to eye, which by
psychological displacement we read as the eye of the woman, is only the
elaboration of a more crucial displacement in the subject, instigated by the
man's view 'about and out across balcony'. This view without an object gives
rise to the replacement, in the subject, of the syntagmatic referent of the
metonymy view/object of view by an imaginary signifier, a paradigmatic
referent for the man's view. This replacment is vehicled by the psychological
displacement underlying projections in the subject.

Situating the metonymical referent in the subject's imaginary is the key
to tracing the inscription of the spectator in the text and is based on the
parallel metaphor/metonymy-condensation/displacement mentioned earlier. Metz situates this parallel in the context of another opposition, the
'force', in the moment of the subject—his impulses—and the 'signification',
in the moment of the figurative articulation.[16] As an agent of the
censorship—the system of defense that determines the passage from the

force to the signification—psychological displacement, rather than condensation, is the process that implicates the impulses of the subject, his desire, in the figuration. An inverse result of this is that the metonymical operation in the text, by signifying an absence that must be filled by the spectator, stimulates a psychological displacement in the latter that terminates in his imaginary, the unconscious configuration of impulses that governs the production of phantasms in the subject. This section of the metonymical operation to stimulate displacements in the spectator constitutes, I believe, what Stephen Heath means when he calls metonymy 'the figure of desire'.[17]

Psychic projection, as conceived by Melanie Klein,[18] is a defense mechanism which functions to displace an unconscious conflict in the subject into the object of his desire. To the degree that a film is an object of desire for the spectator (the desire to enter into the spectatorial game offered by a given film, or to reject it from the outset, varies from one spectator to the next, and is to a great extent psychologically determined), projective displacement is the mechanism governing the implication of the spectator—his desire—in the film text.

In Kleinian theory the sequel to the projection of self into the object of desire is the identification of the subject with the object. Klein calls this projective identification. Once invested with the projections of the subject, the object becomes a sort of mirror for the subject in his imagination, a reflection of his self. It follows that what we call the 'identification of the spectator with the film' is not so much based on the objective or historical similarity prevailing between a character or situation in the film and the spectator, as on the capacity of the film to evoke projections in the spectator by signifying an absence.

In the cinema, the metonymical reference, that is, the metonymy-in-paradigm, is the point of entry *par excellence* of the spectator into the text, since it expresses an absent but contiguously related element that can only be inferred by the spectator. For this reason the suspense film, whose *raison d'être* is the almost visceral assault on the spectator's sensibilities, is filled with metonymies, and one look at the films of Fritz Lang or Alfred Hitchcock confirms this point.

The striking feature of the cuts from viewer to 'viewed' in the slicing sequence from *Un Chien Andalou* is that the elements brought into association by the metonymical operation are situated in obviously disparate time and space contexts. We do not believe, however, that the awareness of this disparity completely breaks down the illusion of contiguity inscribed in the code governing cross-cuts. Nor is the illusion of contiguity of the terms of the association as strong here as it is in narrative manifestations of this code, where the cross-cut serves the logical intentions of the syntagm. What occurs is the movement mentioned earlier, between the code and the uncodifiable, between the symbolic and the imaginary, in this figure. The unexpectedness of the referent 'woman' for the metonymical reference 'view' heightens the experience of lack that is inscribed in the metonymical reference offscreen and that is masked in realist practice by the apparent continuity of the time and space contexts of the terms so associated. The process of identification through the recuperation of this lack, in the spectator, accelerates with the woman's view directly out, in the (imaginary) direction of the spectator. This view inscribes the text with an absent signifier, the imaginary object of the view—the spectator, who passively submits to the sadistic assault of the film on his organ of vision.

NOTES

1. G. Genette, 'Metonymy chez Proust', in *Figures 111* (Paris: Seuil, 1972).
2. R. Jakobson's article, 'Two Aspects of Language and Two Types of Aphasic Disturbances', in *Fundamentals of Language* (The Hague-Paris: Mouton, 1956), is seminal in this regard.
3. P. Ricoeur, *La Métaphore vive* (Paris: Seuil, 1975).
4. C. Metz, *Le Signifiant imaginaire* (Paris: Union Générale d'Editions, 1977).
5. L. Williams, 'The Prologue to *Un Chien Andalou*: A Surrealist Film Metaphor', *Screen* vol. 17 no. 4 (Winter 1977).
6. C. Owens, 'The Primacy of Metaphor', *October* no. 4 (Fall 1977), pp. 21-33.
7. For an analysis of ellipsis as the formal manifestation of the theme of sadistic splitting and fragmentation of the object of desire, see J. Chasseguett-Smirgel's essay on *l'Année dernière à Marienbad* in *Pour une psychanalyse de l'art et de la créativité* (Paris: Payot, 1971).
8. J. Lacan, 'Fonction et champ de la parole et du langage en psychanalyse', in *Ecrits* (Paris: Seuil, 1966).
9. S. Freud, 'The Interpretation of Dreams', *The Standard Edition of the Complete Psychological Works of Sigmund Freud*, ed. and trans. James Strachey, vols. IV & V (London: Hogarth, 1953).
10. Ibid.; (my italics).
11. L. Hjelmslev, *Prolégomènes à une théorie du langage* (Paris: Payot, 1968).
12. Ricoeur, in *La Métaphore vive*, refers to Greimas on this role of metonymy in motivating metaphors: 'If one calls "semic field" the ensemble of elementary constituents of a concept entity, a semic field can be crossed through: "In metonymy, [says Greimas], the mind, crossing through a semic field, focuses on one of the semes and designates the concept entity which is the object of its contemplation by the word, which, in pure linguistic reality, would express this seme, when it is considered as a concept entity" '; (my translation).
13. G. Genette, 'Proust et le langage indirect', in *Figures II* (Paris: Seuil, 1969); (my translation).
14. I.A. Richards, in reaction to the eighteenth century assumption that figures are 'mere embellishment' of a proper sense, says: 'A modern theory would object, first, that in many of the most important uses of metaphor, the co-presence of the vehicle and tenor (the "plain" meaning) results in a meaning (to be clearly distinguished from the tenor) which is not attainable without their interaction. That the vehicle is not normally a mere embellishment of a tenor which is otherwise unchanged by it but that the vehicle and tenor in cooperation give a meaning of a more varied power than can be ascribed to either'. In *The Philosophy of Rhetoric* (Oxford: Oxford University Press, 1936), p. 100; (my parentheses).
15. Ricoeur, p. 239; (my translation).
16. Metz, chapter 8.
17. S. Heath, 'On Screen, In Frame: Film and Ideology', *Quarterly Review of Film Studies* vol. 1 no. 3 (August 1976).
18. M. Klein, 'Envy and Gratitude', in *The Complete Works of Melanie Klein*, vol. III (1957; rpt. London: Hogarth, 1975).

Three Figures of Desire

Linda Williams

I would like to respond to Laura Oswald's criticism of my earlier analysis of the Prologue metaphor from *Un Chien Andalou* by looking again at this metaphor within the larger context of the entire opening section of this film. In my earlier article I intentionally put off any interpretation of the metaphor proper in order to look exclusively at the peculiar *form* of the surrealist metaphor. I never meant to suggest that there was not ultimately what Paul Ricoeur calls a 'metaphorical statement'[1] spoken by this figure, but only that this statement, like the condensations and displacements of dreams, is not immediately translatable in its local context the way the less enigmatic figures of diegetically dominant films are translatable. In the present paper I hope to offer a reading of the Prologue metaphor that can only be discovered through its relation to the two figures which follow. Only by careful attention to the entire figural complex and the dreamlike overdetermination of motifs within this complex can we begin to understand what these figural 'statements' say.

The Progress of the Figures

In the diegetic action following the climax of the eye-cutting, the relationship between the woman whose eye was cut in the Prologue and the cyclist begins. The cyclist, wearing feminine frills and a diagonally striped box, falls off his bicycle. The woman runs downstairs to comfort him. In the next scene, the woman lays out the cyclist's frills, box, collar and tie on the bed in her apartment. This paraphernalia metonymically evokes the absent cyclist in the form of a metonymy placed in paradigm. But the unusual nature of these contiguously related objects lends this particular metonymy a good deal of the artifice usually reserved for relatively 'pure', nondiegetic metaphors. In other words, we seek a similarity between the masculine tie and collar and the feminine frills and the appearance and behavior of the cyclist himself. The cyclist is thus metonymically figured by elements of his dress which are themselves metaphorically similar to his outstanding attributes of confused gender.

This metonymy is closely followed by an intricate series of metaphors beginning with the close-up of the hole in the cyclist's hand. The series proceeds as follows:

> **Shot 1:** Close-up of the man's hand with a *round* hole in the palm, out of which ants swarm. This shot belongs to the diegesis.
>
> **Shot 2:** Close-up of the torso of a female sunbather on her back. The shot is centered on a *round* patch of dark underarm hair. (Extra-diegetic)
>
> **Shot 3:** Close-up of a *round* sea urchin whose dark protruding spines slowly move. (Also extra-diegetic)
>
> **Shot 4:** A *round* iris-framed long shot from a high angle centered on the round head of an androgenous woman holding a long stick. She pokes at the round shape of a severed hand with the stick. The iris opens out to reveal a crowd that has formed a *circle* around the androgyne.

This is the end of the figure proper. Later shots reveal: a close-up of the severed hand as it is prodded by the stick; the swaying crowd; and a policeman who pushes the crowd away from the androgyne. As an interior shot reveals the cyclist and woman standing before a window, we realize that the high-angle shot which first presented the androgyne (shot 4) was in fact the perspective from the woman's apartment and that she and the cyclist have overseen the drama of the severed hand taking place on the street below. While the cyclist and the woman continue to watch from above, the androgyne places the severed hand in a diagonally striped box identical to the cyclist's box. Soon after she is struck by a car. The cyclist's reaction is one of mounting sexual excitement.

The metaphoric series proper is motivated, like the metaphor of the Prologue, by the purely formal similarity of round shapes. The round shape of the hole in the cyclist's hand and the swarming movement of the ants resemble the similar round shape of the sunbather's armpit and its tuft of hair. Thus far similarity of the referents (hole in hand and armpit) combines with contiguity of the discourse to form a metaphor placed in syntagm.

In shot 3 the round shape of the sea urchin with its protruding spines echos the round hole and swarm of ants in shot 1 and the round underarm and tuft of hair in shot 2. But where in shots 1 and 2 the round shapes were concave holes, or volumes, from which the ants and hair emerged, in shot 3 the round shape of the sea urchin is a convex volume from which the black spines protrude.

With shot 4, the round shapes of the preceding three shots are repeated in a much different way. Here it is the iris frame of the shot itself that is round. This roundness is in turn echoed by the round shape of the androgyne's head within the shot. Then, as the iris opens out, its shape is replaced by the round shape of the crowd encircling the androgyne and the small round hand with which she plays.

If we measure the distance between the first and last of these figurations—from the hand with the hole in it in the room to the severed hand on the street below—we discover a marked development from the round concave hole of the hand (1), and the equally concave round cup of the sunbather's armpit (2), to the convex roundness of the sea urchin (3) and the equally convex roundness of the androgyne's head and severed hand (4).

The metaphor, beginning within the diegesis, continues to develop extra-diegetically in the shots of the armpit and sea urchin. But then, in the final shot of the series, the androgyne and severed hand lead back into the diegesis through the subsequent revelation that the androgyne is observed by the cyclist whose own mutilated hand began the series. Thus a progression of similar shapes deviously links the contiguous space of apartment and street, leading us first away from and then back into the diegesis.

The Meaning of the Figures

Each of these enigmatic figures resists interpretation on the local, immediate level. Only by examining the relation between them can we begin to grasp their latent meaning. All of these figures—the Prologue metaphor of the eye-cutting, the metonymy of the garments placed on the bed and the metaphoric series beginning with the hole in the hand—repeat motifs of cut or mutilated flesh along with the signs of male and female gender.

The cutting motif begins with the first trial cut of the thumbnail and the eye-cutting of the Prologue and continues in the mutilated hand and completely severed hand of the metaphoric series. The opposing signs of male and female gender appear first in the diegesis in the combination of male cyclist dressed in feminine frills, then in the metonymic manipulation of male collar and tie combined with these same frills, then in the more abstract concave hollows and convex protrusions of the metaphoric series and, finally, in the person of the androgyne herself.

Frequently, mutilation by cutting leads to the combination of the signs of male and female gender. For example, the initial mutilation of the eye-cutting in the Prologue is followed by the male-female cyclist and then by the fetishized signs of his contradictory gender alone in the metonymies of the garments placed on the bed. Then, in the metaphoric series, this pattern is repeated within a single figure: the initial mutilation of the hole in the hand is followed by a shift from concave to convex roundness culminating in the appearance of the androgyne who combines in one person the same contradictory gender traits as the cyclist.

Most commentators have viewed the Prologue metaphor variously as a symbol of sexual penetration of the female body, an assault on the viewer's own vision and a movement to inner vision, and, finally, a symbol for the process of cinematic construction itself. My own view does not deny any of these meanings, but adds the further notion that the latent meaning of the metaphor can only be castration. This meaning emerges only in the light of the other figures and the way in which they respond to the initial metaphor of the Prologue. For what these subsequent figures do, paradoxically, is to deny the meaning of castration. But as we shall see this very denial becomes itself the confirmation of the fear it is intended to allay.

The woman whose eye is cut by the razor in the Prologue becomes a sexual object of the cyclist's desire in the subsequent diegesis. It is thus reasonable to interpret the woman's split eye as a metaphor for the vagina and the razor as a substitute penis. But if so, this metaphor of male desire is peculiarly condensed. The fact that penetration occurs through cutting opens up the possibility that it is the result of cutting, the result, that is, of castration. But this only becomes apparent in the movement of the following figures to deny the consequences of this castration: sexual difference.

The metonymy of the garments placed on the bed is the first denial of sexual difference. Freud has shown that the function of a fetish is to act as a substitute for the mother's penis, a 'penis that the little boy once believed in'.[2] Freud calls this substitute a 'disavowal' of the fact that women have no penis. These substitutes frequently cover or connect with the part of the body thought to have undergone castration to preserve the illusion of a female phallus. Yet as Freud points out, the fetish is a paradoxical object that, in its very denial of what is most feared, cannot help but assert that same fear. The combination of feminine frills and masculine collar and tie placed on the bed by the woman are fetish objects that wishfully present the cyclist as sexually undifferentiated, simultaneously male and female. Yet this disavowal of sexual difference simultaneously admits, as all fetishes admit, that there is indeed something to be denied.

This process of denial is repeated in the following figure of the metaphoric series. But here the metaphor reasserts the initial fear of castration in the beginning shot of the wounded hand. Just as the wound of the eye-cutting is followed in a subsequent scene by the disavowal of the fetish garments, so here the metaphoric assertion of castration is directly followed by a progression of increasingly convex shapes that attempts to disavow the initial concave wound.

But again, the more the text tries to disavow and cover an initial lack, the more it asserts that lack. For in the final image in the series—the shot of the androgyne on the street—the forms are convex but the content of the convex form is, most disturbingly, a severed hand—a cut-off organ. Not only does this process of disavowal call attention to the fear of castration, it also ironically points out the double nature of the sexual symbols involved: concave and convex are two sides of the same bowl. One side is absence (the concave 'wound', the vagina), the other side is presence (the convex protrusion, the penis). When the convex protrusion turns out to be a severed organ, it becomes a presence that insidiously evokes an absence. Thus even a phallic protrusion becomes an ironic metaphor for the fear that it is intended to allay.

The paradoxical structure of these figures reflects the ambiguous logic of dreams in which the assertion of any thought can be both positive and negative in a perpetual movement between the opposing poles of signification. Contraries act in this film as they do in dreams where, as Freud has observed, the concept 'no' seems not to exist. What is more, causality in general operates throughout the film in a particularly dreamlike way. Freud has observed that dreams can represent causal connection by the introduction of the dream equivalent of a 'dependent clause'. In certain kinds of dreams a clearly separate beginning section—the dependent clause—posits an initial condition or state of affairs which the rest of the dream—the principal clause—then develops. Freud's point is that the seemingly disjointed segments of a dream can nevertheless exhibit the logic of causality.[3] In *Un Chien Andalou* the Prologue metaphor acts as such a dependent clause positing the initial condition of castration-division-absence which the principal clause of the subsequent figures—and the diegesis which flows out of these figures— attempts to deny.

But there is still more to be said about the 'principal clause' of the final metaphoric series ending with the androgyne. The androgyne herself is a dominantly feminine version of the contradictory gender traits of the dominantly masculine cyclist. The cyclist and androgyne are also linked by their mutual possession of the diagonally striped box which in one instance contains a necktie and in another becomes the receptacle for the severed hand. In the first instance, the box appears to let out its secret: the necktie as substitute phallus and fetish working to deny the feared castration. In the second instance the box functions as the container for the counter-secret: as the receptacle for the severed hand which, because it is once again a reminder of castration, must be hidden away. In both cases, the opening and closing of the mysterious box acts to assert the very truth of what it attempts to hide.

Taken together these three figures establish a symmetrical pattern of assertion and denial, the basic terms of which are presence and absence. The Prologue posits a gap-split-absence which the fetish garments attempt to disavow. The hole in the hand posits a similar gap-split-absence which the following series of metaphors even less successfully disavows.

The desire of the text thus mirrors the desire of the subject. It seeks perpetually and impossibly to fill-in, cover-over and otherwise deny an original loss. If castration is one meaning of the Prologue metaphor it is also, as Lacan has said, itself a metaphor for difference, for the fundamental lack-in-being which marks all entrance into the symbolic and which structures all desire.

NOTES

1. P. Ricoeur, *The Rule of Metaphor* (Toronto, Canada: University of Toronto Press, 1977), p. 65.

2. S. Freud, 'Fetishism', *The Standard Edition of the Complete Psychological Works of Sigmund Freud*, ed. and trans. James Strachey, vol. XXI (London: Hogarth, 1953), p. 153.

3. S. Freud, 'The Interpretation of Dreams', *Standard Edition* vols. IV & V (London: Hogarth, 1953), p. 315.

The Primacy of Figure in Cinematic Signification

Dudley Andrew

Structuralism and semiotics of film have been enormously attractive enterprises because they promise to supply procedures capable of dealing systematically with a phenomenon which staunchly resisted systematizing for its first 70 years. The smooth visual surface of the movies could rebuff the advances of all but 'global' scholars ready to fawn over or rebuke her charms. Until the mid sixties, scholars of the art were scarcely distinguishable from popular reviewers. Many performed both functions.

Cinema was adored or feared but in all cases it was deemed inaccessible to scientific or even scientistic labor, this despite such pretentious organizations as the Institut de Filmologie in Paris and America's grotesque and puny copy of it, 'The Society of Cinematologists'. Such groups floundered about in phenomenology, behavioral study, and psychosociology searching for keys to enter the inner workings of the silent screen. Structuralism and semiotics at last opened the door.

The greatest immediate breakthrough in these infant disciplines came in relation to genre films, especially those of the so-called classic American period (1935-55). Here the rewards seemed highest. If ever a cinema consistently guised itself as reality, it was in this era. If ever cinema brooked no challengers, it was then. The goal of structuralism and semiotics, therefore, was to 'crack' this hermetic system, expose its workings and provide social critics with the evidence they needed to perform a symptomatic reading of American culture through a study of the elements and rules structuring its movie-reality.

At the same time, the hopes for success in this enterprise could hardly be higher, for the classic American genre film displayed a consistency which could only be the result of regularization achieved by some hidden application of rules. The sheer accumulation of 450 films a year for 20 years all coming from Hollywood under essentially a single production system foretold an aesthetic system mediating the production situation and the final product. Semiotics promised to track down the units of representation in that aesthetic system, structuralism to account for the specific narrative shape of the values represented. Both derived from structural linguistics, a master discipline which, in 1960, seemed on its way to the complete delineation of the communicative powers of language from its smallest elements to their ordered and 'meaningful' combinations.

If structuralism has run up against resistance in the past few years, it is in part because cultural studies have felt the need to pass from the logical clarity of linguistics to the murkier discipline of rhetoric. Henceforth the study of *figures*, not codes, must be paramount in an examination of cultural artifacts. This is an especially appropriate attitude to adopt in relation to film, which even in the case of the classic American genres has always seemed more a collection of strategies than a well-ordered system. Recent interest in the study of third world films, art films, experimental pieces, and documentaries has confirmed this priority.

In practice this shift to rhetoric has meant supplementing categories of semiotics (codes) and of discourse theory (syntagms, paradigms, aspects of narration) by the introduction of terminology of rhetoric (tropes of metaphor, metonymy, irony, etc.) and of psychoanalysis (condensation, displacement, representability, secondary elaboration, etc.). All these disciplines share a method of organizing a text according to the selection and placement of elements, and if cinema has rules, these can only concern the selection of images or their ordering. It was this vision of the structure of cinema which at first provided such impetus to treat it as a legitimately linguistic system, since selection and ordering make up the very processes of language (dictionary and grammar).

And it is only an enlarged concern for selection and ordering which has forced a semiotician like Christian Metz to shift his categories from those of discourse theory to those of rhetorical and especially psychoanalytic theory. The cynic may find this shift perfectly congruent with the changing intellectual fads in France. The more serious student will see in this shift the recognition by film scholars themselves that film is ordered not as a natural language but at best as a set of practices and strategies which are in some way 'ready-to-hand', but which hardly form a system in any strong sense of the term.

This aspect of *bricolage* at the heart of the medium suggests that meaning in film comes largely by way of conventions which began as figures. A white cowboy hat denotes 'the good guy' today only because it was used as a figure of purity over and over years ago. A dissolve denotes the passage of time today only because for years it figured that passage palpably through the physical intertwining of adjacent but distinct scenes.

While we may be accustomed to thinking of figures as abnormal, disordering embellishments in well-ordered, rational discourse, Metz suggests that they are, especially in cinema, the normal marks of an irrational discourse which becomes progressively ordered. He sees film operating semiotically (through grammar and syntax and an invariant relation of signifier to signified), rhetorically (where figures extend or replace the domain of the signified, thus developing an unstable relation between it and its signifier) and psychoanalytically (where a free play of signifiers responds to dynamic instinctual forces and organizes itself through the processes associated with the dream work—processes, by the way, Freud habitually named after rhetorical figures [antithesis, parallelism, reversal, metallepsis, etc.]).

In his most recent writings, Metz has reversed our conventional order in handling cinematic meaning. Instead of proceeding from the ordered discourse back through figures of discourse to the psychic wellsprings of discourse, Metz has suggested that the true source and referent of all discourse is the 'indestructible' (the drives and processes of the unconscious). The progressive displacement of meaning operating in relation to a censoring process turns a desire into a pattern of flight and detour which surfaces as a discursive form. This form is composed of the figurative movements of the medium which are ultimately constrained into a semiotic matrix which can be rationally exchanged in a communicative act.

Film has freed us, Metz feels, from dealing with figures as instances of disordered speech classifiable by logic or philology. From Aristotle to our own day, figures have been thought of as obscure units replacing conventional units. Taxonomies have enumerated them. But the movement of meaning in film suggests that grammar, order, and semiotic consistency is a last order consideration and that discourse proceeds by way of figures and, through figures, by way of the unconscious. Thus he finds it more appropriate to speak of 'figuration' rather than 'figure', of great processes in which signifiers seek for, attain, extend, and often lose their signifieds.

For Metz, metonymy is the key and most usual figure, the figure of association by which we pass from one aspect or image to a related one in search of a satisfying final picture. When this process becomes fully secondarized and elaborated in logical (i.e., semiotic) patterns, we have before us a filmed narrative. Only the close inspection of the remaining figures which protrude from the otherwise clean path of narrative provide an inkling of the complex detours which were taken in the production of an acceptable story. Thus metonymy does double duty, marking the displacement of psychic energy in its shifting trajectory refracted through censorship, and entering into the sheer contiguity of narrative successivity in which everything is, 'in the end', well-placed. Metonymies are midpoints between force and signification.

Metz' dynamic conception of textuality as a flow, a filtering, and successive detours observable in the struggle between volatile figures and a ruled narrative does not, however, free him from a limited structural stance in the analysis of texts. He calls for the classification of figures in film along four separate axes: degree of secondarization; dominance of metonymy or metaphor; suggestion of condensation or displacement; and the type of incorporation in the text (syntagmatic or paradigmatic). Here once again a closed structuralism dominates its object of research, even though that object is avowedly free and open. In genre study, to return to our clearest instance, the analyst may classify the figurative markers in the texts as they respond over the years to a timeless unconscious source (Lévi-Strauss' 'inherent contradiction') in varying historical contexts.

While this is most assuredly a necessary and valuable enterprise, it is nevertheless insufficient as a final research strategy. For all Metz makes of the unconscious origins of textuality, his is essentially a theory of narration wherein filtering and detour (selection and association) operate to shape a logical and closed story. Classical rhetorical theories of texts represent the inverse of Metz' psychoanalytic view. The text for them stands in relation to a direct prose sense, whereas for Metz it stands in relation to an unconscious non-sense. In both cases figures operate as detours from, and substitutions for, a more direct formulation which the author cannot or will not provide. Thus in both cases the figural nature of a text is a transitional stage through which, as critics, we may try to pass on our way to the recovery of total sense or total energy (the drives).

If our interest is not to interpret what lies beyond the text but rather to classify methods of textual disfiguration, then we may construct a history of rhetorical strategies. The tropology of classical rhetorical theory therefore has its counterpart in Metz' four-axis classification method. The result of both schemas (despite their opposing theories of texts) is a list of genres, practices, and specific tropes by which art carries in its own (artistic) way the force of unconscious drives or the direction toward reasonable signification.

In neither of these cases (passing through the figures or cataloguing them) and from neither point of view (rationalist or psychoanalytic) is the specific figural movement of a given text worth pursuing in and for itself. Structural analysis studies artistic speech without listening to it. It either translates such speech into the 'real' discourse (of the unconscious or of reason) or it treats such speech as a cultural object, a datum for classification.

If figural discourse has anything to say to us by means of its unique form, only a hermeneutic, not a structural, orientation will prepare us to deal with it. It is hardly coincidental that the leading authority on hermeneutics, Paul Ricoeur, has recently published a lengthy treatise on metaphor.

Ever the arbiter, Ricoeur threads his way between a theory of figural substitution for proper meaning coming from Aristotle (conscious, grammatical, ordered, secondary) and a theory of sheer figural process coming from Freud (unconscious, disordered, disordering, and primary). Retaining both substitution and process, Ricoeur emphasizes the *event* of discourse rather than its structure. From this perspective a figure is reducible neither to its proper sense nor to some timeless process it exemplifies, for it has the ability to change the rules of the discursive game in which it participates. Its meaning is not purely substitutionary, nor is it irrecoverable in the indestructible unconscious, for while it depends on rules, sense, and grammar, and while it undoubtedly rests on psychological preconditions, a figural event in discourse expands the space of meaning and invites us to fill in that space through interpretation. Figures alter, but don't dispense with, the dictionary.

Now film historians and genre theorists may very well be content to trace the development of film art in terms of figural markers which serve each generation. In 1920 a superimposition was the appropriate marker to denote the presence of spirits *(Phantom Chariot)* and to connote 'art'. In 1961 the same denotation was carried by an electronic sound accompanying a washed-out photograph of a figure *(The Innocents)*. The history of the cinema and of any of its genres (the ghost film) is not so much a compilation of the tales it has told as a development in the figures it employs to denote such tales and to signal to its audience that this tale is presented 'artistically'.

Without denying the utility of this sort of scholarship, Ricoeur implies that it is unable to attend to the specific world of meaning carved out in a genre film by means of figural operations. More important, neither can it accurately account for the general *process* by which films make artistic meaning. Metz' four categories of figure analysis, for instance, do not provide a dynamic model of the work of figures even though he asserts that figures are dynamic. His is an analysis of the various levels at which a figure may be thought of as working, levels which Metz is at pains to keep separate (the unconscious, the rhetorical, the grammatical, and the diachronic, corresponding to his examination of displacement, metonymy, syntagmatics, and degree of secondarization).

Ricoeur opposes this method of analysis through separation by treating the figural process dialectically. It is not a matter, he claims, of a metaphor being drawn from the lexicon and responding to a certain psychic pressure; the metaphor is an event within which the psyche and the linguistic system adjust to one another. No analysis of this event can afford to neglect this interaction. Perhaps we can see now why Ricoeur privileges metaphor above all figures while Metz demotes it to an occasional and special form of association seldom if ever appearing in a pure state. Every metaphor, Ricoeur claims, alters the discourse (artwork) while changing our sense of (name for) the referent.

Metz' view is an essentially narrative one in which a progressive filtering directs the successive signifying elements, ruling out unrelated connotations from the objects and events we recognize in the images. Metonymy has always been the privileged figure of narrative. Ricoeur, for his part, is anxious to lift poetry, and its prime figure, metaphor, to the summit of artistic activity and by doing so to give metaphor a special function in the life of language.

If metonymy proceeds by redirecting and filtering meanings, we may say that metaphor completely reorients meaning with respect to the situation on which it is used. It is the redescription of a semantic field (let's say, for example, the field of musical sounds) via a statement employing a term transferred from a foreign signifying domain (labels used to cover colors). We not only can speak in a given instance of a 'bright or saturated tone' but the entire system of musical distinctions suddenly becomes vulnerable to a 'chromatic' redescription. This is much more than the redirection of meaning. It is indeed the very birth of meaning as both language and its object are altered in adjusting to one another. It is not a special manner of traversing a semantic field but a way of permanently restructuring it through an 'impertinent attribution' which demands interpretation in order to restore pertinence at some higher point.

Once metaphor is conceived of not as a verbal substitution but as a process resulting in the redescription of a semantic field, it becomes useful to film theory. For we may say that metaphor can occur as the calculated introduction of dissonance into any systematic stage of the film process.

Following Jean Mitry, we can identify three stages in the film viewing process: perception (representation); organization (narrative); and valuation (rhetoric). Each of these stages is constructed by means of a different set of signs and each demands a different operation for the viewer. We might liken each stage to a threshold to its successor as we pass from recognizing objects to the recognition of events, stories, or arguments, and finally to the recognition of a point of view and a system of value.

Cinematic representation (the image itself) is normally an unquestioned mapping of the visible field. Despite its limitations and because of its photochemical origins we accept it as a threshold to the properly narrative and rhetorical levels of discourse. Our sense of the perceptual field can, however, be questioned by a work on the elements of the sign (grain, focus, color, depth, camera stability, etc.). Patterns and games played with these elements, once brought to a level of pertinence for the spectator, might then form a model adequate in itself and suggestive of new relations in the field, relations formerly unmapped and therefore insignificant or nonsignifying.

A figure functions only when it is observed to function, only when it stands in the way of an automatic movement across signs. If, as is usual, nothing halts us at the level of perception, the next potential figural work occurs at the level of narrative. Here, more than at the first level, we recognize the norm as a residue of figural strategies coming down to us through the years as a trial and error process in the attempt to adequately map the field of interlacing actions. But here, more easily than at the first level, we can see at work the concept of the model, the heuristic fiction, which, built in such a way that it is consistent to itself, may give us the terms to redescribe our life-world of objects, actions, and their interrelations.

The conventions of genre and those of the *vraisemblable* make up the norms of narrative. The construction of a fictional world or the introduction of an element absolutely foreign to these norms forces us to reimagine our sense of fictional discourse and the world to which it refers as a model.

Finally, the rhetorical stage involves the codes of discourse and of personal style by which a text foregrounds certain of its aspects. In a film like Robert Bresson's *Pickpocket* we have no trouble construing either the images or the story set before us; but Bresson's importation of seventeenth century music and a literary voice-over narration, not to mention his formal camera movement and obsessive close-ups, halt our easy access to this film. We find ourselves seeking the appropriate level of discourse, that is, interpreting the film at the level its incongruities and obsessions seem to point to. This jump in levels is precisely a metaphoric one, since no literal reading of these marks of discourse is adequate to the work of the film. The film, then, becomes for us a model stance applicable to the world at large.

While in practice these stages in the process of signification in the cinema occur simultaneously, metaphor always localizes itself at a particular stage as it strives to disrupt the system of signification in order to signify something 'other'. What guides the propriety of a metaphorical shift and what guides our subsequent effort to interpret it? I would have to say here that a metaphor only points to a potentially fruitful rapport with the semantic field, a rapport which it is up to the spectator to work out. The metaphor demands close description since by definition no rule or convention can determine or locate its utility and scope. As it is elaborated in detail it becomes a model for the redescription of reality as such.

Only the uncoded manifold of experience can determine the extent of a metaphor's power. Hence the metaphor demands an interrogation between experience and system, between the field and the map, which is largely self-regulating. The point should be clear. A semiotic of film hoped to specify the meaning of its elements. A rhetoric of film hopes to point to its figural moments and initiates an interpretative process which may go on for as long as it is fruitful.

It should be evident now why structuralism can only provide a partial explanation for the workings of film and no real comprehension of the achievement of any given film. For structuralism will not recognize the event of cinematic discourse. It will always and only provide a description of the system which is put into use in the event. If, as I claim with Ricoeur, the system is altered by the event, if (to make a stronger claim) the system was born and exists only as a residue of such events of figuration, then we need a broader vision of the creation of meaning in films.

Semiotics and structuralism taught us to study the system through which signs are recognized as images and stories. We need to focus now on those instances when a sign is not assimilated by the narrative and where therefore a misrecognition occurs.

For Metz such misrecognition arises from the unconscious and points back to it even while a radical filtering reorients the context as the film moves toward its proper closure. All figuration for him is merely displaced narration.

Ricoeur's view is stronger. For him misrecognition forces us to put into play all the possibilities of the sign and then leap to a new possibility, the one which will change the context itself and make us see it through the 'improper and impertinent' sign. This is what produces a seismic shift of the contextual field. In politics we call such condensation 'revolution', in psychoanalysis 'transferal' and in artistic and religious experience 'insight'.

Figures are thus more than shortcuts by way of association and substitution; they have the power to disrupt the relation of context to sign and to reorient not only the discursive event but the system itself, which will never be the same.

The institution of film proceeds not by the routine application of the rules but by a tension between rules and a force of discourse trying to say something. This force overdetermines a sign within a conventional context so that the sign overflows both recognition and narrative positioning, changing the system through misrecognition until, in the tension, we recognize what was meant.

Such misrecognition can occur in the presentation of the elementary cinematic sign, in its placement in a scene, in the scene's placement in the narrative and in the film's relation to a cultural context. While we may be fascinated by the rules of genre, for example, we ought to be still more fascinated by the play of misrecognition which makes a particular genre film interesting to us and which makes it a useful and not merely redundant way to view culture. The great film puts the genre and the culture into question, permanently altering both by means of its defiance of the meaning and its simultaneous search for a true meaning. This can only occur in a process which incorporates structure as one of its constitutive elements, but which could never be exhausted by a study of structure.

This article has also appeared in expanded form in Iris *vol. 1 no. 1 (1983).*

Cinematic Discourse: The Problem of Inner Speech

Paul Willemen

The interdependence of the verbal and the visual in the cinema has been asserted, denied and generally commented upon by film theorists. Yet film theory has tended to avoid the issues that such a recognition of interdependence might raise. The problems are indeed extremely complex, and the implications of their investigation could prove to be far-reaching for the ways we understand and write about cinema as well as for the production and making of films. Moreover, as I will try to suggest, consideration of the verbal-visual nexus inevitably touches on the status of cinema as an ideological practice, which in turn opens up a host of further problems. In the face of this, the safest option would be to avoid the problem altogether, or, if the problem cannot be avoided, to regard the orders of figuration and of verbal discourse as irrevocably separate. In this way, no existing notions about the cinematic fact or institution need be upset and theorists do not need to venture out on a limb too far for comfort.

The commonsense position, shared by dominant and even highly elaborated theoretical discourses, is that language and image shall be regarded as entirely separate, each with its own regimes of specificity. Those who contest the reductionist definition of cinema implicit in the terms 'motion pictures' or 'movies', and who insist on the importance of language as an integral part of cinema, nevertheless maintain a rigorous distinction between the two registers of signification, reducing each to its phenomenal, empirical manifestations. This paper starts from the recognition firstly that 'language is the symbolic expression *par excellence* and all other systems of communication are derived from it and presume its existence', and secondly that 'any human communication of nonverbal messages presupposes a circuit of verbal messages without a reverse implication'.[1] This recognition is founded on previous research[2] which demonstrated that verbal signifiers are present in and have a structuring effect on the very formation of images (camera angles, the figuration of characters and events in narrative films). At the time, I used the term 'literalisms' to designate clear-cut instances of words marking specific figurations in films. However, the many different types of 'literalism' that could be detected suggested that the problem not only needed further investigation, but that the possibility of there being 'considerations of representability' at work in cinema raised issues which went far beyond the mere classification of different forms of literalisms. What follows constitutes a preliminary reconnoitering of the terrain opened up by the introduction of the notions of inner speech and considerations of representability into film theory and attempts to formulate a few theses which may help to focus the issues.

Some Theses

1. *The Audio-Visual Fantasy*

Questions addressed to the relation between language and image tend to be posed as if these two terms corresponded to homogeneous units which can (or cannot) entertain specific, identifiable relations with each other. However, the first requirement when considering this question is to begin by distinguishing between the various dimensions or levels of language, from the phonemic system to the discursive, and between the various aspects of the imaged discourse, from the figurations within the image to their sequential arrangement. The first distinction to be made is that between the verbal signifier, the word (or morpheme) and its corresponding signified. Although there is no signifier without a signified and vice versa, by now it has been established fairly conclusively that the two sides of the sign enjoy a relative autonomy in relation to each other: they do not operate in the same way nor are they structured in the same way. Their relation, in Jakobson's phrase, is one of coded contiguity. Lacan's rewriting of psychoanalysis insists that the coded contiguity addressed by linguists is in fact a special case of coding related to the domain of the conscious, whereas contiguity operates quite differently in signification in general, as can be deduced from the laws of unconscious signification. Consequently, the concept of the signifier in psychoanalysis has little or nothing in common with that of the signifier in linguistics. In psychoanalysis, any element of language, from the distinctive features of phonemes through phonemes themselves to morphemes and discursive units, from semantic features to concepts and their various forms of 'presentation', can function as a signifier. Remaining within the domain of linguistics, verbal signifiers can be seen to be present in cinema in specific phenomenal forms either on the soundtrack[3] or as writing within the field of the image. By restricting language to its phenomenal forms, the currently dominant ideologies, promoting the notion of the audio-visual, assert that the orders of the figure and of the word are two homogeneous blocks that can only be juxtaposed, confronted or combined, but can never be merged in hybrid forms of signification, interpenetrating each other.

According to this audio-visual scenario, a film can be described as cinematic in inverse proportion to the quantity of verbal—crudely identified with the literary—signifiers empirically present in the text. In addition, positions which imply that cinema is a matter of showing rather than telling, of light patterns rather than signification, are also founded on that same scenario, reducing complex forms of heterogeneity to singular homogeneous essences. These views simply ignore that meaning, an inevitable byproduct of any 'mark' in whatever material of expression is itself a verbal phenomenon: it is part of the domain of semantics. As Roland Barthes pointed out:

> To perceive what a substance signifies is inevitably to fall back on the individuation of a language: there is no meaning which is not designated, and the world of signifieds is none other than that of language.[4]

By opposing or juxtaposing the 'audio' element to the 'visual' element, the ideology of the audio-visual engineers a psychodramatic confrontation of the figure and the word founded on the excision of meaning from the realm of language in order to maintain the gap between language and image. All relations between the two blocks become entirely external, formal, optional and ultimately dispensable.

2. The Presence of the Verbal Signified: Lexicalization

Perhaps the most obvious examples of verbal language conditioning ostensibly nonverbal sign systems are instances where words or phrases directly model and determine the signs of a secondary system. Although the terms 'primary' and 'secondary modeling system' are somewhat misleading,[5] in this context they appear appropriate. The 'literalism' operative in the representation of 'looking up to' by a low-angle shot is one example. Another is the verbal metaphor 'flame' for desire, love, passion, etc., being represented by some sort of fire in an image or scene containing a couple (usually young and of opposite sexes). A more elaborate example of symbolization is described by Karel Brusak in his analysis of signs in Chinese theater.[6] Brusak found that makeup constituted 'a self-contained artificial system ... The scheme painted on the actor's face is, in fact, a chart of the moral qualities of the dramatis persona', a system not unlike the typing of heroes and villains in early silent cinema, where white = good, and dark or black = bad. Brusak lists an interesting scheme of colors corresponding to specific verbal meanings:

> Black means simplicity, sincerity, courage and steadfastness; red denotes loyalty, honesty and patriotism; crimson is used with old men as a sign for the calm of old age and prudence allied to these qualities; blue expresses obstinacy, cruelty and pride; yellow indicates ruthlessness, slyness and wiliness; white stands for hypocrisy, irascibility, baseness and viciousness. The extent of the coloured area on the actor's face corresponds to the extent of the moral quality in the character of the dramatis persona ... Green is reserved for spirits and devils, gold for gods.

Brusak also comments on other substitutes for verbal expressions:

> Movement of the facial muscles are conventionalised; binding stipulations govern which facial expression should be used to express a given emotion relative to character type and age and the nature, intensity and duration of the feeling.

Movements such as a particular sleeve-gesture are 'a sign replacing the verbal wish that the other desist from his greetings', and he stresses that Chinese classical theater manifests 'a stock of several systems of lexicalised signs'. Although such conventions cannot be regarded as literalisms, they nevertheless constitute examples of the lexicalization of visual signs, of a kind of verbal score being performed by means of nonverbal signs.

But lexicalization appears to be only one aspect of the verbal presence in the visual. The other is its structuring function in the dynamic of the textual system as a whole. Brusak's examples of the latter, although they refer to theater, are equally applicable to the cinema: all that is required to effect that transition is the filming of a performance. His examples are particularly interesting in that they constitute instances of condensation: the apparent absence of a code or 'language' produces deformations or exaggerations in other sign systems. Brusak noticed that on the one hand 'the use of scenic articles linked to costume comprehensibly delineates the character of the personage while obviating the necessity for explanatory passages in the dialogue'. But as the delineation of character is already coded by the makeup, the linked usage of scenic articles and costume presumably functions as a conventional instance of double coding or motivation. This would suggest that the second aspect of the function is perhaps more important: the replacement of explanatory passages in the dialogue. In cinema, such instances are often referred to as 'condensation'; for example, the need to 'condense' a novel into a film. Brusak suggests that what disappears from the dialogue resurfaces in the combination of costume and scenic objects. This decathexis of one register accompanied by a hypercathexis of another is intensified by a further aspect of the use of costume: as 'Chinese classical theatre is without lighting effects, this gives rise to the magnificence of Chinese theatrical costume', since it must also perform the task of 'forming the scene', of structuring scenic space. The splendor of the costumes is thus the result of two separate but cumulative processes. In it we can trace the 'absence' of lighting and of dialogue. An extension of the argument that immediately suggests itself is that silent cinema can be understood as functioning with similar condensations: heightened stylization as a result of the 'absence' of audible dialogue, noise and color. The same applies to the prevalence of 'dramatic lighting' and 'expressive' styles of montage.

These things seem obvious and have been remarked on by many critics and theorists. But the implications of such remarks are seldom pursued. The question is whether the invention of sound cinema made it possible to absorb and accommodate on the soundtrack all possible manifestations of language that could not in some way be located in the image. Was audible speech really the only extra form of language that needed accommodation in the film text? The actualization of audible speech via the soundtrack did profoundly affect the processes of filmic figuration. But a number of examples of the remaining structuring impact of the verbal can be disengaged fairly easily. In Monte Hellman's *Two Lane Blacktop* the last image of the filmstrip, representing the final 'burn out', looks as if the celluloid catches fire in the projector. But there are also examples where the presence of the word, or indeed of intersecting chains of verbal signifiers, structures aspects of films which are not so easily accounted for as one-to-one substitutions of images for words. For instance, in Sam Fuller's *Pickup on South Street*, there is a camera movement which starts off with a close shot of Skip/Richard Widmark and Candy/Jean Peters, then the camera backs away and travels to the left while keeping the kissing couple in the center of the frame. The camera stops moving when the two chains hooked together in the middle of the image vertically divide the frame. After a few seconds, the camera completes the shot by returning to its initial close shot of the couple, still kissing. This 'hook' appears to function in a number of different verbally determined threads: the two are getting hooked on each other, but Skip/Widmark is also 'on the hook' in the film, as is Candy/Peters. Moreover, the hook also connects chains from which hang the McGuffin of the film. The apparently pointless camera movement thus hooks into a number of different semantic strands. Finally, Terence Fisher's film *Frankenstein and the Monster from Hell* charts the tribulations of a creature which contains the mind of a scientist, the body of a murderer and the soul of an artist and is torn between these different forces. In the end, the creature is literally torn to pieces.

This suggests that the presence of language in cinema cannot be confined to the soundtrack nor even to the occurrence of specific literalisms. Although the discourse of the 'hooks' or of the 'tearing apart' is not explicitly spoken, it is nevertheless an integral discourse of the text. In *The Interpretation of Dreams* Freud came across this form of presence of language with such frequency that he discounted the idea that some peculiar symbolizing activity of the mind was in operation, and argued that all such 'images' were grounded in folklore, popular myths, legends, linguistic idioms, proverbial wisdom and current jokes[7]—all of them, in fact, verbal activities.

3. *Verbal Discourse as Framework*

Another type of verbal manifestation, already hinted at with the example of the code of makeup in Chinese classical theater, is the production of semantic effects apparently not motivated by any of the signifiers underpinning it. This phenomenon has been explored extensively in terms of sound or color symbolisms and is brought about through a mapping of relations of resemblance (themselves culturally determined and possibly formed through the process of synaesthetic thinking that characterizes early childhood) onto the relation of coded contiguity between signifier and signified. Such a process can be provoked by phonemes or even by component features of phonemes. Taking this type of functioning into account, it is possible to conceive of any type of 'mark' which is radically asignifying. As Jakobson wrote: 'Owing to neuropsychological laws of synaesthesia, phonic oppositions can themselves evoke relations with musical, chromatic, olfactory, tactile etc. sensations'.[8] This process can also work in the opposite direction. For instance, in view of the multitude of references to music as the asemantic art *par excellence*, it is of some interest to note that the musicologist J. J. Nattiez[9] identified such a notion as a hangover from mid nineteenth century romanticism. Nattiez insists that it is the social discourses within which music is embedded that determine which sets of selections, of rhythmical patterns, etc., are identified as significant, as constituting the difference between one piece of music and another. Furthermore, all music is shot through with semantic values far exceeding notions of sound symbolism, as can be seen from the various types of musical 'quotes' studied by Zofia Lissa.[10] Jakobson also comments on the phonological, that is, cultural rootedness, of musical systems.[11] This is not to suggest that musical signifiers have stable signifieds and are therefore translatable into a continuous verbal discourse. The point is that it is not possible to abstract music from the discourses within which it functions and in terms of which it is produced. To isolate music from this verbal context and to define it as an autonomous object necessarily means transforming it into 'meaningless' noises or undifferentiated, unorganized sound effects. Even in music, then, allegedly the most ethereal of arts, verbal discourse is implicated from the outset in its production and perception. What semantisms illustrate is that there is no such thing as an essentially asignifying practice and that all signifying practices, regardless of the matter of expression involved, are embedded in and subject to the social discourses that surround them.

As Monique Plaza argued:

> Nothing for human beings escapes the symbolic ordering of language ... Even if one postulates the inscription in the archaic Ucs level of a thing presentation (mother's body) ... this ... becomes psychically meaningful through the inscription of a word presentation 'mother's body'. And, precisely, the phantasy about the mother's body can only appear as a psychic production at the point where the psychic apparatus assimilates the significance that another gives to the utterance 'mother's body'. All these psychic elaborations of the body of the mother rely necessarily on this signifying system limited by a language. When psychoanalysis refers, for example, the castration complex back to an anatomical observation, it is making a theoretical error since it postulates that a thing presentation could be inscribed by a look outside any signifying system.[12]

Meaning, that is, that language cannot be escaped or bracketed, although it can be repressed. Interestingly, and predictably, artistic practices that are claimed to be specific and materialist (in the sense of 'oriented towards their materials of expression'), are always accompanied by verbal discourse, at times verging on logorrhea. What is thrown out of the door returns, with a vengeance, through the window; verbal language has never fared so well as in the so-called civilization of the image. It is instructive to read the writings of painters such as Mondrian and discover the way in which the discursive 'program' determines the figurations produced. It emerges that the painterly practices are closely dependent on the definition of which 'painterly' discourses to reject, transform or develop. In this sense, verbal discourse frames a given painting in the very moment of its production. Paintings must be understood simultaneously—and in a hierarchical order to be determined in each case—in terms of the function and place certain painterly practices have in 'painting', and on the other hand, the function and place they have within a discursive formation that includes and locates 'painting' as an art form. The issue to be analyzed in each specific instance is the interaction between those three terms. Furthermore, due consideration must be given to the fact that such a complex dialectic is itself always embedded in and determined by the encompassing dialectic at work between the three instances that make up the social formation: the ideological, the economic and the political, with the latter providing the articulation of the two others. In the view of this extreme complexity, it is necessary, if only for methodological reasons, also to chart the trajectories of specific component elements or partial sets of interrelating elements. And in this respect, formalist analyses have been and still can be very productive, as semiology has demonstrated. The point at issue there is the place and function of 'formalisms' in any given situation: which discourses or methods of analysis they displace or oppose. It is a question of avoiding the hypothesis of formalisms as 'scientific', non-ideological, etc., and of always thinking of an analytical practice as a social, historical practice of meaning production.

4. *Language and Cinema*

The most systematic account of the location of language in cinema within a semiological model has been formulated by Christian Metz in his book *Language and Cinema*.[13] For Metz, language is present in cinema as recorded phonetic sound and as writing in the image. As such it covers two of the five matters of expression, whose combination constitutes the specificity of cinematic language, the other three being recorded noise, recorded musical sound and the moving photographic image. Metz also gives due consideration to the semantic aspect of language, but confines it to the codes of content which, although an integral part of any film, are not specific to cinema. His conception of cinema is complex and involves both a recognition of 'languages' as technico-sensoral unities and as analytical constructs, that is, as codes or collections of codes at work within these units.

Nevertheless, there is no place within Metz' semiology for hybrid forms of signification nor for a consideration of signification as a discursive process in terms of subject productions and positions. That such processes need to be addressed is signaled by Metz' introduction of the concept of filmic writing to account for the displacements, transformations, substitutions and overlaps affecting the play of codes in any given signifying network, and any particular text. But such displacements are not simply products of random interactions between autonomous and homogeneous codes or homogeneous technico-sensoral unities. As Metz' notion of filmic reading suggests, there is something at work in signification which exceeds the interaction of semiologically defined sets of codes. Metz goes so far as to speak of the destruction of codes in that process, referring to the work of Julia Kristeva as a possible source for an understanding of that process. Presumably, when he cursorily inserts Kristeva's name into the space between cinematic language and filmic writing, he is seeking to invoke her concern with the function of Ucs processes and with questions of subject production in processes of representation. In his more recent writing, Metz concentrates on precisely the shifts and transformations effected in the domain of semiology as a result of the encounter with psychoanalysis. The problem of language reemerges, significantly, as the question of the very possibility of an articulation between semiology and psychoanalysis.

This issue is posed rather interestingly in the collection of essays entitled *Le Signifiant imaginaire*.[14] At one point, in an essay first published in 1977, Metz states that the maintenance of a rigorous dividing line between the orders of discourse and of figuration in effect prevents any possible articulation of semiology and psychoanalysis. Nevertheless, in another essay included in that book, this time a piece first published in 1975, he approves of that very separation, stating that 'the Ucs doesn't think, doesn't produce a discourse, but is figured in images'. In this opposition, images pertain to the domain of the Ucs while language belongs exclusively to the secondary processes, themselves identified with the Pcs/Cs system. The possibility of an agency or instance operating on both sides of the divide between the Ucs and the Pcs/Cs systems receives no mention. The implicit recognition that the crucial problem here is exactly the way the Ucs works through into the Pcs/Cs systems, is presented by Metz in the form of a question: How to understand censorship?[15] or in terms less likely to reactivate the idea of an absolute barrier: How to understand resistance? This question radically shifts the whole problematic set up by the concepts of cinematic language and filmic writing. No longer is the relation between them analogous to that between language system (*langue*) and speech. Now the absolute insistence on the homogeneity of the matters of expression inevitably becomes a little less absolute, and the cinematic codes begin to occupy the place of the symbolic in psychoanalysis. The question as to how to think of resistance can also be reformulated as how to think of the articulation between heterogeneous orders, each of which is itself far from homogeneous, in that symbolic and imaginary always coexist in a necessary simultaneity without any clearly demarcated dividing lines. The question of resistance is also that of the join between the Ucs and Pcs/Cs systems, that of a discourse that articulates, in its very texture, thing- and word-presentations. The fact that the rest of Metz' book can be read as a systematic skirting of that question in no way diminishes the merit of having posed it in the first place.

The problem appears to be that Metz continues to think of cinematic language in terms of technico-sensoral unities. Whenever he addresses the status of verbal language and its relation to the Ucs, he discusses the matter in terms of equations between thing-presentations, film images, the Ucs and the imaginary; word-presentations are equated with the spoken and written appearance of words, without any transitional discourse being considered as articulating both orders. Equally, the possibility of phonemes or phrases having a structuring impact on the formation and sequencing of images is held in suspense or reduced to the viewer's socially determined ability to identify iconic figures as objects, that is, the code of iconic naming. Although he repeatedly refers to the work of Lacan, certain fundamental aspects of that work appear to be left out of the picture. The first is the basic notion of the repressed signifier, with the subsequent point that an image, part of an image or even a series of images can be produced by the repression of a verbal signifier. Such an idea cannot be accommodated in a semiological framework, where a signifier is always manifested in one and only one matter of expression, ruling out hybrid formations.

The notion that the repressed signifier 'can only give itself up under the cover of images',[16] when applied to cinematic discourse, infringes the absolute distinction between language and the moving photographic image. Secondly, the idea that 'a symbol is only an operator in a structure, a means of effecting the distinctive oppositions necessary to the existence of a significant structure'[17] abolishes the definition of the signifier in terms of material specificity, making it into any 'mark' of difference, into the support of the process of differing. This allows for the thinking of signification as operating with heterogeneous signifiers. It also renders it impossible to equate verbal language as such with the symbolic: it is the system of language, imprinted, true enough, by the encounter with the word, which defines the symbolic, but the presence of verbal language is not an automatic indicator of the symbolic, nor is its absence equatable with the register of the imaginary. What is at stake here is precisely the possibility of a discourse which, although structured 'like' a language nevertheless works with the widest variety of signifiers, and thus can be sited at the join of the Ucs and Pcs/Cs systems, the site of the processes of resistance.

The materiality of the signifier does not become irrelevant, it merely becomes a second order factor affecting the movement of signification. The materiality of the 'defiles of the signifier', to use Lacan's phrase, affects the resistance encountered by drives and thus inflects the signifying process. But as signifiers are products of overdetermination, what is resistance in relation to one component drive may be facilitation in relation to another. In this way, the question of censorship that Metz posed as crucial for any theory of signification is reactivated along a different route: this time, what is at issue is the resistance of the discourse as opposed to the intra-psychic resistance of the subject. Both types of resistance have to do with transportation *(Entstellung)* of signifiers, that is to say, with the movement of signification.

5. *Inner Speech and the Ego*

What emerges from these considerations is that it is necessary to think of the articulation of textual systems both with social discourses and with Ucs signification in terms of a discursive form grounded in verbal language but able to operate with a heterogeneous signifying chain.

The function of linguistic processes in the articulation of the Ucs and the social has been addressed by means of concepts such as discourse and the notion of subject production, with the discourse of the Other (the symbolic) producing inescapable subject positions. This conceptual apparatus has been deployed primarily to suggest a unilateral determination by 'the' signifier of 'the' signifying chain pinning subjects in specific positions. In this fundamentally idealist view, subjects are abstracted entities adrift on a sea of discursiveness, helplessly buffeted between discourses whose effectivity operates via the Ucs and is thus by definition removed from any possible area of social struggle. A more nuanced theoretical position insists that the processes of subject production are always already in the social and thus avoids conflating social determination with determination by the Ucs. But although this position recognizes that it is necessary to think of the articulation between heterogeneous orders (the inextricable co-presence of real, symbolic and imaginary in any discursive process), it nevertheless stops short of addressing the terms of that 'embedding' in the social in a way which would open up the possibility of concerted action, that is, struggle against specific forms of social organization. A third position argues that it is necessary to start from the need for struggle rather than from the effectivity of the signifier. Ideologies are seen as contradictory unities which, via the effectivity of institutions, try to hold subjects in/to determinate positions, but it is equally specified that this process of subject production is determined by extra-discursive factors as well as discursive ones.[18] Although such a model comes closer to an understanding of subjectivity in history which does not automatically block any possible concept of struggle, it is nevertheless unsatisfactory in that it still relies exclusively on a model of psychic functioning reduced to a simple opposition between the Ucs and the Pcs/Cs systems. As such, it drastically devalues or even discounts Freud's second topography of instances (Ego, Id, Superego) which must be superimposed on the first one.

Laplanche pointed out that

> what is currently known as ego psychology is, in fact, a conception which makes of the ego an agency of the total person, differentiated ...

essentially as a function of problems of adaptation. [But] ego psychology has the merit—or at least the ambition—of wanting to re-establish the bridge between psychoanalysis and the investigations and discoveries of non-psychoanalytic psychology.[19]

That ego psychology has proved incapable of providing the means to think about the articulation between the subject and the social, substituting instead a notion of adaptation, has unfortunately also discredited the ambition. Opposition to ego psychology has, in the area of the theory of ideological practices, facilitated and legitimized the formulation of an equally crude position: ideologism, using terms such as 'concept', 'discourse' and 'subject' as fetishes to exorcise any possibility of ideological struggle. In its place is posed the total autonomy of the discursive (the signifying chain pinning subjects in determinate positions).[20] In fact, any argument suggesting that the effectivity of the social on the subject is restricted to the impact on the Ucs of the language into which a child is born, overlooks the specific function of the ego as a psychic instance, formed and intervening in its own right at a later stage. Even if the social is reinvoked, in a second movement, as determining the constraints within which discourses are formulated and subjects put into place, the relay of thought processes and their specific function and mode of operation finds no space in that model of discourse production. In this sense the necessary attack on ego psychology would seem to have resulted in a repression or bracketing of the ego as an active instance in the construction of subjectivity.

The ego is a concept relating to that aspect of the dialectic between 'I' and 'other' which, via complex processes of identification (that is, displacements) installs a force field, a reservoir of libidinal energy, a field that binds the free flow of sexual energy and as such can come to be regarded as an active agency. As Laplanche puts it, the ego is a

> specific formation [that] enters into conflicts as a participant by virtue of its double function: an inhibiting function or a function of binding ... and a defensive function, ... through the dual modes of pathological and normal defence. [It is] a kind of relay object, capable of passing itself off, in a more or less deceptive and usurpatory manner, as a desiring and wishing subject.[21]

Furthermore,

> If it is not forgotten that what is at stake here are chains of ideas, the ego turns out to be what introduces into the circulation of fantasy a certain ballast, a process of *binding* which retains a certain energy and causes it to stagnate in the fantasmatic system, preventing it from circulating in an absolutely free and mad manner. Such is the appearance of the *secondary process*.[22]

But Laplanche immediately goes on to warn that there is 'no identity between the secondary process and the ego properly speaking [if we keep in mind the Ucs aspect of the ego—P.W.]. This leads to a distinction concerning the ego between a "permanent portion" and a "changing one" '. A distinction that will be important later in this paper in this connection is L. Vygotsky's distinction between meaning as a relatively stable core and sense as its shifting, mobile periphery.

The 'permanent portion' of the ego concerns that part of the structure which has to do with the Cs system, while the changing part (Freud invoked the image of the mobile contours of an amoeba, contracting and expanding) relates to the Pcs but also to the Ucs. The functions allotted to the ego include

> not only the control of mobility and perception, reality testing, anticipation, the temporal ordering of the mental processes, rational thought, and so on, but also refusal to recognise the facts, rationalisation and compulsive defence against instinctual demands.[23]

This suggests that the ego functions as the site where heterogeneous systems, separated by the bar of repression, and contradictions are articulated, or that the ego is a 'frontier creature', in Freud's phrase.

In *The Interpretation of Dreams*, the account of the functioning of the mental apparatus stresses the topographical distinction between the Ucs and the Pcs/Cs systems: the former working with thing-presentations, the latter with word-presentations. In between the two is located that particular effect of resistance Freud called censorship. In the light of the second topography, involving the notion of the ego, such a rigorous demarcation begins to appear less absolute. Not that the barrier is removed or weakened, but a force field is instituted at the join of these systems, a field that extends—unequally—on either side of the barrier. The traversal of and the consequent deformations operated by this barrier of repression have been described in terms of a movement from a given medium to another one with a different refraction index.[24] This site where resistance works over the join between thing- and word-presentations, where ideational representatives can encounter 'their' predicates according to the transformational laws imposed by the necessity of articulating contradictions and heterogeneity, is precisely the site of the ego. Laplanche describes this passage from one side to the other in these terms:

> The transition of an ucs idea to the pcs/cs level: the verbal representatives are superimposed through a kind of addition, on the ucs representative ... This does not mean that a cs sentence duplicates an ucs sentence as its translation, but rather that isolated representatives individually cathected, induce locally around each of them an energy field accounting for the phenomenon of attention.[25]

In this context, attention itself is a mobile process in that it allows for various degrees of intensity, from daydreaming to focused concentration, from discursive registers on the periphery of the Ucs to different processes of thought and inner speech, and to consciously articulated, logical, grammatical, verbal discourse. It is in this space that the repressed signifier that gave itself up in the Ucs under the guise of an image, refinds a verbal signifier. This movement may pass through indeterminate stages, and the signifier(s) refound will not be the same as the signifier(s) repressed, because of the intervention of resistance, refraction. Suffice it to say that the refound signifier(s) will bear the mark of that transit, which is the process of signification itself. This means that the registers of discourse that operate in the site of the ego may be unequally or incompletely secondarized. The degree of the mix between word- and thing-presentations will depend on various factors (real or desired proximity to the Ucs, the nature of the discourses in play and the degrees of resistance they activate, degrees of 'attention', possible resistance to word-presentations *per se*, etc.), but both will always be co-present, like the often cited recto and verso of a piece of paper. It is also important to realize that such registers of discourse operating at the join of Ucs and Pcs/Cs systems must always be structures in dominance working with different types of signifiers, otherwise no transition process would be thinkable. Just as the Ucs persists in all discursive practices, so does verbal language, even when repressed.

The discourse of attention, thought, has been conceptualized as inner speech (intra-psychic speech, in Jakobson's terminology). Inner speech, like the ego, is a frontier creature. But without its function of binding subject and text in sociality, no signification would be possible other than delirium. The secondarizing work of inner speech, providing the initial stabilization of the signifying process according to the contradictory demands the ego is there to bind, constitutes thought. Thus inner speech constitutes the activity associated with an agency which holds sets of contradictions in socially as well as unconsciously determined balances of forces. In this light, the most perceptive characterization of inner speech was provided by C. S. Peirce: 'A dialogue between different phases of the ego'.[26] This formulation also has the merit of reinforcing the notion that the ego is produced as an imaginary, or rather a contradictory, unity in the dialectic of 'I' and 'other'.

6. Theories of Inner Speech

It should be stressed that inner speech is not to be regarded as speech by the ego. The ego is not the subject of inner speech, nor of any other discourse for that matter. As Peirce made clear, the subject of inner speech is split; it is sustained in that split as the tension between 'I' and 'other'. This suggests that it may be misleading to call inner speech a discourse. It might more accurately be described as a process of signification providing the conditions of existence for any social discourse. Consequently, the production of subject positions via discourses is necessarily always doubled by this particular process. Inner speech lines (as the lining of a jacket helps prevent it coming apart at the seams) any process of meaning production, both at the stage of text-manufacturing and of reading.

This lining accounts to some extent for the difference between the subject-image produced by a text and the historical, biological subject which presided over its manufacture. Neither is more 'authentic' than the other. If the (self) image constructed through discourse never coincides with the subject's sense of identity, this is not solely because that identity is the image of an other, but also because it is split in itself, caught up in an unceasing dialogic process. Perhaps it would be possible to consider the production of a (self) image through discursive practices as an attempt to halt that oscillatory dialogue, to freeze it, to produce a signifier that marks the gap within the structure of the 'differential subject' of inner speech. Nevertheless, inner speech remains a fairly enigmatic concept. Jakobson wrote that

> Besides the more palpable, interpersonal face of communication, its intrapersonal aspect is equally pertinent. Thus, for instance, inner speech, astutely conceived by Peirce as an 'internal dialogue' and until recently rather disregarded in linguistic literature, is a cardinal factor in the network of language and serves as one's connection with the self's past and future.[27]

Some of these terms are questionable, but the thrust of the remark is clear enough.

The importance of the concept of inner speech for cinema was first raised by Boris Eikhenbaum in an essay called 'Problems of Film Stylistics'[28] published in 1927. Eikhenbaum was concerned to account for the way filmic writing—film texts—can be understood. He argued that the sequential arrangement of images produced meaning only in relation to a verbal discourse functioning as a constant ground against which the filmic was marked off or profiled. Thus the verbal in a sense becomes the screen upon which the film is projected, a mapping of the two producing the regime of signification involved. Eikhenbaum calls the verbal discourse doubling—lining—the film, inner speech or thought as opposed to manifested spoken or written language which is the stuff of social speech and literature. He suggested that a film viewer must

> perform the complex mental labour of coupling the frames (construction of film phrases and film periods) . . . or else he will not understand anything . . . Perception and understanding of a motion picture is inextricably bound up with the development of inner speech which makes the connections between separate shots.

The main function of inner speech would thus reside in language's capacity to construct superordinate structures rather than in its lexical aspect. Eikhenbaum is less concerned with the code of iconic naming, with the lexicalization of the image, than with its ability to construct a network of relations.

In contrast, Metz addressed himself to the problem of unenunciated speech in an essay entitled, significantly, 'The Perceived and the Named'.[29] He concentrates exclusively on what psycholinguists would call 'labelling'. He concludes that 'the perceptual object is a constructed unit, socially constructed, and also (partly) a linguistic unit' in that language *(langue)* permanently accompanies vision, ceaselessly glossing it, either 'aloud or simply by calling the phonetic signifier to mind'. Such a notion of inner speech reduces it to the unspoken but formally identical replica of phonetically enounced speech. This, as Vygotsky noted,[30] is to come close to a behaviorism which considers thought a reflex inhibited in its motor part. Although Metz is too perceptive a phenomenologist to allow himself to get bogged down in the morass of reflexology, his code of iconic labeling appears to be haunted by the mythical opposition between thinkers and doers that helped install behaviorism as an ideology in certain social formations. This ghost in Metz' discourse (in the sense that one talks of a ghost image in a faulty tv transmission) is perhaps produced by the temporary convergence of the positivist discursive current shared by semiology and behaviorism. For his part, Eikhenbaum avoids this trap and never reduces inner speech to endophony, the soundless enunciation of words. In his discussion of film metaphor, he specifies that

> Film metaphor is entirely dependent on verbal metaphor. The viewer can understand it only when he possesses a corresponding metaphoric expression in his own verbal baggage [but] the film metaphor is not realised in the consciousness of the viewer to the point of a complete verbal statement.[31]

Inner speech becomes the cement between text, subject and the social. As such, this concept of inner speech inserts an extra discourse into the dialectic of text and subject, opening up a different way of thinking about subject production. The subject production effected by the text, defined as a set of chains of signifiers in determinate relations with clusters of semantic features, will have to pass through inner speech, itself a discursive process determined by the social and the psychoanalytic histories that combined to produce that particular 'individual' in that place at that time. In this respect, inner speech indeed becomes, in Eikhenbaum's words, 'one of the most important problems in cinematic theory'.

Eikhenbaum's intimation that inner speech differs functionally from manifested language was reformulated two years later, in 1929, in the *Theses* published by the Prague linguistic circle. The *Theses* corrected his assumption that 'external' speech predominates in everyday life, pointing out that for most speakers, manifested speech is far less frequent than the use of linguistic forms in thought processes. Nevertheless, the *Theses* tended to reintroduce the notion that inner speech was formally equivalent to manifested speech in spite of Eikhenbaum's rejection of this notion. For Eikhenbaum,

> the very act of thinking consists in the organisation of our inner speech along specific modalities and conditions, ... to the extent that we sometimes find it hard to translate an internal discourse into an external one, as if the difference between the respective codes raised the kind of problems and difficulties of translation analogous to the ones encountered in translation proper.[32]

Although endophony, the calling to mind of the phonetic signifier, can occur in inner speech, the latter cannot be reduced to the former. It also works with images, phonemes, fragments of images, fragments or blocks of writing, schemata, mathematical symbols, etc.; in short, with all the things that can work as ideational representatives in the psychoanalytic sense, as well as with word-presentations in their phonetic and graphic forms. Some of these functional differences between the two 'languages' become clearer when we relate them to Jakobson's representation of social communication, involving an addresser who can exchange messages with an addressee given that they are in contact, if they share a code and are aware of the context within which the whole operation takes place. In inner speech, addresser and addressee are the same or at least intrapersonal, which means firstly, that the context need not be taken into account, no need for redundancies and repetitions, elaborate syntagmatic arrangements and so on; secondly, that there is no need for metalinguistic verifications of the code or even to maintain the process within a given code; and thirdly, that the phatic function, ascertaining contact, can be dispensed with. Of course, this does not mean that none of these things occurs in inner speech; merely that they are not indispensable to it.

Such modifications prompted Vygotsky to concur with the Prague linguists in stressing that 'Inner speech must be regarded, not as speech minus sound, but as an entirely separate speech function',[33] and Jakobson went so far as to speak of a different grammar being involved. Vygotsky continued to point out that

> Inner speech appears disconnected and incomplete ... It shows a tendency towards an altogether specific form of abbreviation: namely, omitting the subject of a sentence and all words connected with it, while preserving the predicate.

Vygotsky is overstating the case here a little, because words connected with the subject (i.e., a great many shifters) do in fact persist in inner speech. But this dominant tendency towards predication and condensation does explain to some extent why inner speech can so freely integrate thing-presentations in its chain of signifiers, a facility it shares with cinema. This convergence also favors the production of the prevalent misconception that verbal discourse is absent from imaged discourse in that some of its signifying configurations appear to overlap.

In his discussion of the relations between thought and language, Vygotsky makes some interesting observations. Firstly, he distinguishes between thought, word meaning (i.e., signifieds) and speech (i.e., the phonetic or graphic practice of linguistic signs). This tripartite order calls to mind Hjelmslev's triad of matter, substance and form, although there are some crucial and productive divergencies. Metz summarized and clarified Hjelmslev's triad in the following terms:

> The material ... represents the originally amorphous something in which the form is inscribed ... and the substance is that which appears when one projects the form onto the material 'as a stretched string projects its shadow onto an uninterrupted surface'.[34]

For Vygotsky, the synaesthetic registration of perceptions (translated in the American version as 'heaps') appears to function as the semantic matter, 'word meanings' or 'concepts' operate as the semantic form, while thought becomes analogous to substance, the locus of the organizing and structuring impact/imprint of language on what Freud calls memory traces. Vygotsky's placing of 'speech', in relation to 'word meanings' and thought, emphasizes the coded contiguity between signifier and signified, thus articulating thought with the phonemic system, i.e., with the spoken discourse, the Word into which we are born. Jakobson's phrase of coded contiguity is a particularly happy one for two reasons. In the first place, it evokes the possibility of variations in coding or even of radically different codes obtaining between signifier(s) and signified(s), while at the same time allowing the possibility of the coding established in verbal language to operate in relation to 'nonverbal' or mixed signifying systems. In this way, 'literalisms', the use of nonverbal stand-ins for verbal signifiers, a result of repression, can be understood as straightforward substitutions of signifiers while the coding of the contiguity is maintained, although the change in signifier makes the sign available for discursive practice in a different manner, allowing it to circulate according to the rules of a different signifying regime and thus satisfying the requirements of resistance. Secondly, Jakobson's phrase is a useful reminder that the relation between signifier and signified is by no means arbitrary, but firmly grounded in the social.

The most productive aspect of the difference between Hjelmslev and Vygotsky, at least in this context, relates to the way they conceive of the 'matter' onto which form is projected. For Hjelmslev, matter is an amorphous but nevertheless homogeneous entity, while for Vygotsky it is a-signifying but by no means necessarily amorphous or homogeneous, as in Hjelmslev's model. In this way, the material can be regarded as being constituted by the free interplay of sensory registration with Ucs drives, the chora in Kristeva's usage (a term she borrows, ironically, from Plato). The form is then provided by the language into which a child is born, and the substance by the imprint of that language on the chora. The production of this imprint is itself to be understood in two phases, logically distinct but continuous in practice: firstly, the registration of difference and secondly, the organization of differences into a symbolic system, the 'becoming meaningful' of the process of differentiation. The gradual nature of this process through which language as a symbolic system is anchored in the chora not only produces the ground of signification, it also accounts for the slack in the system, the lack of fit between the code of language and that which it organizes. This lack of fit, this being out of true, is reinforced by the fact that the material, the chora, is itself not amorphous but constitutes an interplay of perception and drives, a protean mass traversed by libidinal currents setting up energy fields, force lines which both resist and facilitate the structuring impact of language, the join of signifiers and memory traces. In this movement towards coded contiguity, the constituent features of both signifiers and signifieds (distinctive features and phonemes in the former, semantic features or 'atoms of meaning' in the latter) still enjoy a relative autonomy and operate in a dispersed form. Entry into the symbolic then becomes the recognition of a social relation *vis-à-vis* the code of language, an ability to place 'I' in language, an ability that will always operate in the face of and against the pressure of the process of *signifiance,* the pressure of the chora. In other words, the practice of coded contiguity in language will always retain the traces of that movement towards/into the symbolic. In the semantic structure of a language, such traces produce an unstable field around signifieds, a floating periphery of sense around meaning, the cathexis of which makes the chains of signifiers veer off, activating new semantic clusters, and so on. Such a dialectic between signifier and signified determines the production of ideational representatives at the intersection of multiple strands of significa-tion. This process of veering off, of limited drift, has been theorized in terms of the work of the primary processes which, according to Lacan and Metz, are none other than the laws of signification itself.

Vygotsky's second major distinction, that between sense and meaning, can thus be seen to foreshadow the discoveries of structural semantics. Meaning is defined as the lexically fixed core(s) of a signified, its most stable aspect(s), while sense encompasses all the possible semantic features cluster-ing around such a core. In social speech, the meaning functions as the dominant element, while in inner speech—the frontier creature—words are saturated with sense.

> Inner speech works with semantics, not phonetics. The specific semantic structure of inner speech also contributes to abbreviation. The syntax of meanings [i.e., semantic features—P.W.] in inner speech is no less original than its grammatical syntax. [There is a] preponderance of the sense of a word over its meaning . . . The sense of a word [is] the sum of all the psychological events aroused in our consciousness [and Ucs— P.W.] by the word. It is a dynamic, fluid, complex whole, which has several zones of unequal stability. Meaning is only one of the zones of sense, the most stable and precise zone.[35]

'Inner speech is to a large extent thinking in pure meanings. It is a dynamic, shifting, unstable thing, fluttering between word and thought'.[36] Although Vygotsky dismisses psychoanalysis as mystic idealism, his conception of inner speech is perfectly compatible with Freud's description of the way chains of thought (i.e., isotopies) can function in dream processes. Furthermore, the projection of Vygotsky onto Hjelmslev, the notion that thought represents the imprint of language on the asignifying chora, helps to resolve some ambiguities relating to Freud's notion of memory traces, which are at times defined as mere registration, at other times as registration structured under the impact of signifiers (in the psychoanalytic sense of the term). Vygotsky also mentions that 'thought itself is engendered by motivation, i.e., by our desires and needs, our interests and emotions'.[37] In psychoanalytic terms, this can be theorized in terms of the drives determining the pattern of the crisscrossing networks of isotopies traced by the movement of ideational representatives in 'unconscious' thought. However, it must be pointed out that Vygotsky's theory has no concept of resistance other than that offered by the 'adult language' into which the child is born and to which it must submit, a process represented as a linear development of maturation culminating in the fantasy of a language of pure reason. Repression does not appear to exist within his conceptual apparatus, although he does allow for the survival of 'infantile' modes of thought in 'adult' usages of language. Another major point worth stressing is that for Freud, it is the process of signification itself that matters, and not the contents involved as such. The dream work, not the dream thoughts, constitutes the essence of the dream.

7. *Avant-garde Cinema and Language*

Vygotsky's collaborator and disciple, A. R. Luria, continued the investigation of the connections between language and thought, concentrating on the empirical verification of the structuring function of language. In his book, *The Mind of a Mnemonist*,[38] he reports on a study, conducted over a number of years, of a man who was able to perform the most astonishing feats of memory. It emerged that the man, referred to as 'S', transcoded all verbal information into visual figures with due regard for the 'considerations of representability'. Nonsense words or foreign words he would transform through a system of lines and colors corresponding to the phonemic structure of the word in question, producing images akin to 'abstract' paintings. 'S' also reported that he remembered his childhood in terms of vague synaesthetic sensations. Protolinguistic (i.e., pre-oedipal) childhood was dominated by splashes of color corresponding to the perception of phonetic sounds. Later, with the acquisition of language, figurative images would form as distinct, delineated units, but any imprecision in or interference with his perception of phonetic sounds such as unclear pronounciation, overlapping voices or an extraneous noise blotting out a sound, would produce blurs, splashes or puffs of smoke in his ideational representatives. Also, the ideational representatives evoked would set off their own chain of thought and, along the lines of specific isotopies, lead back to scenes from his childhood. The coincidence of this production of clearly delineated images with the acquisition of language is worth noting. But the most important element here is the impact that phonemes are seen to have on the figuration of images, demonstrating that language is present in images not just in the form of repressed/transformed words or as the concatenations of semantic features into isotopies, but also as transformed phonemes.[39] A second study, this time of a soldier who had been shot in the head, proves equally illuminating. Luria writes that

> He referred to his major disability as a loss of speech memory ... Each word was part of a vital world to which it was linked by thousands of associations; each aroused a flood of vivid and graphic recollections. To be in command of a word meant he was able to evoke almost any impression of the past, to understand relationships between things, conceive ideas and be in command of his life. And now all this had been obliterated.[40]

Eventually, the soldier recovered enough to be able to write sentences. He informed Luria that he was

> in a kind of fog all the time, like a heavy half-sleep. My memory is a blank. I can't think of a single word. All that flashes through my head are some images, hazy visions that suddenly appear and just as suddenly disappear giving way to fresh images ... Whatever I do remember is scattered, broken down into disconnected bits and pieces.[41]

Luria also noted that for the soldier, space made no sense and lacked stability. The similarity of such a loss of language to some experimental films is striking, to say the least.

What emerges from Luria's work, amongst other things, is that any firm distinction between the orders of discourse and figuration must be discarded as a fantasy conveying the wish for an Edenic state of 'signification' unsullied by the requirements of the symbolic, a world where difference doesn't exist: in short, a desire to repress language. Luria accounts for the imbrication of language and images in terms of the neurophysiological structure of the brain, and his comments are of considerable interest, even though Freud explicitly located the production of ideational representatives on 'another scene', adding: 'We may, I think, discount the possibility of giving the phrase an anatomical interpretation and supposing it to refer to physiological cerebral localisation or even to the histological layer of the cerebral cortex'.[42] However, consideration of the neurophysiological development of the brain is not entirely irrelevant in this context. It seems reasonable to assume that the processes associated with various aspects of the brain do leave memory traces which are available for reactivation (on 'another scene') under certain circumstances. The development of brain functions appears to fall into three main stages:

> The primary visual cortex ... breaks down images of the external world into millions of constituent parts. The secondary visual cortex converts the individual features of objects perceived into complete, manifold structures ... dynamic patterns. The function of the tertiary cognitive part of the cortex is to combine the visual ... tactile-motor ... and auditory-vestibular sections of the brain. These sections are not even fully developed in the human infant but mature gradually and become effective by age four to seven.[43]

As the ideational activity associated with these different functions must leave memory traces, it follows that, for instance, the repression of language, which is associated with the tertiary regions, may reactivate 'thought' problems. In this way, the symptoms manifested by the brain-damaged soldier (trouble with spatial relations, fragmentation, blurring, images flickering meaninglessly, reduction to blank memory-screens, etc.) can be represented by anyone who, although not in the least brain-damaged, feels compelled to reactivate prelinguistic processes of signification.[44]

Some problems

1. *The Image as Secondary Elaboration*

Because of the connection between inner speech and the ego, one could say that its function is to resist the pressure of the Ucs. As Roland Barthes noted in relation to the captions of photographs, verbal language is there to resist the unlimited polysemy of images: 'The primary function of speech is to immobilize perception at a certain level of intelligibility . . . fixing its level of reading'.[45] From a somewhat different perspective, Laplanche suggested that:

> The ego, if it is the instrument of reality, does *not* bring a privileged access to the real . . . its function is essentially inhibitive: to prevent hallucination, to cut off that 'excess of reality' coming from internal excitation.[46]

But it should be stressed that the images or hallucinations resisted and limited by language were engendered through their encounter with language in the first place. As Monique Plaza insisted, no thing-presentation can be inscribed by a look outside any signifying system. So it emerges that images are constrained by language at both ends of the psychic apparatus, so to speak, which draws into question the firmly established view of the image as a continuous field, a plenitude. It is well known that images always exceed verbal language. Even though each aspect of an image is in itself 'speakable', the sum of its parts is not, being implicated in that excess Laplanche mentions. In this sense, the plenitude of an image can be understood as a product of secondarization, a filling-in operation reconstituting the fantasy of pre-oedipal plenitude, a fantasy always marked by the symbolic incision of the frame. For instance, it would be interesting to know what produced the change from isolated graphic figures towards continuous fields contained within a frame.

Another aspect of this excess can be related to the fact that images, although involved in displacement, are primarily to be understood in terms of condensation. Freud, and Metz after him, describes the translation of the verbal into an image as a process of displacement from one register of signs to another. But this only refers to forms of literalisms. On the other hand, Freud also stresses that each element of a dream text, of a thing-presentation, is rooted in a whole series of chains and can thus be seen as a nodal point, an intersection of significations 'bound to branch out in every direction into the intricate network of our world of thought'. In the same way, the 'infinite polysemy' of images has no ending: there will always be unanalyzed material, although no unanalyzable material.

So, it could be argued quite convincingly that it is the condensation process presiding over image production which guarantees the image as a proliferating nexus of meanings and sense, some aspects referring to Cs or Pcs material, others providing the space for Ucs chains of signifiers to affix themselves to the figurations involved. Moreover, as paradigmatized blocks of discourses massively overdetermined in all aspects, the image is also always 'lined' by two distinct instances of inner speech: one at the time of production, binding image, subject and sense in sociality; the other repeating the process at the time of reading, a change that guarantees the insertion of the image into an entirely different set of discourses. Yet one more process must be taken into consideration in this proliferation of sense provoked/produced by the image: the materiality of the signs/marks in images, their matter(s) of expression and the codes at work in them, also affect the trajectory of meaning production. The cumulative effects of these considerations make for an extremely high degree of indeterminacy, even in the most figurative of figurations. The signifying practices having recourse to images can thus be described, in Mukarovsky's words, as 'designed to render things imprecise', as a movement towards indeterminacy. Mukarovsky saw this movement as indicating a decrease in the communicative function of the discourse and foregrounding the aesthetic (poetic) function. Jakobson echoed this view, specifying that 'the supremacy of the poetic function over the referential function does not obliterate reference ... but renders it ambiguous'.[47] This notion—that a recourse to images connotes a move towards imprecision and the poetic function of discourse—can be counterposed to the commonsense position that the prime virtue of images is that they 'refer' more accurately. Many of the more assiduous documentary filmmakers have become aware of this contradiction, complaining that it is impossible to shoot slums and misery without somehow aestheticizing them—a paradox generated by the widely-held but nevertheless false premise that images represent more 'accurately' than other forms of representation, and that the choice is between imprecise (poetic) 'pictorialism' and precise, referential 'photography of record'.[48] Whereas captions and titles fix levels of reading, images move backwards through language, in an attempt to elude the strictures of resistance, reinforcing the misconception that while 'verbal discourse' is oppressive and authoritarian, images 'speak for themselves' and are more democratic, thus less socially and ideologically determined. Such a belief ignores the full extent of the role of language in helping to determine firstly, what image shall be produced; secondly, the material(s) organized in/by it; thirdly, the social function and placing of imaged discourse in a given discursive formation; and fourthly, the readings produced in relation to it.

2. Ideology and Politics

The idea that verbal language is an important determinant in relation to the formation, function and placing of imaged discourse in a given discursive conjuncture, and thus also in the way it is read, requires a few explanatory remarks particularly because it opens up the question of verbal discourse in relation to imaged discourse in terms of ideology and politics. If we consider a discursive formation (the ideological instance of the social formation) as composed of bundles of discourses in struggle, organized into unities via institutions,[49] it becomes possible to address the problem of the interrelation of discourses, their mutually determining dynamic. As suggested earlier with regard to the 'false' premise of the 'accuracy' of photographic representation, the definition of a discursive practice (produced through verbal discourses) to a large extent—but never totally—governs the discourses produced to oppose or reinforce it. For instance, just as an oppositional ideology which defines verbal discourse itself as somehow suspect rather than analyzing which particular discourses are 'suspect' and how and why they are so, will automatically have recourse to configuration changes (partly as a result of the oppositional practices, or for entirely different, even extra-discursive reasons), so too will the oppositional value/function of the practices in question, and the process will start over again. Such would be a (somewhat overly) schematic representation of the mechanical aspects of the dialectic at work. However, in view of the function of inner speech discussed above, an extra process must be inserted into this dialectic—a process that engages the status of the subject, the binding of text, subject and sense into sociality. This process, which doubles/lines every signifying practice, operates to articulate the laws of Ucs signification (the subject's psychoanalytic history) into the social. What I am proposing here is that inner speech is the discourse that binds the psychoanalytic subject and the subject in history, functioning as a locus of condensation, a site where the two overlap so that the 'mechanical' dialectic must always be read as a function of the productivity of Ucs processes. This is not the same as subscribing to any notion of determination by the Ucs. Quite the contrary.

Finally, it should be stressed that any consideration of the problems of signification in relation to subjects in history will be at best inhibiting, at worst reactionary, if the discourse that attends to those issues is itself not theorized as 'in history'. In other words, theoretical discourses on film must be seen in terms of the same dialectical relations that govern the production of all texts. Such theories of discourse are 'produced' in specific places of the discursive formations, with specific functions in relation to other discourses, the whole caught up in the struggle that constitutes 'the motor of history'. It may be that the moment has come to take distance from a number of discourses which in the not too distant past performed a progressive function in ideological struggles with regard to the cinematic institution. One prime candidate for such a critical distance would be any discourse that essentializes and hypothesizes notions of subject production/positioning, autonomizes the discursive and invokes the Ucs whenever the question of politics and the real is mentioned. The problem is no longer just the thinking of signification in history, it is one of thinking of signification in such a way as to promote an understanding of how specific social formations can be changed. Because, as someone once put it, the point is to change it.

Postscript

In the discussion that followed the presentation of this paper, a number of points were made, two of which in particular engage directly with the issues and theses put forward.

Firstly, it was pointed out by Stephen Heath that the very term 'inner' speech was likely to evoke the binary opposition inner/outer, carrying in its wake the dangers of psychologism, with inner speech being on the side of the individual psyche while manifested, external speech would be on the side of the social. This connotation is indeed present in the way Eikhenbaum, Vygotsky and Jakobson use the terms involved. The fact that inner speech is not phonetically manifested, nor indeed manifested at all except in the traces it imprints in acts of social, (i.e., manifested) enunciations, may tend to suggest that it is an extremely 'individual' discursive activity, located 'within' and thus highly idiosyncratic.

In the paper, the point is made that inner speech is located under the sign of the ego and that the ego participates of the Ucs. Insofar as the Ucs impinges upon the formation of inner speech, the latter is trans-individual, that is to say, profoundly social. The Ucs, if it is to be defined topologically, is a *locus communis* where locutions are indeed 'in common'—something clinical practice constantly attests and which led C.G. Jung to try and extrapolate the Ucs from history altogether through his invention of the collective Ucs with its archetypes and universal symbols. In this respect, Freud's reply that the Ucs is by definition 'collective' and that consequently any attempt to differentiate a special agency called 'the collective Ucs', is a tautology, also means that what conventional psychology designates as the most 'private' is also and simultaneously the most social. At which point the distinction between inner and outer collapses.

The second comment the paper provoked relates to this same issue. Stephen Heath again remarked that 'literalisms' in cinema appeared always to take the form of heavily coded, ritualized and stereotyped formulas and phrases. In other words, the traces of inner speech in the visual, in the figuration of a narrative or a tableau, take the form of, precisely, *loci communes,* of the socially and linguistically commonplace. This would be one more argument why 'images' should be considered products of secondary elaboration, that is to say, displaced enunciations invested by/with Ucs discursive processes, giving the lie to and locating the function of any ideology that insists on maintaining a rigorous separation between the orders of discourse and of the figure. In this way, inner speech, the concatenation of literalisms subjected to specific processes of 'thought work' (in an analogy with the concept of 'dream work') should then indeed be considered as the site where the subjective and the social are articulated, with the 'subjective' being traced in that very process of articulation. In the same sense that the image can be seen as a specific formation sandwiched between two moments of language, so too the subjective can be seen as an articulation between two moments of the social. Film images would thus be closely related, although not for the reasons usually invoked, to dream images: both can be regarded as 'grounded in folklore, popular myths, legends, linguistic idioms, proverbial wisdom and current jokes'.

This article has also appeared in Screen *vol. 22 no. 3 (1981).*

NOTES

1. R. Jakobson, *Main Trends in the Science of Language* (London: Allen & Unwin, 1973), p. 32.

2. P. Willemen, 'Reflections on Eikhenbaum's Concept of Internal Speech in the Cinema', *Screen* vol. 15 no. 4 (Winter 1974/75), pp. 59-70.

3. It is worth signalling in this context that Metz also argued that sound is, in fact, never 'off': 'Claiming to speak about sound one in fact thinks of the visual image of the sound's source', ('Le perçu et le nommé, in *Vers une esthètique sans entrave: Mélanges offerts à Mikel Dufrenne* [Paris: Union Générale d'Editions, 1975], pp. 373-375). Also C. Bailblé, in his article 'Programmation de l'écoute', *Cahiers du cinéma* no. 292 (September 1978), pp. 53-9, makes the point that by virtue of the placing of the speaker behind the screen, sound is located in the image itself. He makes the interesting observation, contradicting Metz' suggestion, that sounds are constructed according to the rules of an aural perspective analogous to monocular perspective. This last remark has significant implications in relation to the recently formulated arguments that hearing is less patriarchally invested than seeing; see, e.g., Luce Irigaray's remarks quoted in S. Heath, 'Difference', *Screen* vol. 19 no. 3 (Autumn 1978), p. 84.

4. R. Barthes, *Elements of Semiology* (New York: Hill & Wang, 1968), pp. 10-11.

5. Yuri Lotman introduced these terms to suggest that 'since man's consciousness is a linguistic consciousness, all the varieties of models constructed on the basis of consciousness—and art is among them—can be defined as *secondary modelling systems*', in *Die Struktur des künstlerischen Textes* (1973), quoted in B. Brewster, 'Notes on the Text "John Ford's *Young Mr. Lincoln*"', *Screen* vol. 14 no. 3 (Autumn 1973), p. 42.

6. K. Brusak, 'Signs in the Chinese Theatre' (1939), in *Semiotics of Art: Prague School Contributions*, L. Matejka and I.R. Titunik (eds.), (Cambridge, Massachusetts: MIT Press, 1976), pp. 59-73.

7. S. Freud, *The Interpretation of Dreams* (Harmondsworth, U.K.: Penguin, 1976), p. 148.

8. R. Jakobson, *Six Lectures on Sound and Meaning* (Brighton, U.K.: Harvester Press, 1978), p. 113.

9. J. Nattiez, *Fondements d'une sémiologie de la musique* (Paris: Union Générale d'Editions, 1975).

10. Z. Lissa, 'Aesthetische Funktionen des musikalischen Zitats', in *Sign, Language, Culture*, R. Jakobson, A.J. Greimas et al. (eds.), (The Hague-Paris: Mouton, 1970), pp. 674-89.

11. R. Jakobson, 'Musikwissenschaft und Linguistik', in *Selected Writings* vol. II (The Hague-Paris: Mouton, 1971), pp. 551-553.

12. M. Plaza, 'Phallomorphic Power and the Psychology of "Woman"', *Ideology and Consciousness* no. 4 (1978), p. 12.

13. C. Metz, *Language and Cinema* (The Hague-Paris: Mouton, 1974), pp. 153, 280.

14. C. Metz, *Le Signifiant imaginaire* (Paris: Union Générale d'Editions, 1977).

15. Ibid., p. 281.

16. A. Lemaire, *Jacques Lacan* (London: Routledge & Kegan Paul, 1977), p. 46.

17. Ibid., p. 281.

18. P. Willemen, 'Notes on Subjectivity', *Screen* vol. 19 no. 1 (Spring 1978).

19. J. Laplanche, *Life and Death in Psychoanalysis* (Baltimore, Maryland: Johns Hopkins University Press, 1976), p. 51.

20. Although still confined to some marginal academic groups in Great Britain, ideologism could develop into a serious threat, especially in the area of film theory, a relatively new discipline that is particularly vulnerable in its struggle to establish itself as a legitimate field of endeavor and to displace the traditions of literary criticism which still massively occupy the terrain of film studies. Ideologism proclaims the total autonomy of the discursive *vis-à-vis* the political and the economic; it abolishes the need to think of politics in any terms other than those of opportunist manipulation, and it effectively abandons any notion of ideological struggle in favor of philosophical meditation and academic careerism.

21. Laplanche, p. 66.

22. Ibid., p. 63.

23. J. Laplanche and J.-B. Pontalis, *The Language of Psycho-Analysis*, trans. D. Nicholson-Smith (London: Hogarth, 1973), p. 139.

24. Ibid., p. 63.

25. Laplanche, p. 126.

26. Quoted in Jakobson, *Main Trends in the Science of Language*, p. 33.

27. Ibid.

28. B. Eikhenbaum, 'Problems of Film Stylistics' (1927), *Screen* vol. 15 no. 4 (Winter 1974/5), pp. 7-34. See also R. Levaco, 'Eikhenbaum, Inner Speech and Film Stylistics', ibid., pp. 47-58.

29. Metz, 'Le perçu et le nommé', pp. 345-77.

30. L.S. Vygotsky, *Thought and Language* (1936), (Cambridge, Massachusetts: MIT Press, 1962), p. 2.

31. Eikhenbaum, op. cit.

32. E. Garroni, 'Langage verbal et éléments non-verbaux dans le message filmico-télévisuel', in *Cinéma: Théorie, lectures,* D. Noquez (ed.), (Paris: Klincksieck, 1973), p. 116.

33. Vygotsky, pp. 145-6.

34. Metz, *Language and Cinema*, p. 209.

35. Vygotsky, pp. 145-6.

36. Ibid., p. 149.

37. Ibid., p. 150.

38. A.R. Luria, *The Mind of a Mnemonist* (Harmondsworth, U.K.: Penguin, 1975).

39. The translation of the phonetic elements of a word into ideational representatives is illustrated by 'S's description of the 'mary-variations': he produced a set of images, each corresponding to a version of the name Mary (Maria, Maryushka, etc.) and each image would be determined by the phonemic structure of the name. Luria added that 'Eisenstein, in testing students to select those he would train as film directors, asked them to describe their impressions of the variations on the name Mariya. He found this an infallible way to single out those who were keenly sensitive to the expressive force of words'. (p. 72)

40. A.R. Luria, *The Man with a Shattered World* (Harmondsworth, U.K.: Penguin, 1975), p. 89.

41. Ibid., p. 60.

42. Freud, p. 113.

43. Luria, *The Man with a Shattered World*, pp. 35-40.

44. It is perhaps worthwhile pointing out that such a regression is not necessarily to be equated with reaction in the political sense. That would be an essentialist procedure which ignores that the political value of a given set of signifying practices depends on its location and function in a given intertextual field, i.e., in a discursive (sub)formation.

45. R. Barthes, *Le Système de la mode* (Paris: Seuil, 1967), p. 23.

46. Laplanche, p. 62.

47. R. Jakobson, 'Concluding Statement: Linguistics and Poetics', in *Style and Language,* ed. T. Sebeok (Cambridge, Massachusetts: MIT Press, 1960), p. 371.

48. P. Wollen, 'Photography and Aesthetics', *Screen* vol. 19 no. 4 (Winter 1978/79), pp. 9-28.
49. Willemen, 'Notes on Subjectivity', especially pp. 64-9.

Subject Formation and Social Formation: Issues and Hypotheses

Philip Rosen

One effect of having a workshop at a conference on cinema and language with words like 'ideology' and 'production' in its title is to raise the problem of the social formation as an explicit theoretical concern. This paper is intended to be a scanning of what I see as certain key problems in a theoretical approach which has had particularly strong impact at Center for Twentieth Century Studies film theory conferences and which has developed as a relatively well-defined position in contemporary film studies. This theoretical approach labels itself materialist, draws heavily on Lacanian psychoanalysis to specify its materialism in relation to language and signifying practices, and desires to describe itself as historical materialism. The extent to which this approach permits and demands a historical materialist analysis is the issue underlying what follows.

Historical materialism insists, among other things, on the inseparability of an understanding of historical processes and contemporary processes, especially contemporary political processes. The nature of historical understanding—what constitutes it and constitutes its possibility—is thus an issue simultaneous with those more explicitly political. Hence, to measure theoretical and methodological formulations against their potentiality for specific sociohistoric analysis is not to revert to a scholasticism.

In contemporary film theory, there has been a great deal of emphasis on the illumination which linguistic structures shed on filmic structures. Since language is traditionally seen as being to some degree transhistorical, the concept of ideology is often called upon to inject more specific sociohistoric concerns into the analysis. The concept of ideology should here be understood not in the sense of an articulated belief system which rationalizes explicitly political actions, but in the sense of systematized and systemic processes of representations which, as part of their historical effectivity, work on and as 'consciousness'. Use of this concept entails the view that knowledge is grounded in and responds to the actuality of social relations, but in such a way that it is promulgated by and promulgates relations which are in some sense distorting or imaginary. Hence, 'consciousness' is treated as being split in historical processes.

The linguistic turn in contemporary film theory brings together language and ideology precisely on the problem of consciousness and unconsciousness. The concept at which the two areas—language and ideology—meet is the subject. The subject is defined as a point of a fixed unity which guarantees knowledge and meaning. It is an impossible and hence fictional freezing of the processes which constitute 'consciousness', especially the interlocked processes of knowledge, language, and psyche.

From the writings of the young Marx through Lenin's formulations on political organization through current debates, the subjective has been a matter of consistent concern for the theory of historical materialism. In fact, recent work on the subject in film theory appears in part as a critique of the concept of the subject in certain famous formulations in the historical materialist tradition. The best known of these, and one which tends to serve as a whipping boy in certain quarters now, is the work of Lukács in his collection *History and Class Consciousness*.[1] Lukács gave the subject a central function in the logic of historical materialism. Considering that function will help one in understanding the difficulties of contemporary theory.

Lukács used the concept of the subject to give epistemological issues political force. For him, Kant had bequeathed to bourgeois thinkers an irreducible split between human understanding and existence. Once eternalized, this gap makes knowledge of the social totality inaccessible to the human subject, and makes rational knowledge of the human possible only through the objectification of human subjectivity. This intellectual alienation of the human is a reflection of the processes described by Marx as the fetishism of commodities, and its existence at the highest philosophical level is evidence of the universal penetration of commodity fetishism throughout bourgeois society. According to Lukács, then, the most significant philosophical problem is the subject-object contradiction, understood as a historical symptom which in turn serves the social formation by limiting knowledge of it.

This view enabled Lukács to attain a certain precision in conceiving of the subject as a concrete force in objective relations.

Since class conflict is the motor of history in classic Marxist analyses, Lukács grounded the concept of the subject of knowledge in the concept of socioeconomic class. His innovation was to investigate historical processes in terms of the potential for rational understanding of those processes by a given class. The historical effectivity of a class was measured by its potential for self-knowledge, the extent to which its position in the relations of production gives it the possibility of becoming an identical subject-object. History would be written as epistemological potentiality and limitation. The political potential of the proletariat in classic Marxist theory was redefined as the surpassing of the subject-object contradiction.[2]

There are a number of benefits for the theory of historical materialism in Lukács' formulations. They include the fact that his elevation of the epistemological subject to central importance serves to introduce a level of determination within historical materialism that obstructs any simplistic economist notions of determination. Another advantge of a Lukácsian position is that the concept of the subject provides a standpoint which supposedly escapes capitalist relations for the consideration of history. It can therefore become the standard for an ethics of history which defines the pertinence of socialism. This ethics of history—the realization of the human subject—is in fact a crucial link between historiography and political analysis. It substantiates the historical materialist claim that the two are inseparable.

Nevertheless, recent work has raised a number of difficulties in such a position. To detail them here is out of the question, but we might consider one disquieting symptom. Lukács conceived of the art work as a mimetic totality and concentrated on art as an area of activity where the subject-object antimony is overtly worked on. Yet, it is notorious that as the preeminent Marxist literary critic of his generation he paid extraordinarily little attention to the effectivity of language as such. Language seems to have been for him a transparency through which the subject, alienated or not, pictures and/or establishes relationships with its world.[3] This is where contemporary film theory in the historical materialist tradition might find an entry into a massive critique of Lukács. The concept of a full or realized subject (as identical subject-object, or at least as a subject in a position permitting knowledge of the world and rational self-knowledge regarding its relationship with the world) has now been called into question precisely by an intense attention to language. The newer theoretical stance focuses on the noncommunicative, nonmimetic aspects of language, precisely those aspects which cannot be attributed to a subject. It then becomes difficult to use the subject as a firm standpoint to measure historical and political processes. Names such as Althusser, Lacan, and Kristeva indicate the direction of this critique.

There is undoubtedly a great gain in specificity for historical materialism in this movement. But given slogans such as 'a signifier represents a subject for another signifier', and 'the unconscious is structured like a language', what happens to the logical functions which the postulated potential of a realized subject previously performed for the theory of historical materialism? Now ideology cannot be conceived as a false consciousness of the social totality imposed on the subject by history. Rather, ideology must be an instance simultaneous with Lacan's Symbolic Order, wherefrom it imports and is involved in the Imaginary Order. How, then, does one now write history, since it cannot be done from the standpoint of the realized subject?

It is clear that there is no need to fear a return of economism. The specificity of signification will serve as an even stronger obstruction to such a conception. With the subject fragmented in language, the human agent is that much less reducible to a personification of an economic motive or position. But new problems may arise precisely because this blockage is so complete. If the signifier exercises such a great degree of determination on conceptions, how can that determination be reconciled with the historical determinations localizable in social formations? To what extent can we maintain this materialism as historical?

Within the contemporary problematic, the configurations involved in the interplay of the two fields of determination are usually described as 'simultaneity' and 'intrication'. A number of pairs such as language and ideology, symbolic and ideology, psyche and sociality, etc., are said to be distinct but simultaneous, specific but inseparable. The overlap of the various pairs is investigated in processes of representation. The point of conjunction of the pairs is the subject.

The resulting difficulties with historical specificity and determination can be seen in two important articles which attempt to incorporate the study of signification psychoanalytically conceived and the study of ideology (or sociality) in discourse. The first is John Brenkman's 'The Other and the One: Psychoanalysis, Reading, the *Symposium*'.[4] Brenkman tries to explain the simultaneity and intrication of the effectivities of the social formation and the history of the individual as subject by equating the locus of the code governing signification—Lacan's Other—with 'the social group'. This is in part explained by the experience of the individual submitted to the institution of the family which supplies a structure through which the individual is inserted into the Symbolic Order.

This kind of formulation leads to a number of comments, revolving around the general problem that the equation of the Other with the social group generalizes that group out of any historically specific situation. The effectivity of the production of the subject can only be defined by language, with no place for sociopolitical/historical shiftings of interests and/or exploitation. As Brenkman sums up his conception of the history of the individual, the lack installed by the signifier 'takes up' the lack in sexuality; that is, biological life is 'submitted' to the processes of subjectivity 'when connected to the action of the signifier, which is itself the heart of the most elementary *social* practices'. (My emphasis.) The universality of the claims being made can be understood when we realize that this last phrase is a reference to the studies of primitive, preindustrial kinship systems by Lévi-Strauss.

The generality of Brenkman's arguments is forcefully demonstrated in his approach to the concrete analysis of a text. He proposes that Derrida's critique of the metaphysics of presence in Western philosophical discourse can be connected to the denial of lack treated by psychoanalysis as a necessary stage in the history of the individual as subject. Disavowal of lack on the part of the individual subject is recapitulated in the positing of a transcendental center by philosophy. If philosophy is seen as ideological discourse, then Derrida's deconstruction of it can be read as a kind of ideological analysis of a text—Western philosophy—which reflects a psychic condition experienced by all humans.

The importation of Derrida as ideological analysis highlights the problem, by emphasizing the extraordinary generality of a transcendental subject constructed to disavow lack, instead of the historical specificity one would expect the concept of ideology to imply. The argument seems to apply to all of Western discourse at least since Plato. The confusion of justification on this point in Brenkman's text is an awareness of the unsolved problem of historicity. He claims historicity in the most classic Marxist sense by justifying the apparently ahistorical existence of philosophical discourse to the present day by identifying ancient Greece with the birth of class society. He contradictorily argues that the persistence of the philosophical text is evidence of the relative autonomy of social practices, thus using an already fragile Marxist concept to evade rather than explain the historically specific. At one point he openly admits the need for a more specific analysis. But his justifications, combined with the appeal to Derrida as ideological analysis and Lévi-Strauss on familial structures, can only work as a blockage of historical specificity. What can it mean in historiographic and political terms to show that the same structure of lack has governed philosophical discourse at least since Plato? This kind of argument seems to make historical specificity almost non-pertinent.

An exactly opposite danger is raised by recent work of Stephen Heath, which explores these problems from an explicit focus on a crucial theoretical and political pressure point of this kind of approach—sexual difference. If psychoanalysis, especially as explicated by Lacan, questions any secure position of knowledge, what is the source of Lacan's own security in certain pronouncements? In his article, 'Difference', Heath argues that, at least in his treatment of femininity, Lacan accepts an immediacy of vision or image, an immediacy which psychoanalysis teaches us to regard with suspicion.[5] The question is how to progress past this suspect immediacy.

Heath's answer ultimately is not a complex one. The difficulty is centered on the issue of lack and castration, where the Symbolic Order fixates on anatomy in order to institute difference. Now, for Heath, the Symbolic is simultaneous with but not identical to ideology. But then these terms, in their simultaneity, can be opposed as a complex singularity to another term in a new binary opposition, namely the biological. The subject is then the point of juncture between biology and psyche.

In this context, the difficulty in Lacan is that his occasional acceptance of the immediate image of woman places sexual difference on the side of the biological, of nature. This must be reversed, by giving the Symbolic a priority over the biological. There is sexual difference in anatomy and sexual difference in the Symbolic. If biological sexuality mandates the structure of lack governing the Symbolic, then the *political* struggle cannot be won. This political requirement is what leads to a theoretical conception of the history of the individual which places sexual difference on the side of psyche as a product of the Symbolic and hence sociality. This inversion returns at a number of points in Heath's article. Its effect is to make a politics of sexuality and the unconscious conceivable.

What happens, then, is that for the sake of political calculation, a binary opposition between the Symbolic and the biological is maintained, and, on the issue of sexual difference, the Symbolic must be given a priority. From the political and ideological standpoint, at least, it seems to me that we can call this priority determination; according to Heath, 'sexuality is always a symbolic production'. But the specific nature of that priority, simultaneity, a question ultimately crucial for historiography and politics, is a question not really considered.

The uneasiness I feel in this formulation is a sense of a theoretical move not completed at the theoretical level. The summary of the political stakes is absolutely correct. But this summary does not result in a theoretical transformation. Instead, at points in the article, there is a displacement of an immediacy of image Heath rightly criticizes in Lacan with an immediacy of politics. This priority of determinations is thus treated as a priority of one immediacy over another.

To understand the ultimate tendency of this kind of operation, we can turn to a more extreme example. In the conclusion of *Marx's Capital and Capitalism Today*, Cutler, Hindess, Hirst, and Hussain answer the theoretical question of the ultimate 'pertinence of socialism' by an appeal to concrete contemporary political concerns. They argue that this general question can only be answered by reference to the particular moment of struggle for non-commodity forms.

> We would maintain that it is at this level that the question of the pertinence of socialist forms and the context of socialist political ideology can be answered, that they are always answered in specific ways which confront the problems of the movement and the constraints it encounters.[6]

The difficulty here is indicated by the fact that if we make the classic equation in historical materialism between political analysis and historiographic analysis, it is possible to assign this view a name: historicism.[7] Historicism functions precisely to eliminate consideration of general issues of determination in the face of historical immediacy. Specificity is attained, indeed fetishized, but only at the cost of a denegation of any theoretical understanding. I would assert, then, that any view which solves theoretical problems with an appeal to an immediacy—that is, which eliminates theoretical understanding from the apprehension of the immediate—is suspect within historical materialism. On this point Marx's *1857 Introduction* seems to me still to be pertinent and a place where, on general issues of method, psychoanalysis and historical materialism can to some degree converge.[8]

Contemporary materialism which draws on psychoanalysis, then, must beware not only of the trap of ahistorical generalities which do not confront the problem of specific determination, but also of the trap of historicism as a solution to that difficulty. The question as to how this can be done, given the terms of contemporary research, is an extremely difficult one. In what follows, I make brief arguments and suggestions in an attempt to indicate ways that we might be able to begin conceptualizing the function of the decentered, fragmented subject in the logic of historical materialism.

It will be recalled that Lukács bestowed on the epistemological subject a central function in historical materialism by assuming that its aspirations were authentic and by positing the possibility of their realization. A psychoanalytic of signification, on the other hand, conceives of that realization as an impossibility and hence makes it an error to construct a view of history or an ethics of history around the realization of the subject. However, it seems to me important to stress that this does not remove the subject as a determinative force from historical processes; the subject may be a fiction, but, as those of us engaged in critical analysis should realize, a fiction is not merely a falsehood. Investigation cannot proceed from the assumption of the coherent subject-position as 'mere' fiction. It must begin from the subject as a component of social relationships.

What I mean can be illustrated by a comment on a statement by Rosalind Coward about the demands of a Lacanian materialist approach to current affairs television. Coward writes:

> It is never a question of what class produces what form or what content of a signifying practice, but rather how systems of representation inscribe (ideological) positions. Nor could it ever start from the assumption of a coherent subject outside the text as a source of plenitude, origin or meanings, either in the form of a coherence of the ideological positions of the producers of the programme, or in the form of its audience.[9]

My suggestion, in opposition to Coward, is that a historical materialist analysis *would* start *precisely* from the 'coherence' of a subject. What it would join Lacanian theories of representation in doing is refusing to *end* with the coherent subject, to 'ontologize' that subject. This may seem to be a terminological detail, but I think it is a crucial methodological point. If it did not appear as if a text is generated by and received by subjects outside of it, and if that appearance did not have some kind of determinative force, then there would be no special virtue in demonstrating how such subjects are processual constructions and heterogeneities, how their unities are fictions.

This is indeed to accept a certain immediacy as a starting point, but only in order to theorize that immediacy for the purpose of understanding its implications as a social phenomenon. Some might suggest that this is a regression to a problematic based on a distinction beween phenomenal appearance (the subject as fixed unity) and actuality (the subject as a production of contradictory processes which remain at work as the subject), i.e., a distinction between the effect of 'consciousness' and real relations. This distinction is often taken as the mark of an idealist problematic.

Nevertheless, I do not think that this kind of distinction necessarily implies an essentialism if it is insisted that 'appearance' is itself an actuality of historical processes. Such a conceptual structure may be inevitable at some point in any kind of materialist discourse which takes the concept of ideology seriously. The paradoxical insight of Marx was that societies are dominated by a kind of discourse which screens out the operations of social processes, yet is a necessary (though not sufficient) condition for the existence of those processes and is part of them. He called that kind of discourse ideology. To locate its operations within a general theory of the relative autonomy or specificity of processes of representation does not permit one to gloss over the historical actuality of the screening processes as 'consciousness'.

This is why Althusser's explorations in the theory of ideology remain significant, despite certain critiques which have their validity and yet seem to me to miss the overall significance of his project. For example, it has been argued that by conceiving of ideology so completely in terms of a closure of a subject position which is for him pure imaginary, Althusser loses the force of the psychoanalytic conception from which he has borrowed to make his arguments. Such a charge is not trivial, but it retains the most weight only as long as one approaches the problem from a 'strictly' psychoanalytic interest in the history of the individual as subject. A concern with the social formation taken as a whole leads not only to questioning the finality of the subject from an analysis of its construction, but also to a simultaneous insistence on its determinative force. Simply to point out the existence of this contradiction is of no help in confronting the difficulties of using the concept of the subject in constructing a logic of historical materialism—a logic which traditionally begins from symptomatic contradictions rather than halting before them. The same kind of response would apply to the argument that Althusser's formula, 'ideology interpellates the individual as subject', presupposes the existence of subjectivity prior to the mechanisms of its construction. This 'circularity', the critique of which rests on a rather positivist notion of causality, seems to me to be productive as a preliminary attempt to reflect in theory the place of subject formation from the perspective of the social formation taken as a whole.[10]

It is the logic of historical materialism which is of concern here. Althusser's points are made in the context of a view which holds, in direct opposition to Lukács, that ideology is always with us and will never be surpassed even in a hypothetically achieved socialist society. This view does dovetail in many respects with the psychoanalytic view of the persistence of processes of subject-positioning, but from a focus which begins explicitly from historic and political analysis. To take any political position is precisely to take a *position*, to declare meanings—to assume, to some extent and however transiently, a knowledge belonging to what Lukács might have called a realized subjectivity. The imbrication of political and ideological practices can first be understood on this level. Hence Jim Fleming's comment earlier in this conference: 'there is always at least a little something of the fantastic in taking a political position'. And hence the necessity for insisting that the coherent subject-position as a historical force cannot be simply eliminated from consideration of the social formation by means of an account of the construction of the individual as subject, even if that account enables us to avoid accepting the subject in its own immediate terms.

Within historical materialism the concept of the realized subject was once able to mediate between ahistorical generality and historicism, or at least that argument could be made. Current theories of the subject inevitably fragmented in language and representation make necessary a consideration of the determinative force of the *appearance* of the coherent subject in its various historical manifestations. This still leads to an examination of discourse, of systems of representations, as they posit subjects, but from the viewpoint of analysis of the social formation. Needless to say, on this view the construction of subjects in discourse as historical phenomena is inseparable from the inadequacies of the unities which the discourses posit.

There are some starting points available for this difficult project. Let me end with a brief reference to a couple of them.

A profitable approach from the viewpoint of individual texts might begin from the now familiar reading of Brecht as being concerned with the transformation of 'consciousness' into a series of subjects throughout the progress of the text in time. This is not the dissolution of the subject, since it presupposes a search for understanding which the text is to put in motion. It can rather be conceptualized as the construction of a series of subjects.[11] From the viewpoint of the social formation, the question becomes one of the determinative forces constraining the production of this seriality of subjects and the predominance of pulling a potential seriality into one for the sake of attaining a 'consciousness' outside of the processes constructing it.

This leads to another approach, which would view the problem not in terms of the individual text, but in terms of a simultaneity of texts and discourses. Historical materialism is nothing if not an analysis of social formations as totalities of many determinations (whether 'totality' is understood in the sense of Lukács' Hegelian concrete totality or Althusser's complex whole structured in dominance). Like the other components of the social formation, representations cannot be taken in isolation (which is not to deny their specificity). From the perspective of the social formation, then, representations must be conceived as a vast network of interlocking and often contradictory discourses. This implies a multitude of addresses and different appeals to subjectivity. Why, then, is there not a seriality of subjects across many texts? Or if there is such a seriality, what happens to its determinative force as a social phenomenon? What happens to the theoretically possible displacement of the singularity of 'consciousness'—the subject in ideology?

Stephen Heath has suggested that an account of 'suturing effects' is crucial for a theory of ideology.[12] This seems important to me, provided that this understanding of junctures among signifiers, to which we attach the label 'suture', refers not only to individual texts and the history of the individual, but also to suturing effectivities among many texts as historical phenomena. To deal with this kind of suturing, in history, I suspect that we need a continuing emphasis on concepts such as discursive formation, sociolect, inner speech, the joint hold of materially heterogeneous discourses on subjects, etc.[13] Some kind of project of this sort is necessary for historical materialism to develop an understanding of the determinative force of text, representation, and subject in sociality.

NOTES

1. G. Lukács, *History and Class Consciousness: Studies in Marxist Dialectics*, trans. R. Livingstone (Cambridge, Massachusetts: MIT Press, 1972). See especially the essays 'What is Orthodox Marxism' and 'Reification and the Consciousness of the Proletariat'.

2. The extent to which Lukács does not here escape the influence of Hegel's solution to the problem he has set himself is well known, for in Lukács the end of the proletarian revolution becomes the end of contradiction, of difference as such. Given the common use of *History and Class Consciousness* in contemporary film theory as an exemplary mistaken project, however, it is only fair to note that in the later part of his career Lukács' position shifted. The end of alienation was no longer the end of objectification. History would now be measured for the potentiality of a class position for achieving the minimum of objectification, not its elimination. And objectification was no longer defined from a purely epistemological point of view, but from one which takes labor into account as purposeful activity marking the human as such. Of course, the human subject remained the main cog in the theoretical apparatus, but the end of all contradiction was no longer envisioned. See the 1967 preface in *History and Class Consciousness*.

3. This formulation might put Lukács close to Stalin's famous view of language as a historically neutral tool belonging to neither base nor superstructure.

4. J. Brenkman, 'The Other and the One: Psychoanalysis, Reading, the *Symposium*', *Yale French Studies* 55/56 (1977), especially pp. 421-424, 438-448.

5. S. Heath, 'Difference', *Screen* vol. 19 no. 3 (Autumn 1978), pp. 51-112. Some of the correlatives of the inversions are on p. 66 ('the individual subject is not constructed from sexuality, sexuality is constructed in the history of the subject, with difference a function of its construction, not its cause, a function which is not necessarily single [on the contrary] and which, *a fortiori*, is not necessarily the holding of that difference to anatomical difference...'); p. 70 ('no sexual revolution will shift dividing lines, the problem is one of social revolution'); p. 109 ('The unconscious is not anatomical, from a given division of the sexes, but symbolic, from a division of the individual as subject in language, meaning, difference...').

6. A. Cutler, B. Hindess, P. Hirst and A. Hussain, *Marx's Capital and Capitalism Today*, vol. 2 (Boston, Massachusetts: Routledge & Kegan Paul, 1978), pp. 258-267.

7. That is, historicism in the classic sense, not the sense assigned the term by Popper. See the introduction in *The Philosophy of History in Our Time: An Anthology*, H. Meyerhoff (ed.), (Garden City, New York: Doubleday, 1959), especially pp. 9-25, and also the editorial comments pp. 299-300. Meyerhoff would associate the term with, for example, Dilthey rather than, say, Marx (as does Popper).

8. K. Marx, *Grundrisse*, trans. M. Nicolaus (New York: Vintage, 1973), pp. 100-101.

9. R. Coward, 'Class, "Culture" and the Social Formation', *Screen* vol. 18 no. 1 (Spring 1977), p. 95.

10. For Althusser on ideology and the subject, see his essay 'Ideology and Ideological State Apparatuses (Notes Towards an Investigation)', in *Lenin and Philosophy, and Other Essays*, trans. B. Brewster (New York: Vintage, 1970), pp. 127-183. For critiques of his work, see

Brenkman, op. cit., p. 447, n. 43; and the more extensive commentary in P. Q. Hirst, 'Althusser and the Theory of Ideology', *Economy and Society*, vol. 5 (Nov. 1976), pp. 385-412, especially pp. 398-407.

11. See B. Brewster, 'From Shklovsky to Brecht: A Reply', *Screen* vol. 15 no. 2 (Summer 1974), pp. 94-95; and S. Heath, 'Lessons from Brecht', ibid., pp. 104-105.

12. S. Heath, 'Notes on Suture', *Screen* vol. 18 no. 4 (Winter 1977/78), p. 74.

13. For discussions of these notions see the following: on discursive formation, S. Heath, 'Notes on Suture'; on sociolect, see R. Barthes, *Elements of Semiology*, trans. A. Lavers and C. Smith (Boston, Massachusetts: Beacon, 1970), pp. 21-22, and R. Barthes, *Image-Music-Text*, trans. S. Heath (New York: Hill & Wang, 1977), pp. 167-169; on inner speech and materially heterogeneous discourses, see the contributions by Willemen and de Lauretis to this volume.